THE GENIUS OF WOMEN

ALSO BY JANICE KAPLAN

The Gratitude Diaries

How Luck Happens

The Genius of
WOMEN

From Overlooked to
Changing the World

Janice Kaplan

DUTTON

DUTTON

An imprint of Penguin Random House LLC

penguinrandomhouse.com

LIBRARY OF CONGRESS CATALOGING-IN-PUBLICATION DATA has been applied for.

ISBN 9781524744212 (hardcover)
ISBN 9781524744229 (ebook)

Printed in the United States of America
1 3 5 7 9 10 8 6 4 2

BOOK DESIGN BY KATY RIEGEL

While the author has made every effort to provide accurate telephone numbers, internet addresses, and other contact information at the time of publication, neither the publisher nor the author assumes any responsibility for errors or for changes that occur after publication. Further, the publisher does not have any control over and does not assume any responsibility for author or third-party websites or their content.

To Pauline and Annie and Matt and Zach.

Your genius minds
and generous hearts inspire me
every day.

Contents

Preface   1

PART ONE

Genius Isn't What You Think

Chapter 1

Why You've Never Heard of Lise Meitner   13

Chapter 2

The Outrageous Bias Against Mozart's Sister   29

Chapter 3

Einstein's Wife and the Theory of Relativity   46

Chapter 4

How a Teenage Nun Painted *The Last Supper*   67

Chapter 5

Why Italian Women Are Better than
You at Math   86

Chapter 6

Rosalind Franklin and the Truth About
the Female Brain   104

PART TWO

The Geniuses Among Us

Chapter 7

Why Fei-Fei Li Should Be on
the Cover of *Vanity Fair*   117

Chapter 8

The Astrophysicist Who Does Not Need Tom Cruise   133

Chapter 9

Broadway's Tina Landau Contains Multitudes   150

Chapter 10

RBG and the Genius of Being a Cuddly Goat   166

Chapter 11

The Dark Lord Trying to Kill Off
Women Scientists   180

PART THREE

How Women Geniuses Fight . . . and Win

Chapter 12

Battling the Ariel-Cinderella Complex   199

Chapter 13
Why Oprah Wanted to Be a Beauty Queen   214

Chapter 14
Geena Davis and the Problem of Being Nice   232

Chapter 15
Frances Arnold Knew She Was Right
(and Then She Won the Nobel Prize)   249

Chapter 16
How to Succeed in Business by Wearing Elegant
Scarves   265

Chapter 17
Why Sally Michel Was a Genius Painter and
Mrs. Milton Avery Was Not   279

Chapter 18
The Game-Changing Power of Genius Women   300

Acknowledgments   309
Notes   311
Index   325

THE GENIUS OF WOMEN

Preface

A cadre of academics—all men—put together a canon of books some years ago that they considered essential reading. These Great Books came to define what it means to be an educated person, and schools including Columbia University and the University of Chicago used them as the basis for a core curriculum.

A hundred or more books made the list. Not one of them was written by a woman.

The men behind the Great Books sanctimoniously claimed that they chose works that contained great ideas, and they didn't care who wrote them. You don't need a PhD in psychology to know that they were fooling themselves. Our decisions about what is great and worthy and valuable are based at least in part on social expectations. We appraise value—whether in intellectual ideas, pocketbooks, or real estate—within a socially accepted context. For the male academics who made the list, and for so many before and since, the expectation was that men were the geniuses worth studying.

My friend Michael Berland, the well-known pollster and strategist, conducted a survey just a few years ago to understand people's attitudes toward genius. Mike has been doing polls for a long time, and he is better than almost anyone at predicting results and then knowing how to use the findings to move forward. But the genius poll floored him. In one question, he asked who was most likely to be a genius—and *90 percent* of Americans said that geniuses tended to be men. When asked to name a female genius, almost the only name anyone could come up with was Marie Curie.

How did we get to the point of ignoring, undermining, and over-looking the extraordinary talents of women? In our current era of assumedly aroused consciousness to gender issues, why do both men and women still believe that men's contributions to society are the ones that really count?

In interviewing dozens of mathematicians, physicists, artists, writers, philosophers, and Nobel Prize winners for this book, I have discovered that the real issue separating men and women isn't talent or achievement or natural brilliance or hard work. It's being in the position to set the rules. Men have had that power, and women have not. Men have been making the decisions about what is good and what matters—and their biases become the status quo, the accepted ethos, for all.

Recognizing genius does not have to be a zero-sum game—and yet it often feels that way. There are only so many Nobel Prizes and tenured jobs at Harvard. There is only so much space for great works in museums and only so many authors whose works can be listed on a core curriculum. You would think that a more aroused awareness in recent years would turn a list like Great Books into a dated relic, but any change gets met with angry resistance. When Columbia University started revising its required reading list to include women writers like Sappho, Virginia Woolf, Toni Morrison, and Jane Austen, even some of the most liberal male professors were outraged. Sure, Virginia Woolf is worth reading and maybe she even redefined the novel more dramatically than anyone else of her time. But which man gets dropped to make way for her?

Men who feel threatened that their work and their heroes may be replaced stop being open to women's achievements. They close ranks and redefine genius. Let me put it bluntly. If you are in power and define a genius as a person who breaks new ground, affects future generations, and has a penis, then you have pretty much given the game away. You can claim that you believe in equality and judge only by performance—but you have rigged the system.

Women have to be aware of how the rules are set. The definitions are never as stark as I just described—unless you read between the lines. When Donna Strickland won the 2018 Nobel Prize in physics, she was celebrated for her groundbreaking research developing a new method of generating laser beams. She had brilliance, originality, and great accomplishments—what she didn't have was a page on *Wikipedia*. An entry about her had been submitted just a few months earlier, but it had been rejected by the mostly white male gatekeepers.

Wikipedia is an impressive undertaking, and I don't mean to point fingers at its failings. Katherine Maher, executive director of the non-profit that oversees *Wikipedia,* was slightly embarrassed when the Strickland story came out, but she explained that *Wikipedia* is simply a reflection of the world's biases, not the cause of them. The massive online encyclopedia is created by a troop of volunteers who represent the values of the society. We can (and will) talk about why women who have different talents than men miss out on the world's applause. But the missing page revealed an even more flagrant problem. Women who have talents the same as or greater than those of their male colleagues (she won the Nobel Prize, for heaven's sakes!) still get ignored. *Wikipedia* guidelines don't specifically define geniuses in physics as requiring a Y chromosome. But by denying Strickland's entry, they basically did.

You don't have to be a genius to have a *Wikipedia* page—you just have to reach the level of "notable," which isn't really a very high standard. But only about 15 percent of the biographies on *Wikipedia* as of 2014 were about women. By the time of the Strickland oversight, the number was close to 18 percent. A measly 3 percent increase may not sound like much, but Maher said that it represented "seventy-two new articles a day, every single day, for the past three and a half years." All that and they still hadn't managed to include the woman who would receive the highest honor in her field.

Do you see what I'm trying to say here? You can do great work. You can be a genius in your field. But the forces of established power can still rule against you. When you are a woman and 85 percent (give or take 3 percent) of the people whom society considers notable are men, you have a tough road to travel.

At about the same time that Strickland was in the paradoxical position of (a) being ignored and (b) winning a Nobel Prize, the Barnes Foundation in Philadelphia opened a show featuring the Impressionist painter Berthe Morisot. You wouldn't normally expect to find a connection between a nineteenth-century artist and a twenty-first-century physicist. But the issues that genius women face have remained constant through the generations. Esteemed art critic Peter Schjeldahl calls Morisot the most interesting artist of her generation, which included huge talents like Manet, Degas, Renoir, and Monet. Those artists considered her part of their inner circle and held her work in the highest esteem. But others were less interested in the powerful form and meaning in her work than in whether Manet, who painted her often, was also in love with her. (She ultimately married his younger brother.) Schjeldahl says with some dismay that despite the breathtaking quality of her work, Morisot was "not so much underrated in standard art history as not rated at all."

What's going on? However much we like to think that we judge work exclusively on its quality, determinations don't happen in a vacuum. Knowing whether a man or a woman created a painting or a physics equation or a great novel changes your view of its value. The Barnes even subtitled its Morisot exhibit *Woman Impressionist*—which just drips of unintended sexist condescension. Is a Woman Impressionist different from a Real Impressionist? Critic Schjeldahl waggishly imagined a parallel case where an exhibit would be called *Georges Braque: Man Cubist*. The suggestion makes you laugh—because it would never happen. Nobody dreams of mentioning gender when great work is done by a man. You note it when the genius is a woman because—well, darn, isn't it amazing? Morisot may be a creative genius. But from the perspective of a male-centered art world, she's just a girl with a brush who happens to paint like the big boys.

There's an old saying that a fish doesn't know it lives in water. And why would it? Whether you're fish or fowl, live in a city or suburb, your everyday surroundings become invisible. You don't know anything else. Your current situation seems like the only possible reality. It's similarly difficult for most of us to realize that we live in a world where men's judgments and perspectives are the very air we breathe (or the water we swim in).

I find myself in many conversations lately with men who have been left slightly confused by the #MeToo movement. They understand blatant offenses and have always been respectful of boundaries. But they don't understand being asked to give up what one man described to me as "the dance"—opening a door for a woman, paying for her dinner, giving her a compliment. One older man I interviewed for this book helped me off with my coat when we first met at a

restaurant and then offered me his arm as we walked to a table to talk. I declined. He rushed to pull out my chair. Honestly,
I'm a grown-up. I have managed to sit down for many years without help.

Many women don't mind the dance at all—and letting a man
take control and help with a few little things may seem like a reasonable way of living in an unequal world. But you have to be aware of
the ramifications. Giving away your power changes how your work
and achievements are seen. You are no longer an equal. You are
Woman Impressionist or Woman Writer or Woman Whatever. The
man who pulled out my chair would have said that he was just being
gallant. But he was also putting himself in control of a situation where
I, the interviewer, otherwise had the upper hand. I didn't say anything
because I didn't want to embarrass him. I'm not sure if that decision
was right or wrong. Women have always had to learn how to cope
within the system—getting their way without being too threatening—
and knowing how to do that is a bit of genius, too.

In the many months of researching this book, I found myself getting increasingly distraught about the huge potential of women that
has been lost over the years, as well as the extraordinary achievements
that have been ignored. It's easy to blame men, but women buy into
the system. We assume the male-dominated water in which we are
swimming is the only possible environment, so we don't allow ourselves to jump out and sample fresh air. We undermine our own
achievements and don't expect to do as well as men. We scare ourselves away from success long before anyone else sends us away.

A recent off-Broadway play called *Gloria: A Life* traced the awakening of Gloria Steinem, who initially saw writing as a way out of her
hometown of Toledo, Ohio. Moving to New York, she won choice
magazine assignments but had some unexpected obstacles. Waiting in
the lobby of the Plaza Hotel once for a celebrity she was interviewing,

she was thrown out for being unescorted. She missed the interview. It took her a while to learn to stand up for herself and fight back. The next time the hotel manager tried to throw her out for not being with a man, she wouldn't leave. The actress portraying Steinem, Christine Lahti (who looked exactly like her), offered the moment of epiphany.

"Finally I understood the radical idea that women are human beings," she said. "It's not just that we live in a patriarchy—it's that the patriarchy lives in us."

The patriarchy lives in us. It's a powerful and potent comment because in the role-changing upheaval that has taken place since the late 1960s, perhaps the greatest challenge for women has been believing in their own worth. Even now, women struggle to fight off the second-class stereotypes that have been ingrained for so long. When you've received the message, overt or subliminal, that you don't belong in the hotel lobby, in the corner office, or at the Nobel Prize ceremony, it's hard to move forward with 100 percent conviction that the world is wrong and your genius has a place in it.

Another question from Mike Berland's genius survey shows how the problem hasn't gone away. When asked if they might be a genius, 15 percent of the men said yes. But not a single woman did. Some of the men answering the survey might have been delusional about their own abilities, but it doesn't really matter. How you answer that question sends a message about your own sense of possibility. Only when you believe something is feasible can you make it happen.

"Do you think you're a genius?" Mike asked me when he told me about the results.

"Of course not!" I said. "Smart, maybe. But not a genius."

Mike shook his head. "I think you're a genius. I think a lot of women I know are geniuses. Why don't they think so?"

Why don't we know how good we are? Why don't we recognize our strengths and potential genius?

Because the patriarchy lives in us.

To be recognized as a genius at any time, you can't be subservient or afraid of your own strength. You have to be able to challenge the accepted norms, try to see things from a fresh perspective, blaze your own path, and make your own rules, no matter the circumstances. Women now have comparatively more opportunities to let their genius shine than in previous generations, but in researching this book, I came to see that the bar is still high and the barriers many.

Geniuses matter because they are the innovators and visionaries who shake the world. You probably know about Leonardo da Vinci, Galileo, Michelangelo, Albert Einstein, and Isaac Newton. But have you ever heard about Emmy Noether, Émilie du Châtelet, Clara Peeters, and Ada Lovelace? Each managed to have wildly original ideas and provide a new view of the world despite the obstacles in her way. The gorgeous actress Hedy Lamarr helped develop a radio guidance system that was used during World War II and is considered a precursor to the Bluetooth technology we all use now. Film mogul Louis B. Mayer promoted Lamarr as the world's most beautiful woman, but aviation tycoon Howard Hughes was impressed for a different reason. He relied on her to design new aerodynamic wings for his planes. He called her a genius.

That there have been women geniuses in every generation fills me with both hope and admiration. Figuring out how they did it—how a woman painted brilliantly in the Italian Renaissance or reimagined physics in the nineteenth century when she was expected to stay home and cook—could change how all of us approach the limits and possibilities in our lives. You don't have to be a mathematician or a NASA scientist or even an academic to be a genius (though I spoke to many women in all those categories). Many women geniuses are working hard in the next office or the next cubicle—but even today, they don't get recognized. It's time that we change our perspective, to see and consider women's talents in a new way.

Genius requires some combination of innate intelligence, passion, and a dedication to hard work. Geniuses tend to have a broad range of abilities—they merge science and arts and throw some emotion into their efforts, too. Walter Isaacson, who wrote terrific biographies of Steve Jobs and Albert Einstein and Benjamin Franklin, found that a common thread of genius is "the creativity that can occur when a feel for both the humanities and the sciences combine in one strong personality." You can find mathematicians and physicists and inventors who fit the bill, as well as entrepreneurs and artists and astronomers. When you start to line up the multifaceted traits, women fit in quite nicely.

Plato said that "what is honored in a country will be cultivated there," and it's not an exaggeration to say that the genius of women is not well cultivated in this country or many others right now. In fact, the genius of women has rarely been socially encouraged or cultivated at all. As exemplars of human possibility, geniuses are an inspiration to others to think creatively and broadly. They consider new paths and don't follow the received wisdom. The genius of women could be transformative in politics and corporate America and education—if only we would allow it to shine through.

The many biases and barriers that have derailed women from exploring their genius potential could fill a book—or two or three. But the bigger fascination for me—and what will fill much of *this* book— is not only the women who have been stopped but also those who refused even to be slowed down. No matter how far back I look—and certainly up to the present—I find women who skirted the obstacles and jumped over the barriers. The real question for me about genius is this: How is it that across the generations, even when they face less-than-perfect circumstances, some women soar so high, achieve so much, and go so far? And what does that say about what we can all do going forward?

I happened on a book by the young writer Sheila Heti, whom one influential critic hailed for "steering literature in new directions." Early in her novel *How Should a Person Be?,* the narrator gives the topic of women geniuses a clever twist.

"One good thing about being a woman is we haven't too many examples yet of what a genius looks like," she says. "It could be me."

The line made me smile—because what could be a better attitude? You can grouse all you want about my friend Michael's survey showing that people think geniuses are men. Or you can see it as a positive. Having been ignored before means women can create who we are moving forward, discover new possibilities and definitions. If people are baffled at the thought of what a woman genius looks like, you can fashion her in your own image.

The model for a woman genius could be me. Or you. Or your daughter.

So join me on my challenging, exciting, and sometimes funny journey to follow Plato's advice and discover how we can explore, honor, and cultivate the real genius of women.

PART ONE

Genius Isn't What You Think

I would venture to guess that Anon, who wrote so many poems
without signing them, was often a woman.

—VIRGINIA WOOLF

I have no special talent. I am only passionately curious.

—ALBERT EINSTEIN

CHAPTER 1

Why You've Never Heard of Lise Meitner

Shortly after I turned nine years old, our family doctor warned my mother that I was reading too much. I remember looking at him, completely baffled. Until then, my voracious love of books had been a point of family pride, but now my mother anxiously asked if all the reading was hurting my eyes. No, he said, the eyes were fine. But maybe I should spend some time participating in girlier activities. He worried that my excitement about books set in far-flung places and trumpeting new ideas could have unintended consequences.

"A girl can get too smart for her own good," he said in a dire tone.

Too smart for her own good. My mother nodded—she understood, but I was shocked. To me it was one of those jolting moments from childhood that stays with you, ringing in your head at the most inconvenient times. I'd like to dismiss the comment as an archaic viewpoint, no longer relevant in a world where a woman superhero movie blasts past a billion dollars at the box office and men are left reeling at the power of #MeToo. But that's wishful thinking. Ideas ingrained in a culture for decades, even centuries, don't disappear in the time that it takes for one smart girl to grow up.

Too smart for her own good. I've thought about that phrase often now as I've pondered the potential power of women to be geniuses and disrupt standard ideas. I grew up at a time when women's roles were changing, which is true for every woman living now or in the remembered past. Women didn't have the right to vote in America until a hundred years ago, which continues to shock me, and I like to think I would have marched and protested if I lived before then. But maybe not. You get used to stuff. People tell you it's not natural for women to vote or be scientists or painters or mathematicians, and deeply ingrained social expectations fight violently against your own deep sense that *this isn't right.*

I had pure confidence when young, and despite that doctor's statement, it never occurred to me that women couldn't do exactly the same things that men did. I attended an Ivy League college that had previously been all male and went on to have a great career as a journalist and television producer. I ran one of the biggest magazines in the country and raised (with my husband) two magnificent sons. But along the way, I started to realize just how much of women's potential got lost, ignored, or abandoned—and still does. The details of discrimination have changed over the years—women tennis players earn a lot more than they did when I started my career as a sports reporter—but the bigger issues remain. Being a talented and ambitious woman in any field is still like riding in the Kentucky Derby while someone pulls back on the reins. You know you have power and ability and a great horse to ride. So what is that unseen hand trying to stop you?

The French philosopher Simone de Beauvoir explained back in the mid-1900s that men see themselves as the norm, the definition of humanity, and since they posit themselves as The One, women become The Other. She called the setup a "miraculous balm" for insecure men—because even the most mediocre get to feel superior when compared to the women they hold down. Women have often accepted the deal because it comes with potential advantages. In the tumultuous past, man-the-sovereign could protect you from the rampaging hordes, and in the unequal-pay present, man-the-executive can pay for the nice house you can't afford on your own. (You can't afford it yourself because men won't pay you what you're worth—which seems like the definition of a vicious circle.)

But not everyone buys into the agreement. On some level, my childhood doctor knew that. Being *too smart for your own good* means you've rejected the pact. You know that men aren't necessarily smarter or more talented, and you're determined to find your own voice and use it. The decision comes with both advantages and risks. Men who feel their position being threatened can be like cornered dogs, and while you can cope with the yapping, you'd like to avoid the more dangerous attacks.

Throughout history, women geniuses have taken the risk of being different. They've followed their own path and accepted scorn and derision because they understood, even when others didn't, that being a genius had nothing to do with gender. Looking at genius women from the past, I was awed by both their brilliance and their ability to push forward despite endless barriers. Talking to extraordinary women right now (and choosing the geniuses for this book) made me aware that the obstacles haven't gone away. Even when talent is a given, you need heaps of temerity and strength to make your mark. Social and cultural pressures determine who we are far beyond the power of any genes or chromosomes. You aren't born a woman genius—you become one. But when the world tries to stop you, how do you prove that you can never be too smart for your own good?

I started my journey to understand the genius of women at Oxford University, which has always been home to a bunch of very smart people. But until 1879, none of those people were women. Oxford has some three dozen colleges where students work and study, and on a sunny day in early fall, I walked down a beautiful tree-lined street to Lady Margaret Hall, which was the first college at Oxford to admit women. It bills itself as the college that was "founded to right a wrong"—though even after it began accepting women in 1879, the university didn't grant them degrees until 1920.

The redbrick buildings of Lady Margaret Hall are set amidst acres of grounds and gardens, and a friendly person at the porter's lodge welcomed me to come in. (Don't you love the idea of a porter's lodge?) A moment later, Professor Susan Wollenberg walked across the courtyard to greet me. She was wearing a longish skirt and cozy cardigan that enveloped her tiny frame, and she had her hair pulled back in a free-form bun. Clutching a sheaf of papers in one hand, she greeted me graciously, and it occurred to me that were I making a movie about a senior Oxford professor, I would cast her immediately.

Wollenberg was the first woman at Oxford to become a professor of music. She was also the first to break away from the standard music canon and study women composers. A lot of firsts, right? As we walked through the pretty college grounds and then sat talking in her office for most of the afternoon, I realized how brave and courageous she had been in her pursuits. Given her humble and soft-spoken style, she would probably never use those words. When we spoke, she stayed focused on her work rather than what it had meant to storm the cultural barricades—or at least push them to the side. But push them she had. If one sign of a genius is someone who thinks in revolutionary and original ways, she was the genius rebel of Oxford music.

Reflecting on her early years as a student at Oxford (she essentially never left), Wollenberg told me that all her work in those days focused on men. She listened to music by men. She wrote essays about men. Nobody ever talked about women composers. "I thought, well, there must have been women. But where are they? They were simply overlooked or ignored."

Once she joined the faculty, she began teaching a course on women composers going back to antiquity, through the Middle Ages, and all the way to the present. She discovered in every period women composers of great talent who had been undermined by men who refused to play their music. Those who emerged had found unconventional ways to be heard. In the twelfth century, Hildegard of Bingen wrote a huge number of musical compositions, which got attention, Wollenberg explained, "because she became an abbess and had her own convent and wrote for her own choir." In a time of limited options for women, becoming a nun didn't necessarily mean you were escaping from the world—it was the one way you could engage with others and let your creativity flow. To be a woman genius, it apparently helped to have God on your side. Or at least to have a lot of other women around who were able to support you. Women geniuses always had to find an alternate path, and for Hildegard of Bingen and others who followed, the convent was one place to try.

As we talked, Wollenberg explained that "genius has always been gendered male," so people simply forgot to notice the women doing great and powerful work. She mentioned professors at other universities who, like her, were trying to reorient traditional thinking and bring attention to genius women composers of the past like Clara Schumann and Fanny Mendelssohn Hensel. Later, it occurred to me that all of the professors Wollenberg mentioned were female—which probably wasn't a surprise. The genius of women might be to recognize the genius of *other* women. Because if we wait for men to do it, we could be waiting a long time.

———

The next day, I was in London wandering through Covent Garden on my way to the restaurant Rules, which opened in 1798 and has served meals to everyone from Charles Dickens to King Edward VII. When I arrived, my lunch companion, Charles Jones, was waiting for me at the bar, drinking something very English. We hadn't met before, but it took just a few minutes of conversation to realize that he was smart and erudite—and one of the good guys. They do exist, you know, and recognizing the genius of women doesn't mean forsaking all insights from men. It's better if all of us can rely on one another's wisdom and talents—so even though we had met to discuss one of his projects, I decided to enlist his perspective on mine.

A Cambridge University professor with a wide-ranging intelligence, Charles shifted our conversation easily from history to ethics to foreign relations. As we moved to our table for lunch, I discovered that he is also an expert on wine. He realized that I am not.

"May I choose something we will both enjoy?" he asked, studying the wine list and getting extra points for emotional intelligence.

As our first courses came, I dipped into my salmon tartare and mentioned that I was spending a lot of time thinking about what makes a genius. Did he have any thoughts?

Charles took a sip of the chardonnay. "Genius," he said thoughtfully. "I suppose that would be where extraordinary ability meets celebrity."

I looked at him in surprise, my fork frozen in midair. Genius as celebrity? Charles's plummy English accent made everything sound smarter. But it also struck me that he had hit on something important that explained a lot—including the extraordinarily talented women Professor Wollenberg had described to me who couldn't get orchestras (then exclusively male) to play their compositions. Of course they had been lost to history. Would Beethoven be considered a genius if he could only play his concertos at home? A lot of people do great work. But the ones we tend to label genius are also the ones who have gotten attention and grabbed our imagination.

"If that's correct, why do you think there have been so few women geniuses?" I asked, suspecting the answer.

Charles sighed and confirmed my thoughts. "Women historically had only half the equation—the ability but not the celebrity. Their talent went unnoticed."

Ah. Now I reached for my glass of wine. (His choice was excellent.) We tend to think of genius as a fixed state—you are or you aren't. But being a genius isn't like being class president, where you get voted in and your name appears forever in the school yearbook. Whom we consider a genius changes over time and in how their story gets told.

Charles is a classic old-school academic, so I knew he didn't mean celebrity in a Kardashian way—he'd probably never heard of reality TV. But he had been in the jungles of academia long enough to know that all brilliance isn't treated equally. Some people gain far greater renown and reputation than their talent seems to warrant. Others do extraordinary work that is applauded by only a small inner circle. And some are stunned to discover their great achievements overlooked entirely.

Throughout history, women have regularly found themselves in that last category. Whether their genius is in the arts or the sciences, they have a tough time getting noticed. Sometimes it's more subtle, as was the case with Donna Strickland's *Wikipedia* entry, but often, men step in and want to take the credit for themselves, determined to vanquish the woman who has taken the spotlight.

For the earliest examples, you can go all the way back to Hypatia, born in about AD 350. She was a genius thinker in astronomy and philosophy and the first female mathematician we know about. (There were probably others whose work wasn't recorded.) Her contemporary Socrates of Constantinople reported that her work surpassed what anyone else was doing at the time. People would gather around her house to hear her speak and many hailed her as one of the most elite scholars of the day. At a time when Christian theologians were trying to silence opposing voices, Hypatia reportedly urged her listeners to "Reserve your right to think. For even to think wrongly is better than not to think at all." Since very little of her actual writing has survived, I suspect those words have been updated (or maybe put in her mouth). But she was surely an example for other women of the time to think outside the accepted dogma and recognize their potential power. A lot of people didn't like that, and some of her mathematical achievement was attributed to her father, Theon of Alexandria. But then came a shocking downfall. Hypatia was attacked by an angry religious mob that ripped her body to pieces and burned the remains.

There has long been uncertainty about who led the attack on Hypatia and why it happened, but it surely had a lot to do with the animus that comes when a genius woman challenges accepted ways of thinking. Over the centuries, Hypatia has become a feminist icon, with plays and novels and artworks about her, and a 2009 movie starring Rachel Weisz—but given the whole angry-mob thing, it's worrisome to consider her as a role model for women geniuses. In the nearly two thousand years since Hypatia upset the men in power by doing better work than they did, men have learned subtler ways to rip women limb from limb. But the generalized anger at any woman who dares threaten or even question male dominance remains frightening. It sends the sad reminder that men's vehemence in asserting their own entitled privilege, by whatever means possible, hasn't changed.

After I left lunch, I wandered around London for a while, and it occurred to me that no matter whom we are talking about or where they may be, genius needs to be nurtured and genius needs to be recognized.

If a woman does brilliant work but nobody notices, can we call her a genius? It's a bit like the tree-falling-in-a-forest question. If the event hasn't been heard by the rest of the world, does it really make a sound?

The celebrity part of the genius equation has ramifications in many directions. It helps explain why we keep rediscovering women geniuses lately—they've been around, but we just didn't see them. The 2016 movie *Hidden Figures* introduced us to three female black mathematicians who were key figures in the early days of NASA. One of them, Katherine Johnson, calculated flight trajectories when John Glenn became the first person to orbit the earth in 1962.

We'd all heard of John Glenn. But Katherine Johnson? It took a movie with a few Oscar nominations to discover women whose math genius quite literally helped launch America's space program.

If I had to pick a purely brilliant mind to put in the category of genius, I might go for Lise Meitner, who turned physics on its head when she discovered nuclear fission. It was an enormously big deal and soon led to the nuclear reactors that could generate heat and electricity.[1] Her understanding of how a uranium nucleus could split into two—and what would happen when it did—was groundbreaking.

But was she celebrated for it? Not so much.

Meitner collaborated for several decades with a chemist named Otto Hahn, working with him on radioactivity and then fission. They were often talked about for a Nobel Prize and, sure enough, in 1944, the Royal Swedish Academy of Sciences came through with an award for the "discovery of the fission of heavy atomic nuclei." But then they announced that the winner was (drumroll, please)—Otto Hahn.

Otto Hahn! Not Lise Meitner. Not Otto Hahn and Lise Meitner

---

1 The discovery of nuclear fission also led to the nuclear weapons that ended World War II and have frightened the world ever since. Meitner refused to be part of the effort to build the first atomic bomb.

together. Only one half of the team—the male half—got the honor and the recognition and the prize money.

Many years later, some physicists reviewed the proceedings of the Nobel Committee (which had just become public) and concluded that excluding Lise Meitner was inexcusable. They described it as a mixture of "bias, political obtuseness, ignorance, and haste." And that was putting it nicely.

Hahn was a good chemist, and from what I have read, it sounds like he deserved a Nobel Prize—but not this one. He never really understood the theoretical basis of nuclear fission and relied on Meitner for the explanations of what was happening. Meitner remained polite after the slight, but as she pointedly explained in a letter about splitting the atom, "how it originates and that it produces so much energy . . . was something very remote to Hahn."

So why was Meitner, a true genius in physics, overlooked? You might chalk it up to confirmation bias. Research shows that when you already have an opinion about something, you look for the facts and information that will support it. If you buy a Volvo because you think that is the best and safest car around, you will no doubt start noticing all the articles about the virtues of Volvos. When new information comes that contradicts your impression, you'll likely find a reason to ignore it. Your neighbor who drives a Volvo says it has bad sight lines and he hit a curb? Well, that's his problem! He's never been a very good driver!

People often think they are being objective and fair, but they are unwittingly swayed by their long-held impressions and sense of how things should be. They convince themselves of what they want to believe. The great thinker Francis Bacon, an early advocate in the sixteenth century of rational explanations and an empirical approach, nevertheless understood that "the human understanding when it has once adopted an opinion . . . draws all things else to support and agree with it." In works like *War and Peace* and *Anna Karenina,* the great Russian novelist Leo Tolstoy explored the theme of how people can get trapped by both their own beliefs and the stifling conventions of society. (Poor Anna, who had to die for her adultery!) In his essays, he was even more direct about the problem of maintaining a fair perspective. He once explained that most men have trouble understanding even the simplest truth if doing so would require them to recognize "the falsity of conclusions they have formed . . . of which they are proud . . . and on which they have built their lives."

Yes, it's tough to challenge the conclusions on which you have built your life. But when it comes to recognizing the talents of women, it's (well past) time. For centuries, men believed that women's achievements couldn't match their own—and sadly, most women felt that way, too. People weren't outraged by the Meitner snub because it simply confirmed their belief that women couldn't perform at the highest levels of science. The position might have been built on a hill of sand, but once it became an ingrained belief, it was (and is) tough to knock down. Bacon's line about the difficulty of changing an opinion made me think of research done back in the 1950s when social psychologist Leon Festinger got involved with a doomsday cult whose leader promised that a spaceship would arrive at a particular time to save true believers from a coming flood. People flocked to wait for it. The spaceship didn't come, and neither did the flood. So the leader announced a new time for the spacemen to arrive, and her followers showed up again. And again. After the fourth time that they continued to ignore the facts in front of them (and the spaceship that wasn't), Festinger concluded, "A man with a conviction is a hard man to change."

Similarly, the men on the Nobel Committee had their own version of the spacemen—a belief that a woman couldn't possibly deserve the most prestigious science prize in the world. So even when they had new information—Meitner had made a brilliant discovery!—they dismissed it. A woman could only support a man's better work. They had to be right. The spaceship would show up.

Meitner had encountered similar situations for her whole career. She got her PhD in physics in Vienna but had no job prospects so moved to Berlin. The situation there was a little better, and she was the first woman in Germany to become a full professor in physics. But still. Despite her position, she wasn't allowed into the main laboratories at the University of Berlin and ended up working out of a carpenter's shop in the basement. The closest ladies' room was down the street. Whenever she was walking with Otto Hahn, her colleagues made a point of snubbing her and saying hello only to him. Forget Mean Girls. The Mean Boys are *really* mean.

Life is complicated, and matters other than gender come into play, too. Meitner was from a Viennese Jewish background, but when the Nazi regime began closing in, she was absorbed in her work and didn't want to leave her lab. Only when Germany was closing its borders in 1938 did she realize that she had to escape. In a touching moment of farewell, Otto Hahn gave Meitner his mother's diamond ring—not for love but for money. She might need it to bribe the border guards. She ultimately crossed into Holland and then went on to Sweden, where she continued her work. Right under the noses of the men on the Nobel Committee, you might say.

Many current scientists are mortified by how Meitner was treated and want to make up for it. A crater on the moon and another one on Venus have been named after her, as have buildings, schools, streets, and prizes. A statue of her now stands in Berlin. She might not have been recognized as a star in her own day, but now she is an asteroid—6999 Meitner is part of the main asteroid belt orbiting the sun.

My very favorite honor for Meitner is one that I think would have made her particularly happy. Remember the periodic table that hung on the wall of your chemistry class in high school? It arranges all the chemical elements according to their atomic number. One writer described a new box on the periodic table as "the most iconic real estate in science." Finding a new element is a big deal, and in 1917, Meitner and Hahn discovered the chemical element protactinium, now number 91 on the chart.

For years, elements were named after mythological creatures or the place where they were discovered. But in the last hundred years or so, new element names recognize great scientists like Albert Einstein and Niels Bohr and Enrico Fermi. One is named for Copernicus, who upended our view of the universe by realizing that the earth revolves around the sun. And in 1997, element 109 was named . . . meitnerium.

It's nice to see Lise Meitner, a woman responsible for great breakthroughs and original thinking, nestled nicely with Einstein and Copernicus. Genius enshrined in the periodic table.

Let's not underestimate what a dramatic change that entails. It's tough to throw over a belief and take a new position. Most people cling to their false beliefs about what women can achieve because it's easier than letting facts get in the way. The scientists who discovered (and named) meitnerium and those who found (and named) the Meitner asteroid and the artists who created the statue in Berlin were okay with overthrowing the status quo. They were eager to point out that a woman had done awesome work and that the conclusions men held about women scientists were simply wrong. They could accept that Lise Meitner was a genius. I have huge admiration for them.

In thinking about women and genius, I found myself with a haunting harmony stuck in my head—a snippet of a song from the award-winning musical *Hamilton*. As far as earworms, you could do worse than something written by Lin-Manuel Miranda. But it was the stirring words that are repeated several times as a refrain during the show that I couldn't shake:

Who lives
Who dies
Who tells your story.

It was becoming very clear to me that genius doesn't stand on its own. How achievements are seen both in the moment and in the greater vantage of history depends greatly on who tells your story—or whether your story gets told at all. And when men control the narrative, as they have for so long, the story of the women geniuses often drifts away. They don't fit the image of the world, the belief system on who should and shouldn't achieve.

Who lives, who dies, who tells your story.

One of my favorite authors, Joan Didion, once said that we tell ourselves stories in order to live. We also tell ourselves stories in order to understand where we fit into the world and how we can make sense of our own talents. Genius women have lived and died, but if nobody told their stories, it was as if they didn't live at all.

The New York Times, which calls itself the newspaper of record, recently admitted that when it comes to recognizing women, their records aren't very complete at all. Since the paper began in the 1850s, only about 10 percent of the obituaries published have been of women. In 2018, the editors launched a series called "Overlooked" to pay homage to women who weren't considered important enough at the times of their deaths to mention. Among the very first group were women we would surely credit now as geniuses in their fields. Charlotte Brontë, author of *Jane Eyre.* The poet Sylvia Plath. Ada Lovelace, who died in 1852 and is now credited with envisioning (and programming) computers a century before Bill Gates was even born. Photographer Diane Arbus.

All of them had extraordinary ability, but it was only decades later that they got enough celebrity to be considered geniuses. Plath couldn't get her novel *The Bell Jar* published in the United States before her death. It has since sold more than three million copies, and she was awarded a posthumous Pulitzer Prize. She died at age thirty of suicide. Would earlier recognition have saved her? She suffered from a serious depression, so the answer is unknown, but it is tragic to imagine that with her talents unnoticed, she simply gave up.

Most of the others never gave up. When Charlotte Brontë was just twenty years old, she sent a sample of her writing to England's poet laureate at the time, Robert Southey. In an infamous letter back to her, he praised her poetic gift but then scolded that "literature cannot be the business of a woman's life: & it ought not to be."

Charlotte thanked him for the advice—and then ignored it. You don't have to be a *Jane Eyre* fan (and I admit that I'm not) to recognize that the book in its time was groundbreaking and important. Her sister Emily went on to write *Wuthering Heights,* and the third sister, Anne, wrote *The Tenant of Wildfell Hall,* often considered one of the first feminist novels. The women started by using male pen names, but then stood boldly by their own identities. Anne ultimately made it clear that she didn't think there was any difference between men and women. "I am satisfied that if a book is a good one, it is so whatever the sex of the author may be," she wrote.

The genius of women is to persist even when nobody believes in them.

Walking through London and thinking about women who developed their genius despite all efforts to suppress them, I changed my course and headed over to Westminster Abbey. Once inside, I spent an hour admiring the impressive tombs of kings and queens—and then walked down the same long aisle that Kate Middleton did when she married Prince William. But princess fantasies will never help women other than Kate (and maybe Meghan) achieve greatness, so I headed over to the Poets' Corner, with its memorials to great writers and other creative artists.

It took me a while to find the memorial to poet Robert Southey, who had tried hard to discourage Charlotte Brontë, but there it was. I guess one misogynist letter wasn't enough to keep him out of Westminster. Nearby, I noticed the memorial to William Shakespeare—and right next to that was the large stone engraved with the names and dates of Charlotte, Emily, and Anne Brontë. I looked back at Southey and wondered how he felt knowing that he hadn't stopped the great women writers at all—and they had far surpassed him in fame. For all eternity, he would look out and see the words on their stone. *With courage to endure.*

For most genius women over the centuries, the merging of talent and recognition never occurred, and the tragedy of their lost potential is the appalling price we pay for generations of sexism and repression. And yet for as far back as you can look—from Hypatia to Charlotte Brontë to Lise Meitner—extraordinary women have been making vital discoveries in science and math, creating brilliant art and music, and explaining the universe in ways that Copernicus could never have imagined. People tried to quash their genius, but the women still wrote great books and ended up in Westminster Abbey. Nobel Committees snubbed them, but they kept working and discovering and asteroids were named for them. That they flourished in less-than-ideal circumstances made me want to find out why it is that sometimes—just sometimes—the genius of women can't be stopped.

CHAPTER 2

The Outrageous Bias Against Mozart's Sister

Even as it was becoming very clear to me that genius needs to be nurtured and recognized and doesn't appear full-blown, I kept running into an opposite view, so romanticized in movies and pop culture that I began to think of it as the Matt Damon Problem. As a young actor, Damon starred in the movie *Good Will Hunting,* playing a janitor from a tough neighborhood in Boston who cleans classrooms at night. When he sees the intricate math problems that a professor leaves on the blackboard, he puts down his mop and solves them. A natural genius! He's untutored but brilliant.

The movie was a hit—and not just because Damon is a fine actor. The genius janitor fit into our popular belief that great insights come as a bolt of lightning, an inexplicable flash of perception that some people have and the rest of us lack. We love the stories of Mozart composing concertos at age five or the mathematician John von Neumann doing complicated calculations in his head at age six. (He could speak ancient Greek, too.) And there was Damon himself, who dropped out of Harvard to write the screenplay for the movie with his childhood friend Ben Affleck—and got an Academy Award. Who needs a college degree when you're a natural genius!

While the concept of spontaneous genius is great for the movies, it's not very accurate. In almost every field, geniuses flourish because of the people and opportunities and expectations around them. The most brilliant natural mind will wither if it's not encouraged. Even Damon's genius janitor needed the help of a kindly therapist (played by Robin Williams) to handle the emotional issues standing in the way of full-fledged geniusdom. Damon's screenplay also didn't spring into existence unaided. He first wrote it for a class at Harvard and later solicited advice on it from Hollywood geniuses like director Rob Reiner and writer William Goldman.

A decade after he got that first Oscar, I spent some time with Damon when I wrote two magazine cover stories about him. By then, he was a huge star with blockbusters like *The Bourne Identity* (and its sequels) and *Ocean's Eleven* (and its sequels) and *Saving Private Ryan* (no sequel). I liked Damon because he was smart and fun to talk to—but also focused and determined and hardworking. After I showed him a draft of one of the stories, he called me three times to clarify small points. He was in the middle of a movie shoot, so it wasn't like he had a lot of time, but he was determined to get every detail right. So maybe the answer to the Matt Damon Problem is that the nitty-gritty of genius is different than it looks. Even if you're born with a halo of smarts and talent, you need to buff it every day, and have others do the same, if you want the glow to radiate. Ultimately whom we nurture and whom we recognize help determine who becomes a genius.

That's even true for a prodigy like Mozart. Yes, he started playing keyboard and violin at age three and by five had performed for royalty. His Symphony No. 1 in E Flat Major may not be his very best, but give him a break—he wrote it at age eight. He followed it with forty more symphonies and some six hundred other pieces.

But Mozart's early talent was also expertly nurtured. His father was a composer and violinist who taught him music, and young Mozart practiced for endless hours. His father took him on tour in Europe when he was young and introduced him to other composers and musicians who helped and encouraged him. He became a court musician in Salzburg, and when that didn't pay enough, he went off in search of better opportunities in Paris and Munich and Vienna. By the time he died at thirty-five, he had worked with energy and purpose for every moment of his life, moving from established positions rather than letting his creativity be stifled. There's a joke in Salzburg that if you tell a friend to meet you at Mozart's house, you'll never find each other. There are too many of them.

Now let's just imagine for a moment what would have happened if our young prodigy were a girl in the eighteenth century. A female Wolfgang might also have begun composing at age five. But it's unlikely that her father would have taken her on that tour of Europe. She wouldn't have performed before royalty or been given opera commissions or been feted as the court musician by the ruler of Salzburg. Instead of being encouraged and given the chance to be great, she would have been urged to stay home and maybe learn some needlework. The genius spark might have ignited despite all odds—but it might also have been stomped out.

I'm not just making that up. Mozart did have an older sister named Maria Anna, known as Nannerl, who was extraordinarily talented, performing on the harpsichord and touring with her brother when they were both young. Some reports say she was better than her little sibling and that he idolized and learned from her. But it didn't really matter. Once she hit her teens, her father deemed it inappropriate for her to perform anymore and sent her home to get married. Can you imagine how frustrating it must have been for her to sit at home, expected to be docile and submissive, after getting accolades for her talents on the stages of Vienna and Paris? She didn't have any options in that society, though, so she married a widower with a bunch of children, had a few more of her own, and continued with perhaps a perfectly nice life. But her potential to be known, centuries later, as a genius? Any chance of that was ended.

I suppose Maria Anna could have stood up to her father and the whole society and kept playing her music. Maybe that would have been a sign of true genius. But it seems overwhelming to demand that if you are an extraordinarily talented woman and want to be heard, you must also possess the stoic heart of a rebel. We never asked Wolfgang to take on the whole world. We just left him alone to do what he loved. His sister never got that chance.

Whatever innate differences may exist between men and women appear to pale next to the bigger question of how each is nurtured and encouraged. If you're looking at talents in any field—whether it's driving, painting, or advanced physics—people usually fall along some simple bell curve. A few people are really terrible, most are clustered in the middle, and then some are the outliers at the far end.

If we draw those curves for something where there is a measurable difference between men and women—like height—the peak curves are in slightly different places since the average man is taller than the average woman. Fine. But that says absolutely nothing about the height of you or me or your cousin Jennie who plays basketball for Notre Dame. The overlap is huge, and the differences *within* the groups of men and *within* the groups of women are a lot more dramatic than the distinctions between them.

People regularly try to make blanket distinctions between men and women. But doing that sucks you into a black hole from which there is no exit. The enormous overlap among the traits of women and men means there is no way you can accurately and fully separate any trait or achievement by gender. If I say that women are better at being insightful and emotional, you can no doubt tell me about a heterosexual man you know who cries at rom-coms and recites Persian poetry. Or about the woman boss you had who was cold and heartless. Generalizations are useless.

My husband and I attended a dinner party recently in Florida where a young couple began talking about replacing the hood of their stove. "We can't seem to agree," said the husband. "The hood a man likes is different from what a woman likes." His wife nodded somberly at that obvious fact, and there were murmurs of agreement around the table. Later that night, I asked my husband what they had meant.

"I have no idea, but everybody else seemed to understand," he said.

"Do we have a male hood or a female hood?"

"We better find out. It's embarrassing not to know," he said. We both started laughing and began making up (slightly dirty) jokes about whether a female or male stove hood would do better in terms of sucking the air. It was ridiculous—but nobody at the table had even blinked an eye. Other gender-based distinctions, equally ridiculous, also get treated as fact rather than foolishness.

Sometimes the most egregious comments *do* get challenged. Academics have been arguing about genius and intelligence for years, and the question of why there are more successful men than women in certain fields can still whip up a pretty ferocious debate. Former Harvard president Larry Summers lost all credibility among many of his colleagues (and added that "former" to his title) after he asked in a 2005 academic conference if "intrinsic aptitude" could explain why there were fewer women than men in sciences. Molecular biologist Nancy Hopkins of MIT walked out in the middle of his comments.

"I just couldn't breathe because this kind of bias makes me physically ill," Dr. Hopkins said later. "Let's not forget that people used to say that women couldn't drive an automobile."

Used to say? In Saudi Arabia, where women were banned from driving until 2018, one common explanation was that driving would put too much stress on their ovaries, pushing their reproductive organs into dangerous positions that would keep them from having children. A top government official made that argument as recently as 2016, making you wonder if Saudi Arabia planned to keep up its fertility rate by making women stand all the time. But don't laugh. A similar explanation was used barely a century ago in America and England for keeping women out of universities—if the blood was going to women's brains, men explained, it couldn't go to their reproductive organs. Men have been well practiced at excluding women under the guise of protecting them—all while using fantastical information that has no basis in science or fact.[1]

So I can understand why Nancy Hopkins felt physically ill at Larry Summers's suggestion. Because it should be obvious that plenty of women have the potential to be stars in science and math and physics. But like the would-be women drivers in Saudi Arabia, if they're not taught and given the keys, that potential will never be realized. Cultural expectations, encouragement, and motivation are ultimately more important than anything else in creating geniuses, basketball players, and Indy 500 drivers.

---

1 The practice hasn't gone out of style. We continue to hear many versions of it among those men determined to diminish women by controlling their bodies.

Looking back over the centuries, it's rather shocking to realize just how little has been done to nurture talented women in any field and give them the chances that they deserve. A poster that I saw while I was in London celebrated 150 years of women at the University of London with the smiling faces of women who had attended the school and been important to society. It was nice to see that recognition in the center of a big city. But it also struck me that 150 years isn't a very long time. Before that, women in Britain simply had no access to a university education. My lovely visit at Oxford reminded me that it is one of the oldest universities around, going back to about 1167. But as I'd learned, women couldn't attend until 1879 and couldn't get a degree until 1920, and a woman didn't become a full professor until 1948. That's almost eight hundred years! How many brilliant women were overlooked in that time and how much talent wasted?

Being an American, I'd like to feel smug about our more democratic country—but we don't have any bragging rights. Harvard went for 312 years before making a woman a tenured professor, and that happened only because the president of the United Fruit Company gave a bunch of money for a chair for "a distinguished woman scholar," also in 1948. To fill the position, Harvard poached a scholar named Helen Cam from Cambridge. It was another ten years before Harvard promoted a woman to tenure from within its ranks. And yet another ten years before women were allowed in the front door of the Faculty Club.

In case you've stopped counting with me, let me clarify. Until 1968, women couldn't use the main entrance of the Faculty Club at Harvard. They were hustled off to the Ladies Waiting Room. Nineteen sixty-eight wasn't so long ago, so while we're wondering where all the women geniuses could be, here's one possibility: Until recently, they may have been trapped in the room next door, shunted off to the side once again.

I was oblivious to most of the boundaries when I was young, and fortunately, by the time I was applying to college, women were being accepted into all the Ivy League schools. I spent a happy four years at Yale knowing that impressive people had walked these courtyards before me—and now I was one of them. Being part of that group gave me the courage to dream big. But what would have happened to my sense of possibility if I grew up a generation (or even a decade) earlier? You can go to many colleges or not go at all and still succeed. But what's harder to overcome is a drumbeat that insists you don't belong and aren't good enough. *No women allowed.*

When I graduated, I moved to Manhattan and joined the Yale Club of New York City with several of my friends. At that point, every graduate and undergraduate school at Yale admitted women and we were very much allowed into the front door of the Yale Club. But—and this still seems incredible to me—we weren't allowed in the pool. When a few of us raised a ruckus, the club manager officiously explained that the rule couldn't be changed because the male members swam naked in the pool.

"Maybe you could cover up the male members with Speedos," one of my friends suggested.

"Or at least something baggy from Brooks Brothers," I added.

The manager didn't appreciate our humor, and he wasn't budging. I dropped my club membership and started jogging in Central Park, where there was no question about men wearing shorts. Women weren't allowed in the Yale Club pool until 1987, which is frighteningly recent. (My husband has ties older than that—and he wears them.) To put this whole story in perspective, the Yale Club wasn't some crazy outlier. Congress has a pool that banned women—*our nation's elected officials!*—until 2009. It was the same story—some of the male representatives liked to swim in the buff. When you look at the saggy, draggy, old men of Congress, you realize this must have been a ridiculous excuse for blatant misogyny. Even they couldn't have wanted to see themselves naked.

Arguments about why women shouldn't be allowed to participate in a school or club or event sound reasonable—until they don't. That the men needed to swim naked now sounds laughable, but it was taken as gospel at the time. At the time I was fighting it, I found the gym issue more amusing than annoying, but I realize now that those girls-versus-boys distinctions have a serious resonance and create a deep divide. To be hailed as a genius of any sort you need to be noticed, and it's tough to get noticed when you're not allowed in the front door. Or when the guys quite literally don't want to play with you and so ban you from the gym. As I look back now, I wonder how much of the intellectual exuberance I felt as a child started to get tamped down by social expectations. Would I be smarter and more successful if I'd had someone encouraging me to ignore all barriers? I think so. I'm proud of what I've done—but slightly peeved at myself that I didn't tell the world to back off so I could do more.

In the blink of an eye that gets us from those locked doors to the present, the change has been astounding and leaves us wondering how we could ever have believed that anything else was acceptable. The Yale Club has renovated its gym and expanded the women's locker rooms. (I am happy to be a member again.) More than half the schools in the Ivy League have now been led by women presidents. More women now attend colleges around the country than men. Drew Gilpin Faust can walk in any front door she wants at Harvard— and she opened a few doors too, since she became president of the university in 2007. As she said at the time, "I'm not the woman president of Harvard. I'm the president of Harvard."

I am in awe of women over the years and centuries who were barred from formal education and managed to become genius intellectuals anyway. The influential French firebrand Madame de Staël stated unequivocally back in the late 1700s that "genius has no sex." And then she set out to prove it. Denied (like all women then) a formal education, she used her ingenuity to defy expectations and create her own centers of learning. Instead of the standard halls of academia, she created "salons" in her home that attracted the great thinkers of the day—most of them men, of course. With brilliant people assembled around her, she gathered both insight and political power.

The stories about Madame de Staël get my heart racing because intellectual courage can be as invigorating as any other sort. She had the advantage of coming from a wealthy family, which surely helped her escape social strictures and create a stimulating and original life. Her father was a banker and the finance minister to Louis XVI, and her mother also hosted well-attended salons, but Madame de Staël's fiery intellect and passionate ambition were really what set her apart. She rallied her powerful friends to take political stands supporting the French Revolution, and she became a major bane of Napoléon. How important was she? The French memoirist Madame de Chastenay famously said at the time that there were three great powers struggling against Napoléon for the soul of Europe—England, Russia, and Madame de Staël.

Napoléon resented everything about Madame de Staël, and he exiled her from France more than once. It particularly galled him to be needled by a woman. Banished from France, she still continued her salons in Italy. Part of her genius was recognizing the limitations of the world she lived in—and finding a way around them. Since her energy and genius already set her apart, she made flamboyance part of her style, wearing colorful silk turbans with bright peacock feathers. One biographer of Madame de Staël, Oxford professor Angelica Goodden, described her as an "argumentative and assertive creature" who refused to follow "the social paradigm of female decorum and male authority." She had been told endlessly that true happiness came from being subordinate to a husband, and at age twenty she agreed to an arranged marriage with the Swedish ambassador to the French court. She imagined what it would be like to close herself off from the world, escape into submissive domesticity, and tell her husband, "I could have shone on the world's stage, I could have received men's applause, but only *you* interest me on earth." She thought about it— but that's not what she did.

Instead, she stayed married but lived mostly apart from her husband amidst a whirlwind life of intellect and influence. She had children, and like so many brilliant women, she struggled to reconcile the personal and public sides of herself and to assert her individuality in a society that demanded women conform to the social codes. Living within a male-dominated society, she knew that she needed to play the game correctly. People described her as a "great conversationalist"— and she was able to attract followers with her quick mind and clever thoughts. The "conversationalist" label always sounds a bit condescending to me—as if it were a superficial charm rather than her powerful intellect that made the evenings at her salons so entertaining. Writers and great thinkers came to be inspired by her—and in turn, she learned from them. Seducing with her genius mind, she had passionate affairs with some of the great intellectuals of the time. There was nothing sexier than her boldly unbounded exuberance and her passionate ideas about liberty and equality.

Men told Madame de Staël that she couldn't have power and Napoléon told her she couldn't live in France and the whole world told her to go home and be a submissive woman. Instead, she was an original, making her own rules while inspiring men to believe in her and listen to her ideas. Call it the great work-around. If you wanted to shine on the world's stage as a woman in the eighteenth century, you had to dance around all the barriers—wearing high heels and bustle skirts. Nobody did that as well as Madame de Staël. She was a great example of the genius of women, conquering the challenges of the time, whatever it took.

Defining genius is complicated in any era. Ancient Romans connected genius to divinity, so saluting a genius meant recognizing the divine spirit—a sort of guardian angel—who offered protection and brought success. By the 1600s, when the saintly became more secular, the men defining genius created it—not surprisingly—in their own image. Dartmouth history professor Darrin McMahon, who studies the history of ideas during the Enlightenment, says that by the eighteenth century genius was viewed "in keeping with long-standing prejudice, almost exclusively as a man."

That long-standing prejudice is now even longer standing, since it continues to this moment.

Some academics worry that we have overly democratized the idea of genius, using the accolade for winning football coaches and top fashion designers. You can find a Genius Bar in Apple stores, a marketing gimmick that has helped make Apple the most financially successful retailer in the world. The company was shrewd enough to realize that when the screen on your computer goes black, you'd rather have a nominal Genius fiddling with your keyboard than a random tech-support guy in a T-shirt.

While we're open to the idea of genius extending in many directions, we've been less amenable to genius—even in name—being female. One woman named Sandy who worked at a Genius Bar told me that most of her counterparts were men—and customers could be condescending. More than once, she'd been asked to have one of the guys check her work. "We all follow the same procedures and guidelines," she told me, but to keep the customer happy, she would have one of the male Geniuses come over and essentially repeat whatever she had just said. "And that made it correct," Sandy said, rolling her eyes.

Even in a moment of mini-crisis (*My iPhone broke!*) our unfounded gender expectations trump all reason. At the Genius Bar, you expect the tech expert will be a guy. When you call the Turkey Talk Line at Thanksgiving, you expect a woman to help you through the mysteries of basting. Neither of these makes any sense. Men can talk turkey, and women can teach tech. Some of the greatest computer programmers were women—including Grace Hopper, a rear admiral in the Navy in the 1940s who helped develop programming languages that are still used today. She was a genius at coding and computer language—and she had the perseverance to get her ideas known. A college at Yale University was recently named after Amazing Grace in recognition of her being a pioneer in the computing world we now take for granted.

We can all probably agree that Grace Hopper was a genius and the people at the Genius Bar are simply well-trained techs. But ever since the ancient Romans, the effort to determine who is a genius has brought one ridiculous conceit after another into vogue. Most of them were meant to exclude women—and did just that. A popular idea in the 1800s held that the shape of your skull determined how smart you were. Then came the variant of measuring the inside of the head rather than the outside, with some claiming that the greater your brain mass, the greater your intelligence. Men on average are bigger than women, so they have bigger body parts—kidneys and livers and brain mass and feet. If you connect brain mass to intelligence you can claim—QED!—that men are smarter than women. But it doesn't make any sense. As Professor McMahon slyly noted, "If it were really true that size alone mattered in questions of intelligence, then the whale would be lord of us all."

The notion that brain mass equates to genius was taken very seriously for a long time and, I'm sorry to say, continues to appear up to this very moment in some articles about how to measure intelligence. You can still read articles positing that since men have a bigger hippocampus or cerebellum, they should therefore be better at whatever activity takes place in those centers. The fact that the measurements are now done through MRI imaging seems to give the whole thing validity. But there's absolutely no evidence that this shopworn theory is true. Maybe we should ask the whales what they think.

Another questionable theory that persists is that genius is based completely on genetics. If you're looking for a culprit, you could blame Sir Francis Galton, the Victorian-era statistician and polymath who was a cousin of Charles Darwin. Galton came up with some good ideas—like using fingerprints to solve crimes—and some notably lousy ones—like trying to improve society through genetic manipulation (also called eugenics). His book *Hereditary Genius* caused a stir in his time, but he had the same problem as the supposed wizards measuring skull size—he started from his conclusion and worked backward.

Galton appreciated the celebrity element of genius, but instead of seeing celebrity as a challenge to his views on inherited talent, he took it as proof. In a wonder of circular thinking, Galton essentially claimed that genius made you famous and fame proved you were a genius. He counted up people who were famous and discovered that they were (surprise!) men from elite families. Professor McMahon points out that treating reputation alone as a sign of genius was "to completely ignore those structures of power that conferred it."

The long-standing nature-versus-nurture debate started with Galton, but he didn't see it as a debate at all. For him it was nature all the way. On that point almost any reasonable scientist would now have a simple response. He was wrong. Genes and environment—the components of nature and nurture—work together, and there's no sense in trying to separate them. Talent is a mix of hard work, natural abilities, social encouragement, and milieu. There is not a single gene for genius, any more than there is a single gene that makes you a good cook. You can be born with an unusually sharp sense of smell or taste, but your skill needs to be nurtured and encouraged. If nobody teaches you how to crack an egg, you'll never make a perfect soufflé.

Galton's dismissal of women's intelligence was particularly dangerous because, like the MRI-measured brains now, it was cloaked in the respectability of science. Galton once walked around counting the pretty women he saw, and based on that he made a "beauty map" of England. Laughable, right? And yet just think what it would be like to be a young woman in Aberdeen, the place Galton ranked the ugliest. Even when facts are just plain dumb, they have an effect on how we see ourselves—and how others see us.[2]

In his influential book *The Mismeasure of Man*, evolutionary biologist Stephen Jay Gould took aim at all the phony arguments that get made to claim there is a genetic basis for inequality. He showed that arguments about supposed "genetic determinism" were more social weapon than real science. He insisted that whether aimed at women or ethnic minorities, the genetic rationales were simply white men trying to prove the superiority of . . . white men.

The next method that came along for defining genius—IQ tests— seemed to have just as many faults and flaws. It should be pretty

---

2   The curator of the Galton Collection at University College London recently wrote that after studying Galton's work, she realized "how bat guano crazy it turns out to be at times."

obvious that you can't capture the range and diversity of talents in a single test. All you can measure is how well someone does answering those particular questions. Despite the great faith put in them, IQ tests don't seem to be predictive. In the early 1900s, psychologist Lewis Terman identified one thousand children with high IQs for a study of what he called "genius in the making." Ultimately, almost none of the would-be geniuses achieved any particular renown, and Professor McMahon has pointed out that the study failed to detect two men who would later be awarded Nobel Prizes in Physics.

IQ tests used to be (and often still are) given to kids with the results adjusted for age. But does getting a high score when you're eight mean you're a genius ever after? *Guinness World Records* used to list the world's highest recorded IQ, but it eventually dumped the category for being unreliable. It's crazy that we would consider IQ to be some holy number. You can get a high score and never achieve anything in life, and you can be a genius without it being reflected in your IQ. Researchers say that most of us credit the scores with being more determinative than they really are. Factors like perseverance and grit and motivation may ultimately be more important than any IQ-measurable ability. If you take two people with the same IQ and encourage one to believe in himself and go to great schools and let the other know that life will be better if she gets married and hides her intelligence—well, then the IQ is the least determinative part of the story.

When I was eight years old, I took that school-mandated IQ test, and a few weeks later, my mother was called up to my classroom. The teacher told her in solemn tones that I had scored a 150.

"That's a genius level," the teacher said, slightly awed.

My mother shrugged. She had three children and we were all bright, but if anybody was a genius, it was my older brother. His IQ score had come in a couple of points lower than mine, so my mom turned dismissive of the testing and discarded the numbers as meaningless. She didn't tell me the IQ result for months. When I finally heard about my 150, I took some secret delight in the result. But I ultimately agreed with my mother. My brother was the smart one.

I still admire my brother and think he is smarter than me. But it took me years (maybe until this very moment) to realize all the extraneous influences that went into my assessment. He was a boy. He was the oldest. He had to be the smartest.

Skull shape. Brain mass. How famous you may be. Heredity. IQ. Being a boy. They are all ways we have judged genius in the past. And it may be that, ultimately, not one of them means a thing. Whatever her hat size, give a smart person the right environment and the right opportunities, nurture her confidence and her talent, and she may become a genius. But don't expect that talent can stand on its own. Even if Mozart's sister, Maria Anna, possessed the most extraordinary natural genius the world had ever seen, it wouldn't have mattered. Because once she was separated from colleagues on the public stage and forced to retreat to a life of domesticity, her creative genius didn't stand a chance. The tragedy for women throughout so much of history has been how often their genius wasn't nurtured, but instead left to ebb and, tragically, fade.

CHAPTER 3

Einstein's Wife and the Theory of Relativity

On a sunny morning, I took a train down to Princeton to wander around the place where the now-iconic genius Albert Einstein lived and worked for many years. You don't have to be a scientist to know that Einstein changed physics with his theory of relativity and came up with the famous equation $E = mc^2$ to explain the connection between mass and energy. By now, the mythic halo around his achievements glistens so brightly that it's almost hard to remember that he was a real person who married, divorced, and married again.

As for that first marriage—was it young love, or more complicated than that? Mileva Marić, Einstein's first wife, was herself a star in math and physics, and the two met at the Polytechnic Institute in Zurich, where she was one of very few women admitted. Some people have suggested that she might have collaborated on the breakthrough papers that Einstein wrote in 1905. One bit of evidence is that Einstein wrote her many letters a couple of years earlier that refer to "our work" and "our" theory of relativity. One report says that her name was included on the original versions of his most famous manuscripts.[1] When they separated, he promised her the proceeds of the Nobel Prize that he expected to win—and he followed through. Why offer her the prize money rather than, say, alimony or child support, unless she deserved it for her contribution?

The mysteries of any marriage are hard to unravel, and I don't have a way to judge how many spirited conversations Albert and Mileva shared about physics and math. But more interesting is the outraged fury that the very suggestion of a collaboration engenders in men who are Team Albert all the way. In articles and academic papers, they will usually agree that she was a sounding board and very familiar with his work. But they steadfastly ignore the letter he wrote saying how proud and happy he would be "when the two of us together will have brought our work on the relative motion to a victorious conclusion!" It can't possibly mean what it says. They dismiss the "our" as the rantings of a young man in love. Maybe it is. Or maybe "our work" means . . . our work.

Einstein was a genius with grand ideas, but he turned to some of the great mathematicians of the time to help with the complexities needed for his theories. Even the Team Albert fans understand that type of collaboration. But that he might have worked with his wife? Several respected scientists and historians have written that Mileva helped Albert with the mathematics of his special relativity paper in 1905. That shouldn't be a big deal—getting support in developing intricate theories is common, and Mileva's help on that one element is usually accepted. But the idea of a woman being involved in the grand theory of relativity seems to make some people crazy. You can find endless rants online about how her math grades weren't even as good as his at the Polytechnic Institute, where they met—though none

---

1   He wrote four groundbreaking papers in 1905, when he was just twenty-six, and one of those papers led to his 1921 Nobel Prize.

mention that he flunked the entrance exam the first time he took it. Why is it so hard to say that Einstein was a genius, but his wife had extraordinary talents, too? Marić never had the chance to fully develop her genius. After she and Einstein married in 1903 and had two sons together, she didn't see a way to sustain her scientific ambitions. Much like Mozart's sister, she receded into the background, devoting herself to her children, her greater talents lost and subsumed.

In Marić's time, a woman's role was behind a man, and there are a lot of people who would like to keep it that way. For many generations, women succeeded by being unthreatening and not letting anyone realize what they were doing. They resorted to `manipulation rather than mastery. Perhaps one trait distinctive to women of genius was recognizing reality and boundaries—however artificially created—and working around them. Like Madame de Staël in Napoleonic France, they could create their own salons and sources of power, and like Mileva Marić, they might whisper ideas to their husbands and watch them flourish. But they rarely stepped into the limelight themselves.

It's time for that to end. A true genius changes the world in a way that other people follow, and that can happen only if you are standing out front, able to be noticed. A genius gives us a new way of thinking about time-and-space or art or motion or how to write a novel. If she is dismissed or ignored, her breakthroughs can't have the resonance through the ages that they might deserve. Women need to be unafraid of making waves themselves. Being a genius means being slightly different from other people. That can be tough for young women who receive the relentless message that they should fit in. As the philosopher Rebecca Newberger Goldstein put it, "If genius is an aberration, then female genius is viewed as significantly more aberrational, since it's seen as an aberration of femaleness itself."

It doesn't have to be, though. A few extraordinary women are integrating genius and femaleness and proving by their very existence that the two aren't at odds. In search of that modern woman genius on the Princeton campus, I headed over to the office of astrophysicist Jo Dunkley, a tenured physics professor who has won a raft of prestigious awards in astrophysics and cosmology. I had tried to prepare for our interview by studying up on her pivotal findings, but when she opened the door for me, I realized I wasn't prepared at all.

Most of us envision a genius in the style of Albert Einstein—crazy white hair, slouchy figure, wrinkled face, and a far-off look in his eye. But who ever expects a genius to look like Jo Dunkley? Slim and gracefully pretty with bouncy blond hair and peaches-and-cream skin, she flashed a lustrous smile as she invited me in. I usually don't describe people's appearance unless it's relevant to their profession. Models and movie stars, yes. Scientists, no. So I hope Dunkley will forgive my wandering into the superficial—because in this case it *is* relevant. Philosopher Goldstein's formulation of genius being an aberration of femaleness is deeply embedded in our unconscious. Even though I had been studying and pondering the subject, I hadn't fully shaken free of that concept, and I caught myself thinking that Dunkley didn't look like a genius scientist at all. Then I remembered the famous comment Gloria Steinem tossed off many decades ago at a birthday party when a reporter told her that she didn't look forty.

"This is what forty looks like," she said. "We've been lying for so long, who would know?"

And looking at Jo Dunkley, I thought—

This is what genius looks like. We've been ignoring genius women for so long, who would know?

"I'm so glad you're here—can I get you some tea?" Dunkley asked. Warm and friendly in her floral dress, she might have come straight from a garden party at the best country club in town.

Instead, she had come to Princeton straight from Oxford, where she was a tenured professor at age thirty-four and considered one of the most brilliant young physicists around. In the announcement when she was hired, one of the chaired professors in the Princeton physics department called her "a fabulous scientist and a wonderful person."

Several academics had already pointed out to me that reference letters for even the most extraordinary women professors usually talk about their personalities and how hardworking they are. Men are simply described by the quality of their achievements. So the "wonderful person" comment may have had a tinge of the unwitting sexism that ultimately hurts women.

On the other hand, Dunkley *did* seem to be a wonderful person. She was wildly excited about her work, but she was also happy to tell me about her two little daughters.

"I love being a mum!" she said, describing some adorable activity her little girls had done the other day. It struck me that she had solved the Mileva Marić problem—managing to be a devoted mom who could also remain devoted to her work.

Dunkley researches vast cosmic questions like "why we're here now, what process got us here, and how we fit into the bigger picture of space." When she was still a postdoc, Dunkley used data coming in from a NASA satellite (the Wilkinson Microwave Anisotropy Probe, or WMAP, if you must know) to estimate the age of the universe better than anyone else had done.

"I was the person who said, 'Right. The universe is 13.8 billion years old,'" she said cheerfully.

"You put an official date on the universe?" I asked in amazement.

"Well, yes," she said.

"That's pretty cool, don't you think?"

"Exactly." She smiled. "We've refined it since then, but I've tried to be at the forefront of making those estimates as we get new data from our biggest telescopes."

Dunkley analyzes light from when the universe was only 400,000 years old, which means she is observing a scene from about 13.8 billion years ago. It is possible because it takes significant time for light to travel from galaxies far, far away—or even from something much closer. When you look at the sun, for example, you actually see how it was eight minutes ago, and the light from the nearest stars takes a few years to get to our eyes. Though most of us learned that in high school science class, the concept remains slightly mind-boggling. It's as if your twelve-year-old daughter complained that you still see her as a six-year-old—and she was right.

Studying light from the earliest days of the universe is a fairly amazing activity, and Dunkley likes using mathematical tools to describe reality and model the universe and answer big questions. But when she was an undergraduate at Cambridge (she grew up in the UK) it never occurred to her to pursue astrophysics. She was the pretty and popular girl who was captain of her college lacrosse team, and her friends were decidedly not the nerdy science students. After college, she set off backpacking in remote areas of South America. At night, sitting under the incredibly clear skies, she read a popular book on physics, and as she looked up at the Milky Way, her mind began somersaulting with ideas. She decided that she would pursue a PhD—and try to get new insights into the universe.

After she got her degree and began rising in her field, Dunkley realized that the modern genius doesn't sit alone in a room trying to be smart. While she could be happy writing computer code and trying to answer questions in a way nobody had ever done before, she quickly learned that the most successful scientists have both very clever ideas and an ability to inspire other people. Concepts in science are too big and theories are too broad for epiphanies to occur in isolation.

"People make progress in science—in the world in general—if they can get others excited about their ideas," Dunkley told me. "I thought my personality would be best working with other people. Inspiring a team is exactly what I do in science."

Dunkley's genius is in creating theories of the universe. She uses vast amounts of data collected from a powerful telescope in Chile to think about how old the universe is, how fast it's growing, what it's made of. In a nicely cosmic twist, the telescope she relies on for data is located just a few miles from where she had gone backpacking after college. At the time, she thought that was the ends of the earth. Now she visits there often.

I had planned to ask Dunkley about the struggles of a woman in science, but as we talked, I realized that for much of her career, her being female had been distinctly beside the point. It never actually occurred to her that she didn't belong or that being a girl should stand in her way. She won prizes and awards early in her career and received big grants to continue her research. She had supportive mentors and never particularly noticed or worried about the lack of women role models in her field. "I feel confident about what I'm able to do, and I think I should be here doing it. Until quite recently, I didn't think about the problems of women in science at all," she told me.

If one woman can become a big star in her field despite all the obstacles, what can we learn from her? Dunkley had the advantage of living a century later than Mileva Marić Einstein, and she didn't think about the barriers of being a woman. She just went ahead with what she wanted to do, sure that being a scientist wouldn't interfere with having the family she also wanted. That positive spirit combined with her tenacity and intelligence and creative thinking made her shine as brightly as the light she studies. Maybe that was one secret of genius. You just keep doing it. Dunkley was exhilarated by her work, so she got on with it and wouldn't be stopped.

Nobody can stop you but yourself, goes a popular quote on Instagram. So why are we stopping ourselves? That's the million-dollar question—but these days, you can get in a lot of trouble for asking it. Sheryl Sandberg, the chief operating officer of Facebook, gave a TED Talk a few years ago describing how women unintentionally hold themselves back from succeeding. She turned it into the huge bestselling book *Lean In,* which offered tips and techniques and inspiring stories for how to make yourself a player and take a (literal and metaphoric) seat at the table. Having worked at Google and Facebook and spent years as one of the few top women executives in tech, Sandberg knew all about bias and discrimination against women. She had seen it and experienced it, and she spent many pages pointing out structural problems that exist in the workplace. But her outlook was positive, and her real goal, she explained in many interviews, was "to change the conversation from what women can't do to what they can." The book sold four million copies, so a lot of people were listening to her advice.

But Sandberg was also widely attacked. Why was she telling women how to change and fit into the system when it's the system itself that needs to change? The corporations and institutions that don't hire enough women and don't pay them equally are the real villains! Focus on them! Tell them what to do, not the women!

Okay, sure. I don't disagree. We'd all like to snap our fingers and make the world equal and fair and honest. But Sandberg wasn't blaming the victims or letting the institutions off the hook. She was just being realistic about how change occurs. Having more female leaders, more women in positions of power, is a key part of the solution. But they have to get there. And maybe that means ignoring the structural issues until you are in a position to do something about them. "The shift to a more equal world will happen person by person," Sandberg said. When you're the boss, then you can hire more women and pay them equally. When you've made the breakthrough in physics or math that can't be ignored, you can bring other women along with you.

If you want to be a genius, the first truth may be a rather blunt one. You can see yourself as a victim because you're a woman. Or you can just get over it and get on with your work. I can't really explain why Sheryl Sandberg had the courage to lean in when she was starting her career or why Jo Dunkley never worried about asking a question when she was sitting in a big lecture hall surrounded by men. It's a common complaint of women that when they are vastly outnumbered, they are afraid to speak up. Dunkley was never afraid to speak. Sandberg wasn't afraid to lean.

For Dunkley, it was simple. *Get over it. Get on with the work. Don't be a victim.* But now that she is in a position to change the system, Dunkley is doing everything she can to encourage the women who don't find it quite so easy to just get on with it. She is aware that not everyone shares her confident style, and if we want to nurture genius in women, "we have to make room for different personalities and not allow success only for the people who shout the loudest." You can be a fantastic scientist and not share the boldness and confidence that she does. Dunkley now makes a major effort to boost other women. She goes to the women-in-science events that once seemed irrelevant to her—and often organizes them. The most extraordinary women in science (or most fields) will find a way to be heard, but it's the next 20 or 30 or 40 percent who can so easily become lost. With Dunkley as a role model, it's likely that more and more women will think about astrophysics. A genius at the very top of an incredibly exciting field, she is happy, brilliantly successful, and joyously fulfilled. If Einstein were still wandering around Princeton, he no doubt would have been delighted to meet her.

Both times that she was pregnant, Dunkley made a point of giving as many public talks as she could. She liked the visual of academic superstar in bloom to motherhood. It wasn't necessary to say anything directly—everyone could see that the roles of mother and scientist got along just fine. Dunkley told me that she and her husband, Faramerz Dabhoiwala, "co-parent completely. We really do it together. That's made a huge difference." Later, I discovered that her husband is a social historian who has written on the history of sex and is an expert on how sexual attitudes evolved. In his view, one of the revolutionary changes of the Enlightenment was that people began celebrating sex as not just any old pleasure but as a key way that we should enjoy life on earth. He also points out that for most of history, women were seen as the seducers, the more sexual beings who led men astray. The Victorians turned that centuries-old position around. Why we continue to believe them rather than the longer historical view is unclear.

"You must have interesting conversations at dinner," I said to Dunkley at one point.

"Oh, there's always a lot to talk about," she said with a laugh.

I didn't bring it up then, but it occurred to me that Dunkley's husband would never wonder if a smart woman can be sexy.

I mention that because many other people do, indeed, worry whether smart can be sexy. In movies and plays, intelligent women are portrayed as some version of Marian the Librarian—with hair in a bun, long skirts, and a repressed manner. When a recent study out of King's College London showed that smart women have better sex lives and twice as many orgasms as their less-savvy sisters, the local newspapers went slightly bonkers.

BRIGHT WOMEN ARE BRILLIANT IN BED, declared one headline.

INTELLIGENT WOMEN ENJOY SEX MORE THAN BIMBOS, said another.

The researcher who led the study is a professor of genetic epidemiology who has published more than eight hundred research articles and is ranked in the top 1 percent of the world's most published scientists. But none of his other work got quite the giddy reaction this one did. Though a serious study, it was treated with humor everywhere it was reported. The idea that smart women are also rollicking in bed somehow makes us laugh.

As a smart woman who likes a good romp, I have a hard time seeing why vacuous and vapid would ever be considered sexy. I suppose a spineless man might crave an even weaker woman to make himself feel better, and usually it is the most inadequate and ego-threatened men who set a standard for "feminine" as being submissive and unchallenging. Fortunately, there are many women now saying enough of that. If the geisha model of female attractiveness doesn't allow for strong and smart women, then good-bye, geisha. Feminist writer Chimamanda Ngozi Adichie suggests that we stop raising girls "to cater to the fragile egos of men." Maybe some men will be put off by a woman with talent and drive and ambition, but so what? As Adichie notes, a man who would be intimidated by her "is exactly the kind of man I would have no interest in."

After I left Dunkley, it occurred to me that ever since I started telling people that I was writing about the genius of women, I got a lot of delighted winks from women and worried looks from men who thought I had found some genius element distinct to being a woman. One man asked me if my message was *the mediocrity of men and the genius of women*! I told him it's a good slogan if you want to march on Washington, but I don't think it's the case. Genius traits are not embedded in either women's distinctiveness or men's. Some people I spoke to suggested that women are better at collaborating and communicating and caring about others—but once pressed, nobody was willing to stand behind those statements. Women and men have big overlaps in ability, and once you try to say that all of womankind (or mankind) is good at one thing, you suggest that all the shes (or hes) are not good at something else. From a global perspective, generalizations are just silliness.

Thinking about the shaky connection between gender and genius, I crossed the campus to talk to the one person I thought would have a good perspective—Shirley Tilghman, the molecular biologist who in 2001 became the first woman president of Princeton University. After twelve years at the top of the university, she returned to a role on the science faculty. One alum I met told me that "everyone loves Shirley," and ever since she left the presidential hot seat, that's probably truer than ever. Tilghman's combination of warmth and smarts and honesty is wonderfully compelling, and she seemed comfy and relaxed as we chatted in her sun-filled corner office. At the question of whether women bring something different to the genius table, though, she gave a sigh.

"I'm deeply ambivalent on the question of a distinct skill set. I get nervous the minute I start down that wormhole. I've gone back and forth on it throughout my career and I can't reach any conclusion in science," she said. Then she paused and gave me a big smile. "But it's not hard with leadership. I think women are much better leaders."

Uh-oh. It was possible that she was about to undermine my whole theory on the fatuousness of gender generalizations.

"Why would that be?" I asked.

"The key to being a good leader is having an idea and then convincing someone else that it's their idea, right? I think women do that more than men," she said.

Okay, fair enough. But if women do that more than men, it's probably because they *need* to do it more than men. Tilghman developed a leadership style that was inclusive, group oriented, and empathetic. She focused on team building and was more willing to share credit and yield credit. When women do that it's not an innate ability—it's a style they have figured out will work. Male leaders don't need to prove that they are unthreatening. They can take credit without being called nasty names behind their back. Women leaders, in politics and elsewhere, are expected to be likable. Just what that means is hazy, but clearly being smart, capable, and competent isn't enough. They still have to make the men feel good and convince them that all the top-notch ideas were theirs. It's noble to be willing to share credit, but you just have to hope that men will return the favor. Often, they don't. The result is that men's egos are salved—and women's own genius ideas go unacknowledged.

When Tilghman was starting out as a molecular biologist, women in top labs were still viewed with skepticism. She was determined not to be drummed out by fear or to let stereotypes affect her. She played a little game with herself where she closed her eyes and tried to picture a really great scientist. Once she got to the point where she pictured a woman as often as a man, she knew she was okay. The practical result was that when she organized scientific meetings, she invited a large number of women to participate. She wasn't making a point of equality—she had just learned to recognize genius, however it was clothed.

She carried her gender-blind flair for finding talent into the president's office. When she appointed several spectacularly qualified women to top positions at the university, it should have been an exciting model of how talent can triumph regardless of gender. But most people on campus had never taught themselves the close-your-eyes game, and when they tried to picture academic leaders, all they could imagine were men. The mainstream student newspaper editorialized in 2003 that it was "implausible" for so many women to be the most qualified candidates—and students across the political spectrum debated the fairness of the appointments. Tilghman was stunned. Implausible that women were as qualified as men? Was that still an argument at the beginning of the twenty-first century? She expected that Princeton's women undergraduates would rise in outrage at such a preposterous, sexist statement. But it didn't happen.

If you want to know what keeps women from becoming geniuses, the answer might be right there, in that lack of protest. Tilghman thinks that on an unconscious but heartfelt level, some of the smartest undergraduate women in the country had absorbed the much-hammered-in social message that men deserve top positions and women get them only because of unseemly machinations. There was much discussion on the campus about "quality versus diversity"—as if a man would get a job because he had the ability, while a woman was hired only for diversity. How offensive and how wrong. The women Tilghman appointed were brilliant and original thinkers who went on to be some of the most respected academic leaders in the country.[2] "The notion that I bent over backwards to find or hire them is just laughable," Tilghman told me. But instead of cheering, the women students were uncomfortable.

Tilghman asked Nan Keohane, a faculty member who had previously been the president of Duke, to help her figure out what was going on. Keohane did a study that uncovered a self-confidence deficit, with women students less certain of their place in the universe than their male colleagues. Many women were doing magnificent work behind the scenes, but they were uncomfortable taking any credit. They had learned the lesson of being nonthreatening, no matter how good they were. Tilghman didn't want women leading from behind—she expected them to step out front, just like she had done.

Like many strong women who came of age during the gender

---

2 Four of Tilghman's appointees became college presidents themselves—Christina Paxson at Brown University, Amy Gutmann at the University of Pennsylvania, Maria Klawe at Harvey Mudd College, and Valerie Smith at Swarthmore College. Another, Anne Marie Slaughter, held a high position in the State Department under Hillary Clinton and has written powerfully about the need to rethink gender roles so both men and women can flourish in careers and at home. Not a shabby group.

equality movement of the late sixties and early seventies (then deri-
sively dismissed as "Women's Lib"), Tilghman had a pioneer spirit.
"We knew we were going to have to prove ourselves, and we went out
to set the world on fire," she told me. She had a strong backbone and
the courage to believe that "when you reach obstacles, you just power
your way through them." Now she worries that young women expect
to find no barriers to success. Parents and professors coddle them and
cheer them on—and then the real world hits them as a surprise.

"We treat the women here now like poodles," she said. "When
they get out and encounter the obstacles that are out there, they don't
know what to do."

Poodles. It made me laugh. But she is absolutely right about the
need for women to charge ahead with strength. People who see
themselves as fragile creatures who need to be protected don't end up
flying into the genius firmament. People who see themselves as victims don't, either. To be a genius, you have to feel it in your bones. You
have to believe that your work counts and is as good as any other.
Women have often been denied that feeling or been forced to fight
hard for it. The women geniuses who can break through may be the
ones who find a way to close their eyes and, despite all input to the
contrary, see themselves as the geniuses.

When I left Tilghman's office, I felt buoyed by her bravery. Walking just a couple of minutes from the science building, I came to the
newest residential college on campus, named for Meg Whitman, who
forever changed online retail as CEO of eBay. The company had
modest annual revenues when she started in 1998 and was mostly
known as a place to scoop up Beanie Babies.[3] When she left ten years

---

3   Beanie Babies were wildly popular and so hard to find in retail stores that people were willing
to pay a fortune for them. They accounted for 10 percent of eBay's revenue at the time. Now you
can grab one on the site for a few bucks.

later, it was a global powerhouse with $8 billion in annual sales; owned companies like PayPal, Skype, and StubHub; and sold anything you could dream of buying. She went on to other impressive CEO positions. While Tilghman was president, Whitman (class of 1977) made a $30 million gift to the new college, and I felt a delicious thrill stepping onto the grassy courtyard of Whitman College.[4] The classically built building has strong, traditional lines and looks like it has been around forever.

Tilghman had told me that some of the male donors to the university had been wary when she first took office, but even those "who started off thinking that I was a crazy, radical, liberal feminist nutjob" quickly came around. She was smart, she was doing a great job, she loved the school, and they loved her. Only one major contributor insisted that as long as a woman was president, he would never donate another dime. And he didn't. As I looked around, it struck me that Whitman College was the perfect answer to the guy who wouldn't give. If you look at a person running a university and can see nothing except the fact that she is a woman, your name will be forgotten to history. Instead Meg Whitman and Shirley Tilghman are the ones who will be remembered—with Whitman College a lasting tribute in stone to the genius of women.

Over the last few years, there has been a kerfuffle at elite old-line schools from Princeton to Oxford about the paintings of important alums that line the walls of dining halls and public spaces. Almost all of the pictures are of men, and some people worried that the visages would make women students feel unwelcome. But it's all in your

---

4 Princeton and Yale call their residential complexes "colleges," much like Oxford and Cambridge. Harvard calls them houses. I don't know why.

perspective. One Yale undergraduate told me that rather than being intimidated, she liked having dinner in the Commons (which looks a little like the Great Hall at Hogwarts) amidst the glowering formal portraits because all those famous people had once been students here and now she was, too. Greatness could be in her future! I felt the same way in my student days at Yale. I imagine that Jo Dunkley and Shirley Tilghman also looked at the oil paintings on the walls at one point or another and thought with satisfaction, *I'm now part of this! My painting could end up there.*

An inner certitude that you belong seems to be a common factor for genius women. Instead of counting the number of women in their class to decide if they should be there, they *assume* they should be there and get energized and excited by the work. If they think about it at all, they recognize the intellectual strength and powerful curiosity they share with their peers. Anything else—like whether they prefer tacos or Big Macs, play soccer or tennis, or are female or male—is not particularly relevant to the work they're doing.

As I left the Princeton campus, another song buzzed in my ear—a tune from *Sesame Street.* The groundbreaking show had moments of sheer genius, but one of the sketches always irked me. If you ever had a four-year-old (or *were* a four-year-old) you probably remember the tune:

> *One of these things is not like the others*
> *One of these things just doesn't belong . . .*

Pictures appear on the screen, and you're supposed to pick which one is not like the others. There might be three shoes and one rain boot, with the correct answer being that the boot was different. But wait a minute. How about if you ask how they are all the *same*? They are all footwear. Now you have a wider perspective on how things are related and interrelated. Isn't that a much more creative way of thinking? For a show that celebrated diversity, this little game extolled a limiting view of the world. Another time I remember three pairs of sunglasses and one hat. A three-year-old might say that the hat is the different one. But an adult should have a more inclusive view. Sunglasses and a hat are all things that you wear outside in the sunshine.

How we see boots and shoes or sunglasses and hats or women and men depends on how we frame the questions. The famous behavioral economist Amos Tversky did a study in the 1970s where he gave people lists of paired countries. Using the same sets, he asked some of the people which of the pairs were most similar and asked others which were the most different. For example, one of the sets had you choose between "East Germany and West Germany" or "Ceylon and Nepal." In the "most similar" group, about 67 percent picked East and West Germany. In the "most different" group, about 70 percent made the same choice.

You might protest that the result makes no sense! How can one pairing be seen as the more similar and also the more different? The answer turns on what it is that you're primed to think about. The people who were asked about differences might have considered the opposing governments East and West had at that time and their at-odds philosophies. Those who were asked about similarities probably remembered that the people in both countries speak the same language and are descendants of Germanic tribes that go back a couple of thousand years.

Different? Yup. The same? Absolutely.

Similarly, Dunkley told me that she never attended the women-in-physics events when she was in graduate school because they didn't seem relevant. She saw herself as a physics student like every other physics student and no further categorizing was necessary.

For women geniuses, the music needs to be different.

All of these things are just like the others.
All of these things belong . . .

Wouldn't it be nice if we could all have those lyrics circling in our heads? Dunkley and Tilghman know it hasn't happened yet, and they work hard mentoring women to bring them into the fold. But perhaps the reason that women like Dunkley and Tilghman are able to reach the peak of male-dominated professions is that they already believe with every fiber of their being that they belong. They know they are just like the others—or possibly a lot better.

A couple of weeks earlier I had met Helen Wilson, who, like Jo Dunkley, is the mom of two little kids and a star in her field. Wilson researches fluids that don't follow a standard Newtonian model—meaning they behave differently than water. Think about toothpaste or egg whites or mayonnaise or mud. It's an extremely complex field, but that doesn't mean it can't be fun and relevant. She and one of her students wrote a paper on why chocolate fountains behave the way they do.

"I definitely had a lot of chocolate in my office for a while," she told me when we met.

"That already makes you a genius," I said with a laugh.

Wilson is small and slim with a runner's body—so it makes sense that she spent a few years doing her research at a lab in Boulder, Colorado. ("If you're not a runner before you go to Boulder, you will be when you leave," she explained.) Now Wilson is the first woman head of the mathematics department at University College London.

As an undergraduate, Wilson went to a class one day in a different department, just to get a glimpse of the person giving the lecture: a woman who was a full professor. It was such a rarity at the time at Cambridge that Wilson had never seen one before. Going to that lecture was like hunting for a unicorn. You just want the experience.[5]

But Wilson didn't worry that the college walls were lined with oil paintings of distinguished men with nary a woman in sight. As per our new song, what she saw was that all of these things were just like the others. Now she was one of them—no different from the portraits on the walls. Of course she belonged.

"It never really crossed my consciousness that there was a problem," she said. "I didn't associate my gender with my potential to do the work." Everybody has doubts starting out, but hers had nothing to do with being a girl. "My only question was, 'Am I good enough to do this?' Which is a perfectly sensible question to ask," she said.

When she went to one professor as an undergraduate to ask if she should consider pursuing a PhD, he asked to see her test results. After looking them over, he said, "Well, of course you should do it." His completely factual, objective approach was incredibly reassuring to her. He wasn't trying to be encouraging or nice. He was evaluating her brains and nothing else.

As down-to-earth and centered as she may be, Wilson also understands that being a top woman in math and non-Newtonian fluids makes her a little . . . different. Or maybe being a little different is what allows her to do creative and mind-bending work. She finds that she's not quite like the "sea of moms at the school gates"—but that doesn't worry her. Top women in math are a self-selected group.

---

5   Wilson got her PhD in 1998, so it wasn't really all that long ago. But to be fair, full professors in general used to be rarities at Oxford and Cambridge. The system has since changed.

"The tiny things, the micro-aggressions, those of us who have succeeded to this point are the people who don't even notice them," she said.

Not noticing. Feeling like you belong. Having confidence in your work. These traits seemed to be crossing over to many of the extraordinary women I met. Studies show that women are much more likely to join a field like physics or math or computer coding if they see people like themselves already involved, and I cheer the efforts of Wilson and Dunkley and others to make women feel like part of the existing community rather than outsiders.

But maybe a true genius needs that innate centeredness to see things most people would never consider. Looking at the night sky, many people might wish on a twinkling star. Dunkley thought about how she could use the light from that star to determine the age of the universe. Eating a bowl of tomato soup, most of us would focus on the taste. Wilson noticed that if you stir the soup and then stop stirring, the top will recoil as it slows down because the polymers in it get stretched.

Women geniuses still have many struggles with being accepted. And, yes, we need more role models and more pictures of women on the walls. But the one great advantage in being a woman who thinks about new ways to see the world is that you don't waste a lot of time thinking about how the world sees you.

CHAPTER 4

How a Teenage Nun Painted
The Last Supper

Have you ever heard of the artist Clara Peeters? Unless you have a PhD in art history, probably not. And until recently, neither had I. She painted in the early 1600s and was one of the few women artists from the Dutch Golden Age—the time of Rembrandt and Rubens. Ever heard of *them*? Yup, me too.

Peeters's work is exquisite—lush still lifes of food and fish and flowers with a stunning intricacy that evokes a rich culture. But as recently as 2009, you could have bought one of her paintings on auction at Christie's for about $150,000. That may not sound like a bargain, but the work of her male contemporaries was going for tens of millions.

Then in 2016, Peeters was given an important show at the Prado Museum in Madrid. It was the first time the Prado had ever featured a woman in a solo exhibition. Clara Peeters was suddenly an international star. Good luck trying to buy one of her paintings now. Only forty are known, and most are in museums.

The curator of the Prado exhibit, Alejandro Vergara, praised the brilliance of Peeters's still-life paintings—rich layouts of sumptuous meals on elegant tables. He pointed out that if you looked closely enough, each of the paintings included a miniature self-portrait—a reflection of Peeters's face on one of the shiny goblets. "She's really trying to be seen," he said.

Women artists and writers and scientists and mathematicians have always had a hard time being seen—and in her own day, Peeters was scarcely seen at all. Her life is pretty much unknown other than that she probably lived in Antwerp and maybe Amsterdam. Why did she do so few paintings? It's possible that after she got married, social pressures required her to give up her brushes. Nobody talked about her work until the curator at the Prado made her a celebrity.

It's thrilling to think that the Prado finally recognized a previously forgotten genius. But the better-late-than-never excitement is kind of discomforting, too. Her pictures had been hanging around for more than four hundred years. If she was a genius who did great work, wasn't she always a genius who did great work?

There's the rub—because there's no clear definition for genius in art or science or any other field. What counts as great is what those in power *say* is great. For hundreds of years, men have been the arbiters—and they didn't even bother to think about a woman artist in the genius category. It's nice that the Prado finally changed that. The solo exhibition was a way of saying: *Welcome to the ranks of genius, Ms. Peeters. Apologies that it was a little late.*

When the Whitney Museum opened its new location in New York a few years ago, I went with my college roommate, Anna, to the opening exhibition. In one airy and light-filled gallery, we stopped to admire a huge painting by the artist Lee Krasner. A much smaller work by her husband, Jackson Pollock, was nearby. There were also great pieces by Joan Mitchell and Georgia O'Keeffe.

"With all this space, I guess they finally brought the women out of the basement," Anna said, slightly sardonically.

I laughed, but it turned out she was completely right. Many museums are now bringing women artists out of the basement and into the light, quite literally. At the famed Uffizi museum in Florence, Italy, director Eike Schmidt discovered great works of early women artists moldering in the storage rooms when he arrived in 2015. He dragged them upstairs and put them on the walls to be seen.

That was the same year that the Guerrilla Girls celebrated their thirtieth anniversary of shaking up the art world. The feminist-artist-activists wear furry gorilla masks to protest gender inequities in their field. Staying anonymous themselves, they use the names of great women artists as their aliases. One of their famous posters from the 1980s asked, DO WOMEN HAVE TO BE NAKED TO GET INTO THE MET MUSEUM? It pointed out that less than 5 percent of the artists in the modern arts section were women—but 85 percent of the nudes are female. Another poster listed the paltry number of women artists on display at certain galleries and museums, and yet another printed the text on a half-empty page to point out that without the vision of women artists, YOU'RE SEEING LESS THAN HALF THE PICTURE. One of the founders of the group, who calls herself Frida Kahlo, wisely pointed out that when you ignore the work and voice of women, you're not giving a fair view of the culture at all. You're just telling the story of who is in power.

When the Guerrilla Girls started, they were scorned and scoffed at as attention seekers who weren't good enough to be in museums themselves. You have proof right there of what they were protesting. Nobody knew the identity of the separate Guerrilla Girls, so the quality of their individual artistic work was impossible to guess. But since they were women, critics with zero information were quick to undermine them. Now, in a lovely twist, posters and art projects from the Guerrilla Girls are in the collections of more than sixty museums and cultural institutions, including the Whitney. As women gain more power, work that was once scorned is hailed as genius.

The Guerrilla Girls are famous as icons, not individuals. An artist named Petah Coyne, who has created extravagant sculptures of women, spent years photographing the fifty or so women who were part of the original group of Guerrilla Girls. Each photo shows the artist wearing her gorilla mask and portraying the long-dead artist she represents. Coyne also took photos of each artist unmasked—but promised not to show them until after the artist had died. It's fairly amazing, isn't it? Brilliant women artists so committed to the bigger issues that they are willing to live in anonymity and be celebrated only after their death. It's sad to think that for women, genius is sometimes celebrated only in the rearview mirror. You will be ignored now. Your fight is for posterity.

My husband and I have collected lithographs and etchings for many years (since we can't afford originals), and we have some big-name artists. One day, after I started being aware of the male-female inequities in the art world, I walked around our house and counted up the number of pictures by women artists on the walls. Three. Not so bad. I gave a sigh of relief. Then I counted up all the other pictures and plugged the numbers into my calculator. Whoops.

"We have to buy more work by women artists," I told my husband at dinner that night. "Only fourteen percent of our collection is women. That's terrible."

He looked at me dubiously. "I don't buy according to gender," he said. "I buy what I like."

We all like to think that our choices are independent, but the forces on our decisions are both subtle and strong. The next afternoon, my husband and I went over to a local gallery that we often visit, and as we walked around admiring work that we'd love to buy,

I pointed out that not a single lithograph, sculpture, painting, or pho-tograph was by a woman artist.

"Do you think that there are no women doing better work than this?" I whispered, as we stood in front of a not-very-interesting col-lage by a well-known male artist.

My husband looked confused, especially since the owner of the gallery is a woman. We sauntered over to her desk to ask about the dearth of women artists on her walls.

"Oh, I know, I think about it a lot," she said. "But it's all about market forces. I can only show pictures that will sell."

She left the rest unstated, but we got it. In the art world as in so many other fields, you can't be a genius on your own. A dealer has to take the pictures from your studio and hang them in a gallery, and enough people have to buy them to create a market. There are no absolutes of quality in art—it's all about perception and critical ac-claim and prices at auction. A woman artist today might have a somewhat better chance of being seen than Clara Peeters did, but it's often men who have the big money to splurge on art, and their un-conscious bias is very real. As our friendly gallery owner knew, a big buyer may not admit that he's only interested in a male artist—but his deep expectation is that important art is done by men.

In an earlier day, it helped to be the wealthy wife or daughter of a great artist if you wanted to make a mark (quite literally) as a woman painter. The artists' guilds were all male. No women could apprentice. You could only learn the craft if you had someone at home willing to teach you. The other option was to be a nun, since, as was also true in music (with Hildegard of Bingen), women in convents had ironically more freedom than many of their contemporaries and could control their work and artistic endeavors. A young nun named Plautilla Nelli painted a huge *Last Supper* in the 1570s that is a startling twenty-three feet long and six feet high. It's believed to be the first painting of the subject ever done by a woman, and it has a richness and artistry that put it in a league with some of the other great Renaissance renderings. At the convent, Nelli essentially had her own guild of apprentices—a group of eight nun-artists she had taught. You can't paint something that large without a little help, and a convent was about the only place where a woman at that time could get people to work with her.

The great piece was hidden from public view for 450 years—hanging in the convent's refectory and later the friar's private refectory. Now it is being restored and getting international attention. At least one art critic has marveled at Nelli's artistic skill but asked if she got the bodies of the apostles just right. The question made me laugh because, really, how could she get them right? Before Leonardo da Vinci painted his *Last Supper,* he learned the details of anatomy by dissecting corpses. He reportedly paid grave robbers and doctors to bring him dead bodies that he could study. Michelangelo used to sneak into the Santo Spirito Church at night to study the cadavers there and try to understand the bones and structures under the skin. You need to be able to study to be a genius. There is no gene that teaches you the body structure when you are born. You have to learn it. Nelli became a nun at age fourteen. She not only never dissected a male body; it's a good bet that she never saw a man's body at all.

Men's efforts to shield women can often be fronts for controlling them and keeping them out of power. If a woman can't get access to a paintbrush, a lesson in perspective, or a chance to understand anatomy, it's a rocky road to becoming an important painter. When the men suppressing all her opportunities claim that they're doing it for her own good, she's less likely to notice how wrong it is and object. Meanwhile, if people keep telling a woman (or anyone) that it's dangerous or wrong for her to do something she loves—like paint or draw or exist outside of a man's control—there's a good chance that after a while she'll believe them and stop trying.

Somehow Clara Peeters and Plautilla Nelli and other creative geniuses were able to ignore the messages. The more you look, the more you can find women artists throughout the centuries who found a way around the limits imposed on them and let their genius in art shine through. Most have been ignobly overlooked. The Renaissance produced artists whose names everyone still knows—like Michelangelo and Raphael and Botticelli. To that list, you can add superstars like Sofonisba Anguissola and Elisabetta Sirani and Artemisia Gentileschi. Don't recognize those names? Famous during the Renaissance, those women artists were slowly written out of history by critics creating the myth of the Great Male Artist. The women's work is now being rediscovered as both extraordinary and important. But you still won't find it front and center in most museums.

The women breaking rules and creating art didn't have an easy time. Elisabetta Sirani's father was an artist, but he was at first reluctant to teach her. Maybe with good reason—once she started painting, she became far more renowned than he was. She did hundreds of drawings and portraits, and her paintings of saints and biblical scenes were often groundbreakingly original. Not bad for a seventeenth-century woman. But it didn't end well. Her triumphs came to an abrupt end when she died suspiciously at age twenty-seven. Though it was never proven, a maidservant was charged with poisoning her.

Artemisia Gentileschi also did amazing work in seventeenth-century Italy (it was a great time and place for painting), and she was the first woman to be accepted into the art academy in Florence. As a young teenager, she learned about color and technique in the workshop of her father, who was also an artist. Proud of her enormous talent, he hired a well-known artist to tutor her privately. It also didn't end well. One day in the studio, the tutor brutally raped her. During the trial, Artemisia was tortured with a thumbscrew to prove that she was telling the truth. Her rapist got a sentence of exile from Rome that was never carried out. She moved to Florence and went on to do bold and important work, often showing defiant women bonding together or triumphing over men. Her famous *Judith Beheading Holofernes* is at the Uffizi, and the National Gallery in London recently bought a self-portrait by her and is planning a solo exhibition of her work—its first ever by a woman artist. (Their collection of more than twenty-three hundred pieces contains about twenty-three by women. I'll do the math for you. That's 1 percent.)

Artistic brilliance often comes with severe trials—to wit: Vincent van Gogh cutting off his ear. But rape, torture, and potential poisoning seem off the scale. For women geniuses, it was (unfortunately) all in a day's work.

If you get a chance to see the work of any of these Renaissance women, I guarantee you'll find them powerful and interesting. I'd declare them to be just as good, if not better, than some of the paintings of the genius men of the time. Before any art critics wrinkle their noses at me, let me point out that I think it's high time we disrupt their accepted narrative about the masters (never mistresses) of art. Because how do we judge genius in art? When we look at a painting to determine its genius or originality or value, what standard are we actually using?

I love the work of Judith Leyster, who painted in the 1600s during the Dutch Golden Age and did exuberant figures similar to those of the much-celebrated artist Frans Hals. She was known at the time but then forgotten. A work considered to be one of the best paintings by Hals, *The Jolly Companions,* hung in the Louvre until 1893—and then something surprising happened. It turned out that the painting was by Leyster. Hals's false signature had been added on top of hers.

There were lawsuits and embarrassment all around. A painting praised for two centuries as a masterpiece was suddenly worthless because it was by . . . a woman.

We rarely use just our own eyes to evaluate a piece of art. We rely on what critics have said and the celebrity of the artist. If we've seen an image before, we like it more. The *Mona Lisa* is one of the most famous paintings in the world, and nearly seven million people crowd in front of it every year at the Louvre in Paris. But the piece wasn't particularly popular until it became the center of an international hullabaloo and a juicy scandal when it was stolen in 1911. Even Picasso was briefly implicated. (He had nothing to do with it.) The thief turned out to be a disgruntled employee who had hidden in a broom closet and then simply walked out of the museum with it. For a day or so, nobody even noticed the painting was gone.

When I went to the Louvre recently and visited Room 6, throngs of people were snapping selfies in front of the *Mona Lisa*. To avoid the crowd, I wandered around looking at the stunning works by Veronese and Titian and Tintoretto that are in the same room—and I liked some of those much better. But the *Mona Lisa* was the one under thick bulletproof glass with special LED lights and its own security guards. It struck me that what we call great or genius in art isn't always tied to obvious, objective talent or achievement. We are back to celebrity. Put images of one of Elisabetta Sirani's portraits under bulletproof glass, and you'd have a hit. Could we change our view of art by treating the work of women artists with *Mona Lisa*–like reverence and attention?

I chatted about that question one afternoon with Linda Gordon, a history professor at New York University. She was one of the pioneering historians in the 1970s who started studying women and gender and family as academic topics. One of her books is about the genius photographer Dorothea Lange, who snapped the unforgettable images of Depression-era families. Gordon knows how difficult it is for women artists to get attention. She told me that when Dorothea Lange was married to her first husband, famed Western painter Maynard Dixon, her powerful photographs dramatically influenced his style, but all the celebrity focused on him. She earned the living and took care of the house and children so that he could be free to be the artistic genius. "I privately think of him as the husband from hell, but a lot of people like his paintings, so those were the trade-offs," Gordon said. Only when Lange remarried did her own genius finally flourish. Her second husband was a professor of economics who "worshipped and supported her, even though she could be pretty difficult." After Lange died, he ardently promoted her work. "He was a very, very unusual man," Gordon said.

As we sat in her office near Washington Square Park, I mentioned Clara Peeters and the *Mona Lisa* and my surprise that the goalposts for greatness seemed to shift.

"Think about who defines what counts as great," Gordon said with a little smile. "It's always been men, of course."

Men (of course) are likely to pump up their own achievements rather than anyone else's, and that's true even when the women are working in the same genres and with the same skill as the men. Gordon was also interested in what happens when a woman's style is *different* from a man's. Could it be that we always celebrate the things that men are good at rather than what a woman might do well? Gordon herself loves going to exhibits of weaving and pottery and quilts. They can be beautifully intricate and wildly original—and they are traditionally done by women.

"So why are crafts not considered art?" Gordon asked. "Is a woman who has no formal training but creates great pottery a genius? We might say so."

We might say so, indeed. But *they*—the critics and influencers and men who set the prices—have a different view. Since crafts are associated with the home and usually created by women, they are the macaroni and cheese of the art world—tasty and appealing but not haute enough to be haute cuisine. Since women weren't accepted into the distinguished art institutes like the École des Beaux-Arts in Paris, their work got treated as outsider art. It's pretty amazing when you think about it—men ban half the population from the mainstream and then call them "outsiders."

Even art that has some distant connection to traditional crafts gets shunted aside. When a sculptor named Ruth Asawa had an exhibit at a New York gallery recently, an art reviewer for *The New Yorker* called the pieces "ethereal" and "diaphanous wonders" and credited Asawa with reshaping art history. But Asawa, who died in 2013 at age eighty-seven, didn't get the attention she deserved in her lifetime for her stunningly beautiful pieces. What went wrong? The reviewer, Andrea Scott, pointed out that Asawa had developed her unusual technique of crocheting wire after a trip to Mexico where she saw baskets being made.

"That domestic association has led to her work being marginalized," said Scott.

Just think of it. Original and exquisite sculptures credited with reshaping art history don't get their full due because they have "domestic associations." They make reference to the work that women traditionally do, and therefore they are of questionable value. If only Asawa had based her sculptures on things that men do well. Like start wars. Museums are very fond of paintings of men fighting bloody battles, after all.

Once you start realizing how women and women's work get implicitly undermined, it's hard not to fall down a rabbit hole of being pissed off. That, of course, is useless. But unfortunately, it is also hard not to start wondering if the ignoring and undermining and writing out of history might actually have some speck of reason to it.

That insecurity holds in many fields, not just art. When actress Claire Foy starred as Queen Elizabeth in the Netflix series *The Crown,* she won international praise and rafts of awards. After the second season of huge accolades, news got out that Foy had been paid less for her stunningly good lead performance than Matt Smith, the actor who played her husband, Prince Philip. It was blatantly wrong, unfair, and even shocking. How could the actress starring as the queen—the Queen of England, for heaven's sakes!—not be the most valuable person in the cast? Once the controversy was public, the producers apologized and made up the difference. All over social media, people wondered why Foy (or her agent) hadn't negotiated more forcefully in the beginning. In an interview, Foy admitted that it wouldn't have occurred to her. She's an actress. Young women are always being told in one way or another that they're not worth as much as men. "So you go 'You're right, I'm not [worth more].' Because that's what you say to yourself when someone tells you that, and you absorb it," Foy said, by way of explanation.

Whether you're a woman artist or a weaver or an actress playing Queen Elizabeth, you unconsciously absorb messages undermining your value. Foy was happy to snare an Emmy and a shiny Golden Globe Award for her work, but she also didn't question whether she was as valuable as the man who played a secondary role to her. When told that you're not a genius, your work isn't great, or you don't deserve more money, not too many women are likely to turn around and shout, *You're wrong!*

But before any more of us head down that particular soul-destroying tunnel of believing we're unworthy, let me offer some objective proof to change the picture. Like art and acting, music was long considered more valuable if done by men. If you went to a concert at one of the top symphony orchestras in America back in 1970, you would have seen a sea of black-tied men playing the instruments. Only about 5 percent of the musicians were women, and some influential conductors thought that was too many. Zubin Mehta, the esteemed musical director of the Los Angeles Philharmonic, who would later lead the New York Philharmonic, was blunt in his assessment.

"I just don't think women should be in an orchestra," Mehta said. "Men treat them as equals; they even change their pants in front of them. I think it's terrible!"

Let's pause for a moment to take that in. The man responsible for giving opportunities to some of the greatest virtuosos in the world *complained* that male musicians treated their female counterparts as equals.

Unfairness may last for generations even when there is no reasonable explanation. But once reason does arrive, a different truth can start to emerge. In the early 1970s, many orchestras decided to start holding blind auditions, with candidates playing behind a screen so that the judges couldn't be influenced by anything other than musical skill.[1] Surely no audition judge would ever think that he was swayed by whether the violinist wore a skirt or pants. *It's only the quality of the music, of course! Not my fault if most of the better players are men!* But once the judges couldn't see who was playing, a funny thing happened. The women musicians seemed to get a lot better. The economists Claudia Goldin and Cecilia Rouse published an academic paper in 2000 called "Orchestrating Impartiality," which analyzed the data from top orchestras. They came up with the stunning

---

1 The original idea of blind auditions was to open up the process so that conductors didn't just select their own friends and students—as had been the norm. The whole women thing was a nice side effect.

conclusion that auditioning behind a screen increased by 50 percent the probability that a woman would advance from a preliminary round. And it increased "by severalfold" the likelihood of a woman's winning a seat in the orchestra.

Though it is filled with charts and graphs and complicated math, Goldin and Rouse's paper hit a cultural nerve—and it has gotten huge popular attention. It has encouraged people in all fields to understand that how we think we're judging talent isn't actually how we evaluate it at all. Before the study, it was reasonable to think that men dominated orchestras because they played better. But now we couldn't fool ourselves anymore. The research showed that simply hearing high heels clicking as a candidate walks onstage for an audition can affect the judge's evaluation. The solution is pretty simple. Most orchestras that do blind auditions now also put down rugs to muffle the footfalls—or have candidates take off their shoes.

The impact of all this has been so dramatic that if you go to a concert now at one of the top symphony orchestras, you'll see a relatively even mix of men and women. At the New York Philharmonic, fifty men and forty-four women fill the stage—a pretty spectacular change from the all-male orchestra of the 1960s. Turnover is slow at most orchestras since you don't add musicians; you just replace those who leave or retire. Goldin and Rouse suggested that some of the increase comes simply from a bigger pool of women auditioning. But a significant percentage—they estimated it at 30 percent—has been a direct result of the blind auditions.

The proof that we are influenced by gender even when we think we are judging by talent is so persuasive that many other professions are picking up the idea of the blind audition. The writers' rooms for most of the nightly talk shows on television have famously been all-boys clubs. Back in 2008, executive producer Steve Bodow of *The Daily Show* on Comedy Central (then starring Jon Stewart) decided to ask that material be submitted to him without names—just iden-tifying numbers. On that first anonymous round, he hired three new writers—and two of them were women. In a short time, he found himself hiring more women and minorities. They were funny. They wrote great jokes. He had uncovered the kind of prob-lem that happened at all levels of creative hiring. If a man saw a woman's name on a joke, he might not have been primed to laugh. But when the material came from candidate number 42—well, it was a killer.

So, bravo! Progress. Brilliant women in music and comedy are get-ting their chance. But hold your applause. It's like the old game of Whac-A-Mole—you knock down one problem and another pops up. The New York Philharmonic has a lot more women—but it still re-quires those women to wear floor-length black gowns or flowing skirts. Pants that may make it easier to play? Nope. You try being a musical genius when you're worried about one of the keys of your instrument getting caught in your skirt. That happened to an En-glish horn player named Julie Ann Giacobassi when she was in the San Francisco orchestra back in the 1980s. Rather than risk it again, she bought a set of formal tails, just like the men wore. She got a few jeers at some foreign concerts, but the orchestra saw the light and made tails part of the accepted dress code for everyone. You want genius? That's the genius of a determined woman.

With the issue of women in orchestras (mostly) solved, the next problem is the powerful position of conductor. You can't hold blind auditions for that role since every move and facial expression is part of the performance. The very first woman to lead a major American orchestra got her post in 2007, when Marin Alsop came to the Balti-more Symphony. She said at the time that she was "honoured to be the first," but "shocked that we can be in this year, in this century, and there can still be 'firsts' for women."

Here's what else is shocking in this year and century—a Russian conductor named Vasily Petrenko complained recently that "a cute girl on a podium" was a distraction to the musicians. One wants to laugh (or snort) at such dumb and dated comments, but they have an impact. The conductor is the very visible leader of the orchestra, and men who want to protect their own positions continue to come up with oddball reasons for why women shouldn't be in the forefront in boardrooms, platoons, or symphonies. Alas, even comments as ludicrous as the Russian's become part of the received wisdom. Women conductors are still as rare as songbirds in wintertime.

Women have also been excluded from writing classical music, which puzzled me more than the conducting. What is gender specific about notes on a page? To find out, I checked in with Robert Beaser, the longtime chairman of the composition department at Juilliard. He has been called one of the most accomplished musicians of his generation, but I still call him Bobby because we went to high school together. When we met for lunch at a restaurant across from Lincoln Center, I had to remember to call him Bob.

Beaser's talent was obvious even in high school—he wrote a major orchestral composition at age sixteen and conducted its premiere with a Boston symphony. He was the youngest person ever to win the esteemed Rome Prize. His wife, Kati Agócs, is also a composer, and he proudly claims that their five-year-old daughter, Olivia, shows great talent. But he quickly adds that what matters is how you use the talent and what you make of it. People shouldn't be praised for the things they're born with, but for how they optimize them.

Beaser understands that "it's been hard for women composers for basically six hundred years," but he is convinced that the problem has everything to do with cultural expectation and nothing to do with innate ability. It drives him crazy when people try to generalize about male versus female styles in composing. He had been working that morning with a student "who writes the most ball-busting music" and also happened to be a diminutive young woman from Singapore. "Talent isn't a single thing—it has many tranches and celebrates the uniqueness of the individual," he said.

I mentioned Susan Wollenberg, the professor I had met at Oxford, and a paper she told me about written many years ago asking why there have been no women Beethovens. Beaser shook his head in frustration. It was a ridiculous premise. "Maybe we need a little perspective. There haven't been any more male Beethovens, either—and we wouldn't want anymore," he said. Beethoven was just fine as he was. What we really hope for are composers—men and women—doing new and original work. "Let's just go for that," he said. Beaser pointed out that every genius has a different process, and Mozart and Beethoven are good examples. Mozart wrote with ease and spontaneity, and his musical inspirations flowed like water. He didn't revise much and reportedly stayed up the night before the opening of the opera *Don Giovanni,* writing the brilliant overture in just a few hours. (The same story gets told about *The Marriage of Figaro.*) Beethoven, in contrast, worked laboriously to get his music just right. He struggled and honed and chiseled and was never satisfied. His notebooks show the endless changes he would make. Yet Beethoven was among the first artists to inspire the romantic modern belief in genius—an almost mythological view of natural talent that played into what Beaser called "the self-nurturing syndrome of male dominance."

Great artists in any field know what talents they have and what they don't, and they work around the difficulties, taking the snippets that are best, developing their techniques and their artistic personality. Beaser tells his students that creating art is about working around obstacles. From the many musical geniuses and near geniuses and some flameouts that he has seen over the years, he knows that any natural talents and skill sets need to be nurtured and developed. The few women who now write the music or wield batons for important orchestras have musical genius combined with unbreakable tenacity. They may have more obstacles, but overcoming them becomes part of the beauty of their work.

After my lunch with Beaser, I watched a YouTube video of a young conductor named Alondra de la Parra leading an orchestra, and she was so full of joy and energy, and the music sounded so alive, that I would be happy to crown her as a conducting genius. She has conducted prestigious orchestras around the world and was recently named the musical director of the Queensland Symphony Orchestra. She is (get ready) the first woman in Australia to be the conductor of a major orchestra.

Marin Alsop is right that now, in this year and this century, it's almost too sad to have to report a "first" like that. But de la Parra's path was its own kind of genius. She was born in New York and grew up in Mexico City, and she was just twenty-three when she figured out that being a girl genius with a baton didn't mean that anyone would give you a chance. A champion of Latin American music, she founded a group that she called the Philharmonic Orchestra of the Americas— which is in itself a kind of genius. The name makes it sound like it has been around forever. The group's first album got both critical acclaim and popular attention and turned platinum within a couple of months. De la Parra was praised for charisma and imagination and for changing classical music with a new style and energy.

New, different, and bold. A genius of musical innovation and reinvention. One article I read described de la Parra as one of the most exciting new conductors in years, describing her creativity, her musical style, and her inspired originality. And in the last line it asked, "Did we mention she's a woman? No? Good."

Good, indeed. If we could truly not notice, or at least not care, about the gender of a horn player, conductor, or artist, we might see their work and achievements from a more balanced perspective. But the not caring doesn't come naturally—and it is very, very hard to achieve. So one more story. One of the genius composers of our time is surely Kaija Saariaho, who famed music critic Alex Ross described as creating "an oceanic expanse of sound, one that shifts before one's ears and quivers with hidden life." Her opera *L'Amour de Loin* is so brilliant and original that Ross said it seems "to resound not only in space but within the mind." And yet when it was performed at the Metropolitan Opera in 2016, it was their first work by a woman composer in more than a century.

Saariaho expressed shock at how slowly things change. She described how when she was just starting out, her teacher at the academy in Helsinki told her to stand in front of a mirror ten times a day and say, "I can do it."

She could do it. She did do it. Her musical genius got seen and noticed. I find these brilliant and tenacious women inspiring. But discovering them, I found myself wondering why it was so difficult for their genius to shine. Why do we need blind auditions and carpets to muffle high-heeled shoes? Why do men not want women to be conductors—and why would it possibly take a hundred years for the Metropolitan Opera to perform an opera by a woman?

Men once dominated the world because of their (usually) greater brawn, but we have moved many centuries past the days when physical size was all that mattered. Genius in music or comedy or art requires a very different kind of strength. Women can possess it as well as men—but they need a forum where it can be nurtured and recognized. Entrenched interests are hard to upend. But maybe once you recognize the barriers, you can start to knock them down.

CHAPTER 5

Why Italian Women Are
Better than You at Math

O ne of the most popular genius role models in the world is Sherlock Holmes—the fictional detective who can make amazing deductions from the slimmest evidence. Growing up, I read all the Sherlock Holmes stories from a thick book that my dad bought for a dollar at a fire sale. Given that it was a literal fire sale after an inferno at the local bookstore, the pages were all charred and the cardboard covers smelled of smoke. I loved the book for being as uniquely special as the genius in its pages.

Holmes, the quirky, edgy genius who might save your life (or at least find your diamond) has been an irresistible lure to many. And, yes, he is fictional, despite many people's insistence otherwise. When Holmes died in a story in 1893 (author Arthur Conan Doyle brought him back a decade later), fans protested in the streets, wearing black armbands of mourning. A stellar collection of writers and intellectuals formed the Baker Street Irregulars in 1934 as an elite forum to discuss art and literature and Sherlock Holmes—and they didn't allow women until 1991. The old boys were considerably more sexist than their hero. Maybe they resented that in one story, Holmes was outwitted by the smarter and even more cunning Irene Adler. Holmes forever after called her "the woman." As with centuries of men before them, the Baker Street Irregulars realized that if you exclude all women, you never have to confront an Irene Adler again.

Sherlock Holmes remains a pop culture hero, his genius portrayed recently by Robert Downey Jr. in the movies and Benedict Cumberbatch in the brilliant BBC series. (I could watch Cumberbatch all day.) The deductive genius who sees things the rest of us miss has become part of our collective unconscious. We immediately understand genius types like Dr. Greg House, the star of the TV series *House,* whose Sherlock Holmes–style deductions saved lives and got eight seasons of high ratings.

If you're looking for a brilliant woman genius in pop culture, it's a little harder to find. Shows that feature geniuses all focus on men. When Jodie Foster directed and starred in the movie *Little Man Tate,* about a single mom raising a son who is a prodigy, some critics wondered if the little boy was a stand-in for Foster's own experiences as a wunderkind. If so, I can understand why they didn't make the child a girl since (a) girls don't get portrayed as geniuses and (b) the social problems of a girl genius would be way, way more complicated than even that movie could handle.

The most-loved woman genius of pop culture lately may be Amy Farrah Fowler, the nerdy genius on TV's *The Big Bang Theory.* The show ran for twelve seasons and was the most popular comedy around for many years. It initially focused on the brilliant but socially awkward scientists Sheldon and Leonard (the terrific actors Jim Parsons and Johnny Galecki), a couple of their nerdy genius buddies, and their pretty neighbor Penny (the talented Kaley Cuoco), who lived down the hall. Amy came in after a few seasons as a love interest for Sheldon. Perhaps unwittingly, the show set up diametric possibilities of what it is to be a woman. A young girl watching could imagine herself as the girl next door like Penny—a sexy blond waitress at the Cheesecake Factory who inspires lust in all the boys. Or Amy, the nerdy neuroscientist with a good heart and a bad wardrobe who can spar with the smart guys because she's a genius in her own right.

Who would you rather be?

I gave a call to Mayim Bialik, the actress who played Amy, to get her perspective. Bialik didn't just play a genius on TV—she has a PhD in neuroscience from UCLA. She's also the mom of two little boys, the author of several books, and a huge presence on social media. Funny, talented, and thoughtful, she's the real-life smart girl anybody would like to be.

As a teenager, Bialik was the star of a TV show called *Blossom*. When it ended after five years, she went to college and then spent seven years studying and doing research to get her PhD. She jokes that she only went back to acting because she needed health insurance. Her agent got her an audition for *The Big Bang Theory,* and she auditioned for the role of Amy. When she handed the producer her headshot and résumé, it listed her acting credits, and under "Other" she had written: "PhD in neuroscience."

"Is this a joke?" the producer asked.

"No, it's real. I have a PhD. I just didn't know where else to put it on my résumé."

Bialik laughs heartily when she tells that story. She loves science and took her research seriously (you can't get a PhD otherwise), but she also knew that on a Hollywood résumé, her academic achievements carried about as much punch as "likes yoga" or "knows how to skateboard." She did get one bonus for her hard work. When she won the role, the producers decided to make Amy a neuroscientist.

"They must have figured I could correct any science mistakes that the writers made," she joked.

But Bialik took her role—and her role modeling—seriously. "It's profoundly important to me that girls look at me and say, 'I can be a scientist, too,'" she said. At one point, she insisted that being able to inspire conversations about female role models in the sciences was more important to her than going to the Emmys or learning how to put on fake eyelashes. (Both of which she has also proudly done.)

Bialik told me that as a neuroscientist, she believes that there are some differences between men and women, but that "it's more interesting finding the common emotions and the common psychological processing and understand that we are fundamentally made of the same things." Encouraging boys to talk about their feelings or encouraging girls to be smart and stand up to boys "is not going to disrupt the pattern of *Homo sapiens.*"

I asked Bialik about the Amy-versus-Penny divide. Was it easier to be the slightly dumb but good-hearted Penny than the unusual, sometimes awkward genius Amy?

Bialik sighed. "We have to allow both types of females and both types of males as well," she said. She understands that there are people who, as she put it, seek to be appreciated only for their appearance. But she pointed to another character on the show, Bernadette, played by actress Melissa Rauch, who was also a scientist and "gets to wear cute headbands and cute clothes while Amy is very frumpy. But both of them have exciting and gratifying careers. They are both in fulfilling and satisfying relationships that they've chosen. We need to show all those different possibilities to our girls."

At the end of the eleventh season of the show (an eternity in TV time), Amy and Sheldon got married. The couple were late getting to the ceremony because they got excitedly distracted while solving an important science problem. Amy had been thrilled to go wedding-dress shopping earlier with Penny and Bernadette and, after trying on pretty gowns, had picked an abomination of frills and lace and high-necked ruffles. Her friends were horrified, but when she finally walked down the aisle, all that really mattered was that we all knew how beautiful she felt.

As far as TV weddings go, it was one of my favorites ever. I loved that the writers made the science as important as the ceremony—but they also let the genius girl have the classic pleasures of the day. The vows Sheldon and Amy wrote to each other were tear-jerkingly touching, and ultimately we saw that two people who are complete in themselves can also be human and emotional as they decide to join hearts and minds forever after. Their bond further paid off the next season when the show ended its run with Sheldon and Amy winning the Nobel Prize.[1] In her brief speech accepting the prize, Amy (dressed in a long gown and tiara) urged young girls to go after the joys of science. "If anybody tells you you can't, don't listen," she said. More than eighteen million viewers watched the episode, and maybe some realized that in a fictional show, that message was true and from the heart.

Bialik told me that "you don't know what you can be until you see it."

The more we see women geniuses in books and movies and TV, the less shocking the great variety of human experience comes to seem.

Our perceptions of what men and women can do is largely based on myth, tradition, and context. Are there biological influences? Well, sure. But they can be either overpowered or exacerbated by the context—where we grow up, who is around us, what is expected. We all like to think that we are in control of our choices, so it's unsettling to realize just how much of what we do is influenced by cultural

---

1   Only in TV land can you win a Nobel Prize so quickly. Twelve years is an extremely long run for a sitcom—but it usually takes decades to be recognized with a Nobel.

expectations. I had started to understand that theoretically—but it hit me viscerally when I visited physicist Carla Molteni at King's College. The day we met, classes weren't in session and most of the professors had escaped to country homes or seaside vacations. The campus was quiet, but when I made my way to the seventh floor of the physics building, Professor Molteni was waiting for me by the elevator. She led me toward her office, and as we passed row after row of empty desks, I asked, "Are you the only person working today?"

"Oh, I don't think so," she said. But then she laughed. "Well, maybe."

Only about 7 percent of the physics professors at elite universities are women, so it's not a surprise if Molteni instinctively works harder than anybody else.

When we sat down, Professor Molteni told me that she grew up in a small town in Italy and was part of the first generation in her family to go to college. She got her PhD in Milan, then did postgraduate work at Cambridge and the Max Planck Institute in Germany. Her research—which looks at how atoms interact and react to stimuli like light and pressure—had been described to me as brilliant.

I asked Molteni how she had the courage as a young woman to go into a field like physics, and she gave a little shrug.

"Where I grew up in Italy, women were expected to be able to do math and physics," she said. "I have a sister and six female cousins, and most of us have science degrees. We have an engineer and a physicist and a chemist and an architect. Nobody told us we couldn't do it."

I was surprised that a small Italian town would be so open-minded. But it turned out that the people in Molteni's town weren't groundbreaking feminists—they simply had a different notion of what men and women do well. Cultural expectations are often based on scant reality, but they are so deeply ingrained that they have an oversized effect on achievement.

"In the Southern Mediterranean, it's more unusual for men to do math than for women," she told me. "I never even heard these things about women being bad at abstract numbers until I got here."

King's College is smack in the middle of London, but not one of Molteni's female colleagues is from the UK or the US. There are only three women on the physics faculty (out of thirty-five total), and two are from Italy and one is from Greece. "If you want women physicists, that's where you need to look," Molteni told me.

I sat back, trying to understand how where you are born could determine whether or not you're good in math and science. But it makes sense. Had I been raised in Molteni's hometown, I would speak Italian, gesture with my hands, and have a great recipe for pasta primavera. It's not a big leap to say that I also wouldn't be intimidated by calculus and might develop some deep understanding of photons and wave-particle duality. On every level of learning, we are influenced by what we see and experience.

Even as I write about the Italian paradox, I know how hard it is to feel deep in your gut that you aren't just *you*—but a person who has been molded by pervasive social influences. Changing our perceptions of what is innately male versus female (much less than you think) and what is cultural (much more) is tough. Even when the data and facts are inexorable, they are hard to connect with how we feel about ourselves and our own abilities. It's easy enough to understand that women raised in Mediterranean countries are good in math and physics, but much harder to make it personal. You're more likely to think, *I am not good at those subjects, and it has nothing to do with where I live! It's just that I am. . . . not good at them!*

I've only been able to understand the power of mind-set and expectations by thinking of them like a societal placebo effect. We all know by now that if you take a sugar pill that you are told will make your headache go away, there's a very good chance your headache will go away. Our belief systems are powerful enough to change our physical functions. They are also powerful enough to change what we can achieve.

The placebo effect works in medicine—and some variant of it works equally well in achievement tests. If you think you're not smart or you have a disadvantage because you're a girl, you will do worse than if you're primed to think otherwise. In one study that always amazes me, Asian girls do well on math tests if reminded just before-hand that they are Asian. They do less well if reminded that they are girls. You might think that a math test is a math test—either you know your calculus and your two-plus-two or you don't. But the at-titude and confidence you bring to solving any problem are crucial to your success. Tell me I'm a genius, and I'm more likely to stick with that thorny math equation and actually solve it.

Back when I was in high school, I studied hard for the SAT, was confident on test day, and aced the exam. My mom gave a big sigh of relief when the scores came back and told me that she had panicked when I got my period the night before. She'd heard that the hor-monal cycle makes girls do worse on tests. "I didn't mention it that day because I thought it would just make you nervous," she said. Not sharing her panic at that time no doubt saved me several points on those SATs. There is absolutely no valid data connecting achievement to a woman's monthly cycle. But there is endless data showing the power of our mind-set. If you think that you will be worse in math at the beginning, middle, or end of any month, then surely you will be.

Women can't shine in a field unless they are *in* the field, and a host of academics and public figures and actors (including Mayim Bialik) are trying to encourage girls to study science. Connecting girls to the so-called STEM subjects—science, technology, engineering, and math—has become something of a cottage industry in itself. You can find STEM summer camps and after-school programs and books. Walking through a toy store recently, I saw all sorts of pink boxes with stickers on them guaranteeing that the contents would promote STEM talents. (One said it was STEM-approved, even though I can't seem to find any STEM-approval agency.) One that caught my attention was a home spa set for girls that promised to teach "the beautiful science" behind making glitter lip gel and other beauty products. It seems a bit dubious to me, but if whipping up an avocado face mask will (somehow) lead to a Nobel Prize, I'm all for it.

Further investigation, though, shows that the stumbling block for girls' genius isn't as neat as STEM versus non-STEM classes. Enough has changed over the last couple of decades that certain sciences—including molecular biology, genetics, and neuroscience—now attract large numbers of women. In graduate programs in those fields, women now get more than half the advanced degrees. Amazing progress! The flip side in the drive to equality, though, is that certain subjects in the humanities remain overwhelmingly male. There are stunningly few women in philosophy, and men so dominate in music composition (home to Beethoven and my friend Bob Beaser) that women get barely 15 percent of the advanced degrees.

What's going on? To find out, I sat down with Sarah-Jane Leslie, a philosophy professor and dean of the graduate school at Princeton. At a conference a few years earlier, she and NYU psychologist Andrei Cimpian began chatting about different ways of conceptualizing ability. Some people attribute their success to hard work and others to innate ability—and it struck them that different fields think about the balance differently. Philosophers overwhelmingly talk about how smart and gifted someone is, as if you are born to be a philosopher. "A philosopher who says that a colleague 'worked really hard on that' probably means it as a slight," Leslie told me. Psychologists, on the other hand, admire hard work and are skeptical of innate brilliance. They have many studies showing that it's better to praise a child for working hard than for being smart. If you think that grit and perseverance helped you get an A on a math test as a kid or create a $100 million start-up as an adult, then you have some control over the future. You can do it again and again. Attributing the success to being naturally smart means it could be a onetime flash in the pan that you can't re-create.

At a dinner that night, someone posed the question of why philosophy has so few women and psychology has so many. Leslie and Cimpian immediately looked at each other and thought of their previous conversation. Was it something about perceptions of hard work versus natural brilliance? They teamed up to investigate, eventually putting together a survey that they sent to eighteen hundred professors and graduate students at top schools around the country. Their hypothesis was that certain subjects, whether in the sciences or the humanities, are considered to require sheer brilliance and intellectual firepower. Others are seen to be conquerable by determination and intense work. They guessed that the more a subject was considered to require innate brilliance, the less likely women were to be involved and to get advanced degrees.

The research proved them right. Subjects considered to be in the hard-work category—like molecular biology and psychology—are roughly half women by now. Subjects seen to require natural gifts and inexplicable flashes of insight—like philosophy and physics and music composition—still have only tiny percentages of women.

"We've found that these beliefs about brilliance predicted women's representation above and beyond all other factors," Leslie told me when we chatted in her office.

Her conclusion was that women know that they are capable of hard work but they rarely think of themselves as natural geniuses. How can they? The images of geniuses in popular culture are mostly male—hello, Sherlock Holmes and Dr. House—and women don't see themselves mirrored in those roles. They stay away from the subjects that require sheer brilliance and are therefore associated with genius. They pick a different field.

It's an intriguing idea, and maybe because academics love research about academics, the findings have swept across campuses and even generated their own acronym—FAB, for field-specific ability beliefs. The generalizations get repeated as fact. One extremely successful microbiologist I interviewed told me only half-jokingly that she had succeeded because "I work very hard and I'm in one of those fields where I don't have to be brilliant."

"You *are* brilliant," I told her.

She smiled. "But according to that new research, I don't have to be, right?"

Her self-deprecation made me wonder if there was real validity to the distinctions Leslie and Cimpian found—or if this was just another way of undermining successful women. Is it really true that you can conquer molecular biology and psychology through hard work but that you need natural gifts and insight for philosophy and physics? Leslie said she wasn't sure that any research could actually justify the divisions, but once people believe them, "they become self-sustaining sociocultural phenomena." Her research has given them even more sustenance.

As I thought about this research afterward, it occurred to me that you could also turn the findings upside down and come to a very different conclusion. Could it be that once a field has more women, it's less valued and not considered as an area that requires true genius?

Neuroscience and molecular biology probably have better representation because a few bold women managed to succeed early on and become role models, inspiring and encouraging other women to join them. As far as I can tell, those subjects require just as much innate brilliance as the still-male-dominated fields of philosophy and computer science—but there we go with that self-sustaining sociocultural phenomenon. However nasty and wrong, the message gets sent that if women are succeeding in a field, it must be less challenging and not requiring of any natural genius.

What's true for perceptions of genius is also true for how jobs are paid. Considerable research has shown that as more women enter a field, *any* field, the pay scale drops. The whole field starts to seem less important and everybody gets paid less. As women started becoming biologists over the last couple of decades, the salaries in biological sciences dropped by about 18 percent. Did biology get any easier or less important? I don't think so. It works the other way, too. In the early days of computers, when women did the programming, it was considered a low-wage, menial job. Once men moved in, the salaries and the prestige soared—as did the belief that you had to be a genius to be a computer programmer.

The sociology professor Cecilia Ridgeway at Stanford had chatted with me a few weeks earlier about "status belief"—the idea we hold that certain people are more worthy of respect and better at the things that count most. When that gets embedded in a stereotype, we start seeing certain groups as more valuable than others. Status tends to be granted by the groups in power. Get the point? We reward the things that men do and value them more highly. If men are the philosophers and computer programmers, well, then, philosophical reasoning and computer programming must require some brilliance. Because social expectation says that men are the geniuses.

The bias begins very early. At age six, to be exact. At least that was the finding from another recent study Leslie and Cimpian conducted, where they told little children a story about a person who was "really, really smart." Then they showed them four pictures—two men and two women—and asked who the story was about. Up until age five, the boys and girls pointed to the grown-up who looked like them—the boys picked one of the men and the girls picked one of the women. But at age six, it changed. Asked to identify the "really, really smart" person, the boys picked a man—and the girls did, too.

"Little kids are these incredible statistical processors," Leslie told me. "At an implicit level, they pick up statistical regularities in the environment. They pick up which sorts of things go together with which other thing." By age six, they have been exposed to enough social learning to internalize "this entire ecosystem of stereotyping— the language that gets used to describe different people and different professions and who is portrayed as being brilliant."

In other words, even though they might be doing better than boys at school (as is often the case), girls have gotten the message that the boys are supposed to be the smart ones. "It's not just that girls have internalized the stereotypes and think they're not smart. Everyone has internalized the stereotypes. A girl is less likely to be perceived as exceptionally talented by a teacher, by a parent, and, later on, by a professor." If she wants to be a philosopher or a physicist, she has a lot of convincing to do—for herself and others—to believe that it's possible.

One of the biggest problems in social science research is that findings often can't be replicated. But in this case (sadly), Leslie's finding is so brick solid that you can copy it with a group of kids in your own living room. I saw a news feature on TV based on Leslie's research where six-year-olds were told the story about the "really, really smart" person and shown the pictures—and sure enough, the girls pointed to the men's photos over and over again as the likely genius. The girls' mothers, shown the videos afterward, were both mortified and dumbstruck. They thought they were raising their girls to believe they could do anything! They had GIRL POWER T-shirts and brought them to see *Wonder Woman*! But somehow the deeply ingrained social message had seeped through.

Ironically, despite all her research on subjects that require brilliance, Leslie doesn't much believe in the natural genius.

"What we see again and again is that any achievements that are worthwhile also take incredible amounts of hard work and dedication. I really reject the idea that anything worthwhile is accomplished by just showing up and being brilliant," she told me.

She pointed out that it's fun to talk about "how so-and-so is a God among men" and everything is so easy for him. It's less exciting to hear that he woke up at six A.M. every day, went to the lab, and worked really hard. That he had social support and recognition and someone handling the daily details (cooking, cleaning, shopping) so he could devote himself in an intense way to a particular undertaking. Give women that kind of backing and a lot more of them will look like geniuses.

A Barbie doll programmed to say, "Math class is tough," caused a tempest in the toy world when it appeared in stores in 1992—and the unfortunate line has been repeated (with accompanying rolled eyes) so often that it has become a shorthand for ingrained sexism. Many people pointed out at the time that Barbie's flip comment was just one more example of how girls get undermined in school. History is tough too, and so are sewing and knitting, but girls are told they can master those subjects, and so they do.

I never played with Barbie when I was little—I guess even at age five, I didn't put much stock in big breasts and a tiny waist. I'm surprised that of all the questionable social messages associated with an oddly shaped fashion doll, it's her aversion to math that has remained a sticking point. The toy creators at Mattel probably hadn't thought twice about the phrase because it just captured the zeitgeist. Barbie wasn't creating a position; she was reinforcing what social expectations already held true. I'd have to say that the egregious canned line turned out to be a good thing—because hearing Barbie echo a ludicrous attitude made it clear that expectations matter and what we say has consequences. Math class is tough for girls largely because girls *think* math is tough. Stock Barbie with a different phrase—"Computer programming is fun!"—and you might change both expectations and actual ability. (You won't do anything about the ridiculous size of her waist, though.)

One sideline to the story is that after Mattel responded to the uproar by pulling the doll from the shelves, CEO Jill Barad explained that "we didn't fully consider the long-term implications of telling girls that math is tough." Galling, isn't it? Barad was the first woman to run a major toy company, and when she left Mattel sometime later, after thirteen years in the corner office, she got a reported $50 million severance package. Somebody was learning math.

Social possibilities, expectations, and opportunities create or limit the genius of women far more than any genetic potential ever could. Yet for many women (including me) all the data and research are hard to relate to personal experience. We don't know—and often can't envision—the person we *might* have been given different circumstances. You can't start again as a little girl in a small Italian town and see if you end up good in math. When you struggle to figure out which investment will give a better yield to your 401(k), you blame yourself for being bad at numbers. You never think how much better you might have been given a more encouraging environment. When you do try to overcome social expectation and fulfill your own potential, you still have to deal with the men who are effectively (sometimes too effectively) screaming, *You're a girl! You can't do that!*

Because we endow genius with a mystical, Holmesian aura, it's hard to recognize (or understand in your gut) just how affected it is by social pressures. The whole question reminds me of the controversy in sports when women were told for decades that they were too fragile to compete in marathons, too weak to lift weights, and definitely not candidates to play hockey, lacrosse, or soccer. Then Title IX passed in America in 1972 and schools started to open playing fields and sports teams to women. The sea change in opportunities didn't give women different bodies, but it sure seemed that way. In almost no time at all, women were running marathons, lifting weights, and playing every team sport around. They went from being uninspiring in sports to breaking barriers that were once considered insurmountable.

If you want proof of how social dictates affect our bodies and minds, consider Kathrine Switzer, who tried to run the Boston Marathon in 1967, at a time when women weren't allowed to compete in any race longer than 800 meters. She entered as K. V. Switzer and wore a baggy, gray sweat suit. But a few miles in, a race official realized a woman was running (OMG!) and chased after her, ripping at her number and trying to physically push her off the course. Switzer got away with the help of a body block from her boyfriend and—yes, she persisted. She finished the race with a time of four hours and twenty minutes.

Five years later, women were finally accepted in the race and Switzer went to the official starting line with several other women. Now she had support. It was okay to be there. The social belief in what she could do had changed. When the race was over, she had improved her time by *fifty minutes*. The women's winner finished well over *an hour* faster than Switzer's first marathon.

Now, a few decades later, the top women marathoners are another hour faster. *Two hours* of improvement! That is an eternity in a sport where improvements are measured in minutes and seconds. The top man in 1972 finished in two hours and fifteen minutes—which is what women now run.

How could women improve so dramatically in such a short time? It was all about expectations. When Switzer ran for the first time, people snarled at her and she was told at the finish line that "women don't run marathons." There were whispered fears that women would faint or die or (certainly) never be able to have children.

"It was considered dangerous—we were too frail and our uterus would fall out, our legs would get big, and maybe we'd grow hair on our chest," Switzer says now. "But running made me feel free and powerful. It was what I wanted to do, so I did it."

In a recent article about the best women's slalom skier in the world, a young American named Mikaela Shiffrin, *New Yorker* writer Nick Paumgarten pointed out that we often think "of prodigies as embodiments of peculiar genius, uncorrupted by convention, impossible to replicate or reengineer. But this is not the case." Shiffrin, he explained, was a "stark example of nurture over nature, of work over talent." She became great by wanting to be great and believing she could be. Her parents led her on a step-by-step process to create excellence. Her father wasn't concerned with where she started—only with where she ended up. "Kids with raw athletic talent rarely make it," he said.

In sports, the women who believe they can achieve are the ones who do—and that turns out to be similarly true in physics and music composition and neurobiology. I am inspired by the brilliant and tenacious women who ignore social expectations and prove their own power. They aren't necessarily very different in abilities from you and me, but they have experienced their talents differently. Natural talent is nice whether you want to be an astrophysicist or a slalom skier. But far more important is that when you're a six-year-old girl and get asked who is the star, the genius, the person likely to be on top, you point to the grown-up who looks most like you.

CHAPTER 6

Rosalind Franklin and the Truth About the Female Brain

We have gotten to that point where we can't talk about men and women and genius without facing the elephant in the room. The bright pink and blue elephant. However much we agree about discrimination and power and how talent can be overlooked, about bell curves and individuality and social pressures, there is something else lurking in the shadows. I see it when I talk to many people about unconscious bias, and they nod but give themselves away with a wariness in their eyes. They don't want to say it to me, but the uncertainty in their expression telegraphs the question.

Sure, yes, all that is fine . . . but isn't there a basic difference in men's and women's brains?

Before I try to answer that, let me tell you about a day recently when a friend entrusted me with her fourteen-month-old, and I stepped into the elevator in their apartment building holding him in my arms. Fourteen months old is a squishy and delicious age, and he is a particularly irresistible baby, with big eyes and light hair and a smile that lights up the immediate surroundings. Dressed in blue jeans and a sweatshirt, he was clutching a sippy cup that happened to have a pink top. I don't know why his parents got him a pink sippy cup—they live in the liberal bastion of the Upper West Side of Manhattan, so maybe they didn't even notice. But the woman who got on the elevator on the next floor did notice.

"Oh, so adorable!" she said. "Boy or girl?"

I started to answer, but then I thought, *What difference does it make?* "It's a baby! Fourteen months old!" I said brightly.

She ignored my reply. "I thought at first 'he,' but then I saw the pink cup, so I'm guessing 'she.' Is that right?" she asked.

"At this age, just a baby!" I said with a smile.

She stroked the baby's foot, but I could see she was befuddled about what to say. If the pink cup was the giveaway, then she would coo that the baby was sweet and beautiful, but if the jeans ruled, then she'd admire how big and sturdy he was. Without a hint on which way to go, she was stymied and uncomfortable and didn't say anything.

I felt her pain, and when we got to the lobby, I told her about my book and my research showing that so many distinctions in ability between men and women (and girls and boys) are strictly cultural. Wouldn't it be nice to start erasing some of those? She told me she had four children, ages ten through seventeen, and had tried to raise them without gender stereotypes. The two girls were very different from the two boys—which she always took as proof that "they are wired differently." But the brief elevator ride and our conversation had been eye-opening.

"I guess we send signals even when we don't mean to," she said.

I was glad that I had won her over, but the idea that males and females are wired differently, that some of the differences between them are natural and inborn, seems to be deeply accepted in our culture. But from various research studies I had been reading from neuroscientists, it didn't seem like it was particularly true. I needed more

information. So on a chilly Tuesday morning, I went to the leafy suburb of Lake Bluff, Illinois, to have lunch with Lise Eliot, a neuroscientist who researches the differences—or lack of them—between
male and female brains. After graduating from Harvard and getting
her PhD at Columbia, she is now a professor at Rosalind Franklin
University.

As we sat down at a pretty restaurant on the main street of town,
I admitted to her that before we connected, I had never heard of the
school where she works.

"Proof of what we're here to talk about?" I asked.

"Ironic, at least," she said with a laugh.

The gifted chemist Rosalind Franklin was one of the key figures
in the discovery of the structure of DNA, but for many years, she
didn't get any of the recognition. James Watson and Francis Crick
walked away with the credit and the Nobel Prize—and they never
fully admitted that her findings allowed them to make their great
leap forward. Using a technique that she developed herself, she took
X-rays that showed DNA's helical structure, and Watson and Crick
built their model based on her research.[1] One scientist at the time
called Franklin's images, including one known as Photo 51, which
clearly showed the structure of DNA, "amongst the most beautiful
X-ray photographs of any substance ever taken." Watson didn't bother
to mention the importance of Franklin's findings in his book about
the discovery of DNA, *The Double Helix,* but her equal participa-
tion in the discovery has become more and more clear. She had presented her findings at a lecture and in papers before Watson and
Crick made their model, and they had studied her X-ray images.

---

1   They had been secretly given Franklin's image of DNA by Franklin's colleague Maurice
Wilkins, who later shared the Nobel. Wilkins reportedly wasn't excited about having a woman
in his lab at King's College and was happy to collaborate with the rogues from America. The true
story emerged slowly, years after Franklin's death at age thirty-eight from ovarian cancer.

Science is cumulative, findings building on each other, so there is no shame in admitting someone else's contribution—but Watson tried very hard to write her out of history. Some scientists have called it the most egregious snub of a woman scientist in history—but honestly, I think there's a lot of competition for that position.

I had the chance to talk with Dr. Watson once at a party when he was ninety years old and presumably somewhat mellowed. The party was noisy and his voice was low, so I had to lean in to hear him—and discovered that he still enjoyed being the provocateur. He complained to me about feminists being wrong and claimed that his opinions on racial differences "got me in trouble but are probably true." I was gracious for a while to keep him talking, but finally I got tired of it, and as I got up to go, I asked him what he thought the truth was about Rosalind Franklin.

"She didn't know what she was looking at," he said. "She had to give the X-rays to me to make sense of them."

Did she really? When Watson made a similarly patronizing comment directly to Franklin in 1953, she told him that she knew exactly what her data said. He didn't hear it then, and he had conveniently forgotten it again. Fortunately, history seems to have been revised correctly, and despite the efforts of Watson and his peers, Rosalind Franklin is firmly installed in the canon of geniuses.

Now here I was with a professor from Rosalind Franklin University—who had a thing or two to say about how women's work and brains can be misunderstood. After we ordered Cobb salads, Eliot told me that she has a daughter and two sons, and when they were little, she got interested in "pink brains versus blue brains." A lot of research coming out at the time purported to show the physiological differences between male and female brains—and how those created distinctive strengths in men and women. She thought she might write a book explaining how brain structure and hormones and evolutionary trends impact who we are and what our innate abilities might be.

"But then I started looking at the actual brain data, and it just wasn't coming together. I was looking for the proven scientific difference between adult male and female brains and I realized—I got nothin'!" she told me.

At that point her research and her thinking took a sharp turn. She saw that a lot of what passed for scientific evidence was politics in disguise. For example, back in the 1980s, some sociobiologists tried to make the case for the role of evolution in distinguishing the abilities of males and females. Some studies at the time showed that men were stronger in visual-spatial ability and women better in verbal skills. Why would that be? The sociobiologists explained that our male ancestors were off hunting while the women were raising children and communicating around the campfire. Women evolved with social skills to protect their families! Men became good at roaming the land and seeing predators—or they didn't become our ancestors!

"It's a nice explanation, but there's absolutely no empirical evidence," Dr. Eliot said. "You can make up a story to explain anything—but it doesn't mean it's right." The explanations thoroughly ignored any social or cultural influences that came into play. The popular Harvard scientist Stephen Jay Gould debunked the evolutionary explanations by comparing them to Rudyard Kipling's *Just So Stories*. In his view, the scientists' tale of "How Men Became Good at Math" made about as much sense as Kipling's fable of "How the Leopard Got Its Spots." The latter is a charming tale that involves black paint but isn't very high on the veracity scale.

Eliot shared Gould's disdain for the evolutionary explanations. But even more galling to her were the supposed proofs from neuroscience that purported to explain everything from the scarcity of women electrical engineers to the overabundance of boys who don't like to read. Neuroscientists used hi-tech imaging techniques like MRI machines, which can outline specific areas of the brain, and fMRI scans, which can show the brain in action. (They actually show the blood flow to different regions of the brain, which gets interpreted as what part of the brain is in use.) Researchers would give women and men a set of problems, put them in an fMRI, and see which part of the brain lit up as they worked. They took the results and extrapolated to say that differences in brain size and physiology explained male versus female achievement.

Eliot started taking a closer look at some of the data and doing what is called "meta-analysis"—or studies of all the studies. For example, one researcher in the early 2000s looked at the hippocampus a part of the brain linked to depression, anxiety, and Alzheimer's disease—and concluded it was smaller in women than in men. The study was widely accepted as an explanation for why women are more susceptible to all those conditions. But once Eliot and her students collected data on other experiments and looked at thousands of measurements, they found no meaningful gender differences in the hippocampus at all.

As Eliot looked more and more, the gender-based brain evidence held up less and less. She became infuriated when she realized that very small and essentially meaningless variances were being blown way out of proportion and repeated over and over as fact. One study out of India claiming that males and females rely on different pathways for thinking made headlines in newspapers and on TV shows and websites around the world.

"It's sexy to talk about sex difference," Dr. Eliot said, "but it turns out not to be true."

I was so fascinated hearing about her work that my salad sat untouched as I furiously scribbled down notes. She was very convincing, and her research was compelling and exciting. But was she right that men's and women's brains aren't really very different? I'd had many parents tell me that no matter what they did, their sons and daughters seemed like different species. The boys wanted to play with cars and the girls wanted to have tea parties. I quoted my new friend from the elevator, who felt like her children were wired differently.

Eliot put her head in her hands. She'd heard similar comments before and they drove her crazy.

"Whatever parents are telling each other, we're not hardwired for anything above the brain stem!" she said.

The brain stem, which is attached to the spinal cord, is the basic center that controls breathing and heart rate and all the instinctive reflexes of the central nervous system. It is already in place in the second trimester of fetal development. Then there's what we consider the "higher brain"—the cerebral cortex. It gets involved in the stuff that we're more conscious of controlling, like talking and reading and deciding whether you want to play with Tinkertoys or American Girl dolls. That part of the brain has only a basic structure in a newborn. As Dr. Eliot explained it, the cerebral cortex has twenty billion neurons that have some initial wiring but aren't connected at birth. The synapses and neural pathways between them are formed only as learning occurs.

"The gift of higher mammals is that we are essentially left as blank slates to learn from the environment," she said. "Most of learning is social—and babies are largely social creatures that copy what they see."

As I thought about it afterward, I realized that we attribute "hardwiring" only to things that are gender related. We understand that babies gobble up signals from the people around them. They learn faces and emotions and what foods are okay to eat. In just a little over a year, some toddlers speak Spanish and others babble in French. If I reported that the French-versus-Spanish dichotomy so early in life proves that language is hardwired, you would simply laugh. Of course not! Language skills are learned! Babies may quickly separate into those who say *hola* and those who say *bonjour,* but we all know that if you give them different input and encouragement, they'll come out in the other group.

And here's the point. If it's so obvious that nobody is hardwired to eat croissants and recite French poetry, why should we ever think that loving Legos or not is determined by genetics? Sorting out the social clues necessary to learn language is a whole lot more complicated than picking up whether you are expected to wear frilly dresses or denim overalls.

This could all seem like a nice academic argument, but it has profound implications. Once you tell yourself (or your kids) that boys and girls are wired differently, you treat them differently. And once you treat them differently, you reinforce, encourage, and teach them to act exactly the way you initially expected. We now have the definition of a self-fulfilling prophecy.

"Teachers come into a classroom and say, 'Hello, boys and girls,' and we think it's fine. But what if they routinely said, 'Hello, whites and blacks'?" Eliot paused and looked at me meaningfully. "When you divide people, you announce that you have different expectations for them—and that's just wrong."

The waiter came over to tell us that the restaurant was closing, so we paid our bill—and then sat and kept talking. We agreed about the social issues and power dynamics that kept women from being seen as geniuses. But I told her that I worried about exhibiting a bias on the other side. Could there be some brain differences that did matter? The subject continues to be controversial.

The next day, Eliot emailed me studies from other researchers about sex differences in the human brain. One large study had eighteen researchers' names listed and included important academics from around the world. It was long, technical, and scientific—and she had (kindly) highlighted some of the most important findings. Underlined in yellow on page eight was the information that "the human brain cannot . . . be described as 'sexually dimorphic.'"

I had to look that one up. Sexual dimorphism turns out to be exactly what it sounds like—a difference within a species based solely on sex. Think of the male peacock with its brightly colored tail display versus the smaller brown female and you understand sexual dimorphism. All male peacocks have that fancy plumage, and the females simply don't. But that dimorphism doesn't exist in human brains. There are greater differences within the groups of human males and females than there are between them. Some women have the intellectual equivalent of vibrant plumage, and so do some males. But making generalizations about their brains as a group? Forgive me, but that explanation is for the birds.

A large contingent of neuroscientists now share Lise Eliot's position that brains are not inherently male or female—and neither are abilities. By now I've looked at so many studies about male and female brains that my eyes are a little sore—and the main thing I've learned is that we have a great attraction to categorizing things. When it comes to neuroscience, we need to get over that particular problem, because researchers around the world are starting to agree that brains are rarely completely male or completely female. They can't be neatly categorized. Daphna Joel, a professor of psychology and neuroscience at Tel Aviv University, analyzed large data sets of brain scans and found that an individual brain is almost always a "mosaic" of features. Some features of structure and size are more common in males and some more common in females, but the classifications become meaningless when you look at a particular person. She found the same when she looked at a range of personality traits. Writing with Cordelia Fine, a professor at the University of Melbourne, she concluded that on a large range of variables, "not a single person had only feminine or only masculine scores." That's all to the good, isn't it? A mosaic is a lot more interesting than a boring blue wall.

Look, I'm not trying to go crazy here in terms of making definite pronouncements. Scientific research is never quite as determinative as we would like, and people can slice and dice various brain studies in all sorts of ways. Those who want to make a point on one side or the other will find data that supports their position. But the research seems clear that whatever minuscule differences can be found (or claimed) are essentially meaningless on a practical level. It is wrong— if not downright deceptive—to blow them up into generalizations that simply aren't true on any individual level. As Joel and Fine bluntly explain, "The notion of fundamentally female and male brains or natures is a misconception."

One day after I read a huge batch of articles and research studies on men's and women's brains, I went outside to take a walk and try to make sense of it all. Deep in thought, I found myself staring down at my size 8 boots. It suddenly occurred to me that we could move from brains to feet and make the same arguments. Men on average have bigger feet than women—so are those feet more capable? Surely someone could do an experiment to find that larger feet are helpful in walking on slippery pavement and smaller feet better for frolicking down stairs. But we end up at the same need to separate the individual from the group. My mom wore a size 10 and a guy friend of mine wears a diminutive men's size 7. Even if averages did tell us something, no innate difference is going to matter nearly as much as whether you are wearing stilettos or running shoes. Bone structure and gender and genetics may all have a role in how well you walk—but nothing will hobble you quite as much as a set of narrow four-inch heels.

In the brain debate, we are arguing about the edges, the smallest differences in what makes us different, when it is really the social pressures—the metaphoric pair of Jimmy Choos we feel compelled to wear—that turn any tiny distinctions into major ones. Women are not hardwired to wear high heels or to think that math is hard. We take social constructs as fact and then try to work backward and explain them by neuroscience. You want to be smart, no matter your gender? Invest in the intellectual equivalent of a pair of Nikes and say to hell with what's expected—I'm just going to do it.

PART TWO

The Geniuses Among Us

Ought not every woman, like every man,
to follow the bent of her own talents?

—MADAME DE STAËL

When men are oppressed, it's a tragedy.
When women are oppressed, it's tradition.

—LETTY COTTIN POGREBIN

CHAPTER 7

Why Fei-Fei Li Should Be on the Cover of *Vanity Fair*

Visiting Paris for an academic meeting, I went over to my favorite bakery, Pierre Hermé, and waited in a long line to buy a sampling of their amazing macarons. French macarons are best eaten the day you buy them, so I put two of my favorites—a rose and a chocolate—into a separate bag and brought them to one of the professors I was interviewing. She looked at the pretty bag and graciously thanked me (she's French, after all), but I thought she gave a little sigh.

"Is something wrong?" I asked.

"The world is divided into people who like Pierre Hermé macarons and those who like Ladurée," she said, referencing another Paris bakery.

"And you like Ladurée?" I asked.

"*Oui,*" she said. She held up the perfect rose macaron. "But I will enjoy this anyway."

I laughed at the idea that there are two kinds of people in the world, separated by the kind of pastry they eat. (In the name of research, I went to Ladurée that afternoon. Trust me, Pierre Hermé is better.) But I understood because we have a tendency to like neat divisions. Cat people and dog people. Yankees fans or Red Sox. People who like mountains and those who like oceans.

And then our most persistent determination in the "two kinds of people in the world" theorem—men and women.

Given that there are about 163 million women in America right now (half the total population), it's obvious that we're not all the same. But the expectations of what it means to be a woman can be rigid and restricting. I wear a lot of dresses to work, and my close friend Candy, who ran a color and fashion consulting business, defines my style as "classic ingenue." But I don't follow the other conventions that seem— inexplicably to me—to go with being a woman in my circle. I don't wear nail polish, I've never had a pedicure, my ears aren't pierced, I have no interest in expensive pocketbooks.

The messages of what a woman should be are transmitted at an early age. A woman I know told me that her three-year-old daughter loves to parade around holding a baby designer pocketbook while her older sons never expressed a similar interest. Isn't that proof that some behaviors are innate? I told her that although scientists have decoded the entire human genome, nobody has yet found a gene that makes girls like Chanel and Hermès.

"You worked at *Vogue*!" I reminded her. "Don't you think she's just picking up your subtle cues about what to like and how to behave?"

I suppose I shy away from the pedicures and pocketbooks because they strike me as outward manifestations of a culture that still expects women to be pleasing, slightly submissive, and ever friendly. When I was young, I liked talking about hair and makeup with some of the beauty-obsessed girls in my class, but I was also editor of the newspaper and captain of the debate team and had a lot in common with the ambitious, hardworking boys in the class. Why should there be an either-or? When I tell you that there are two kinds of people in the world, those who like Pierre Hermé and those who like Ladurée, you might laugh because it is obvious that there is so much more to a person than the kind of French macaron they like.

And there is so much more to a person than whether they are a man or a woman.

Many of the genius women I spoke to realized early on that they didn't fit—didn't *want* to fit—the conventional stereotypes. And why should they? Back in the eighteenth century, the early feminist philosopher Mary Wollstonecraft argued that social pressures crush women so that they lose their "strength and usefulness." Backed into a corner without independence, women become "anxious only to inspire love, when they ought to have the nobler aim of getting respect for their abilities and virtues." She thought that marriages would be better if women were strong and respected by their spouses rather than just protected. "When 'innocent' is applied to men or women, it is merely a polite word for 'weak,'" she said.

We are better educated than women were in Wollstonecraft's day,[1] but women who care about being strong and successful and smart still feel themselves at odds sometimes with the prevailing winds. For their genius to shine, they need to avoid the conventional paths. Genius women—and indeed successful women of many sorts—are baffled by the narrow boxes that society creates around men and women. They know they aren't men, and they don't want to be. They also can't see themselves inside the narrow boundaries we create for someone to be feminine and female. They don't necessarily fight the stereotypes so much as ignore them. They cross boundaries and expectations and see themselves as original and distinctive. It's as if they

---

1 Like so many women of her time, Mary Wollstonecraft died from complications of childbirth. She was just thirty-eight. The daughter she left behind followed her mom's advice that women could achieve and flourish. She became known as Mary Shelley and wrote the great classic *Frankenstein*.

take the Ladurée recipe and the Pierre Hermé packaging and mix them up into something new. Instead of two categories, they see at least three: Men, Women, and Me.

On a trip to the Bay Area recently, I sat down with Fei-Fei Li, who has been called one of the world's leading scientists in artificial intelligence (AI). Just about everyone describes her as a brilliant leader in the field that is going to change how all of us live in the future. Many people had told me that to write about genius, I *must* talk to Fei-Fei, and I had tried contacting her several times. But she was very busy as the head of artificial intelligence at Google Cloud, a sought-after tenured professor at Stanford, the devoted mother of two small children, and the leader of an international movement to teach machines how to see the way humans do. A mutual friend at Stanford finally connected us. (Thanks, Stephen.)

When we met, Fei-Fei was thoughtful, intense, and very focused. Because I had heard so much about her, I felt like I was in the presence of celebrity—but she humbly told me that she had been a normal kid and "I'm still a normal person." She wasn't being coy—she is forthright and straightforward—so it was actually encouraging to think that a woman in her early forties now considers it normal to be one of the great leaders in her field.

But not everyone considers it normal that a woman is a leader in this male-dominated world. She ran the Stanford Artificial Intelligence Laboratory for five years, and the breakthrough work she has done teaching machines to see has had an impact on transformative technologies like driverless cars. But when I mentioned her renown in the field, Fei-Fei told me about an article that had appeared a couple of years earlier in *Vanity Fair* magazine, with twenty thought leaders discussing the future of AI. She wasn't included. No women were included. As we talked, she pulled up the article on her computer.

"Look, literally all men," she said, pointing to the twenty little headshots on the page. "I know all of them because they are either my colleagues or peers. I just wonder why no women were even contacted."

My guess is that if the editors even thought about Fei-Fei and her female colleagues, all they could see was a blaring light that said "Woman." The designation blinded them to any further subtlety or nuance.

Fei-Fei's friends have told her that she needs to promote herself more, but that's not her style. She wants to focus on the work rather than the credit. Her personal value system says it's the execution that matters, not the awards. She does the former brilliantly, so does the recognition really matter? Yes, I told her, it does. She is a role model. Young women need to see her getting the public kudos she deserves. It's also a classic problem of smart women—we think that if we put our heads down and just do the work, it will get noticed. It doesn't. Fei-Fei was surprised recently when one well-known guy in Silicon Valley tweeted that she was this generation's Rosalind Franklin.

"My thought was, 'Oh no, I hope I live longer,' because she died very young of cancer, right?" Fei-Fei asked me.

I confirmed that Franklin had died at age thirty-eight of ovarian cancer, but I expected that the tweeter was referring to Franklin's not getting the Nobel Prize for her discoveries in DNA.

"Has someone else been getting the credit for the work you did on ImageNet?" I asked, mentioning one of Fei-Fei's great achievements in machine learning.

"I honestly don't think that way," Fei-Fei said.

Fei-Fei grew up in Chengdu, China, and is ever grateful to her parents, who "created a home environment that did not tell me to conform." They encouraged independent thinking, and while she says that she was "not a rebel in the traditional sense," she was able to ignore the gender expectations of teachers and others in her community. Moving to a small town in New Jersey at age sixteen, Fei-Fei spoke almost no English but learned and adapted quickly, got a scholarship to Princeton, and graduated with high honors.

"The fact that I was let free to be who I am without any gender consciousness in the early stages helped a lot," she said.

It struck me that Fei-Fei, like so many of the other genius women I met, unconsciously divided the world into Men, Women, and Me. She wouldn't necessarily describe it that way, but how else to explain being a person with many facets in a world that prefers to limit and categorize? Like astrophysicist Jo Dunkley (mom of two) or molecular biologist Shirley Tilghman (same—plus some grandkids now), she wasn't trying to be a man. But she also knew from a young age that she didn't fit into the gender conventions that diminish and restrict what a woman should be. The only category left is the person who is uniquely you, the one who can transcend the male-female dichotomy and succeed on her own terms. The one who doesn't conform. The one without gender consciousness in achievement. Me.

I raised the question with Fei-Fei, and she agreed that in the early stages of finding her passion, she saw herself simply as a scientist. The identification as Woman Scientist came later, when she was able to look back and see the challenges that she had previously ignored. "Now in my career I've become more conscious of the issues and I feel I have a responsibility to lift other women with me," Fei-Fei said.

It was a trajectory I had heard before. As a genius woman, you put on blinders and focus on the work. If you start out seeing the world as limited because you are a Woman, the possibilities for who and what you can be are immediately reduced. Only if you can ignore the implicit restrictions and climb high are you then in the position to use your distinctive position for good. All of the women I had interviewed had done exactly that. They walked through closed doors—and once they were on the other side, they looked for ways to push them wide open. I thought about how Jo Dunkley told me that she never thought twice about raising her hand in her all-male advanced science classes and didn't attend the women-in-physics seminars when she was at Oxford because they didn't seem relevant. *Woman in science? No, I'm just a scientist, thanks.* Only when she had achieved a rarefied level of success did she look back and see the implications of the bias she had previously brushed off. Fei-Fei recognized and understood those gender expectations when she was young, but she disregarded them. Once she was established, she was determined to change what she had previously ignored. She cofounded with a former student named Olga Russakovsky (now an assistant professor at Princeton) an organization called AI4ALL to promote diversity and inclusiveness in the field.

Fei-Fei has made the point often that machine values are human values. If you want to use AI for good—and that is her whole goal—you need people with different perspectives creating the applications. "It took a left-handed person to create the left-handed scissors," Fei-Fei told me. "The right-handed people had been using the right-handed scissors and never seen that the technology was lacking."

The advantage of seeing yourself outside of categories and boundaries, of feeling comfortable with the Me designation, is that you let yourself think creatively. Unbounded, out-of-the-box thinking is almost a requirement for genius. When Fei-Fei got into AI, scientists were coming up with more and more complicated algorithms to teach computers to see and recognize objects. As Fei-Fei explains it, if you were trying to get a computer to identify a cat, you'd tell it in mathematical language that a cat has round eyes, two pointy ears, a long body, and a curvy tail. But what if the image showed a curled-up cat, where all you could see is a blob of fur? Or how about a cat that's leaping off a chair? There were an infinite number of parameters for the computer to learn.

Fei-Fei started thinking in a completely different direction. What if she could teach computers to learn the same way babies did—by experiencing the world around them? She realized that if you think of a child's eyes as being biological cameras, by age three, a child has seen hundreds of millions of pictures of the real world. Fei-Fei was inspired. Instead of creating more and more parameters and data sets, as most computer scientists were doing, she would just show the computer as many images as possible and let it learn. Everyone told her she was wrong and her idea would never work, but in 2007, she launched a project called ImageNet, collecting and sorting nearly a billion images on the internet. She then connected them to a kind of machine learning based on neural networks—and the results were compelling. Her computers could look at an image and tell a simple story about what they were seeing.

Fei-Fei's technique is now used everywhere in AI, but it was radical at the time. I asked her how she got the courage to go ahead amidst all the doubters, and she politely reminded me that she's a scientist. She's not melodramatic. She wasn't getting threatening calls on stormy nights telling her to back off her plan. Rather, she listened to the objections people expressed and analyzed them and didn't find anything convincing enough to make her give up.

"I had enough reason to believe this is a fruitful direction and we have to give it a try," she said. "I wasn't able to say I was absolutely right and you guys are absolutely wrong. But I didn't mind other people telling me no. The harder task is to execute it well. How do I go ahead and get it done?"

Wow. I tried to imagine any point in my entire life when I would have had Fei-Fei's nerve. I couldn't think of one. I like to believe that I am independent and strong, but I grew up with traditional parents holding traditional suburban values, and I was infected with agreeable-woman disease. I want people to like me. I always figure someone knows more than I do. Tell me no and I probably won't argue or assume that I'm right—I'll disappear and try something more likely to get accepted. I see little girls on the street wearing T-shirts that say THE FUTURE IS FEMALE or GIRLS CAN DO ANYTHING, and I wonder how much the messages mean when set against the sparkly tiaras they are also wearing. To believe, truly believe deep in your bones, that you should stand up for yourself and challenge the status quo is difficult for anyone. For a woman, it is almost impossible. But it is an absolutely vital step if you want to make waves as a genius.

Fei Fei told me that even as a child, she recognized the explicit gender expectations of society, but she did whatever she could to avoid them. She never stayed within boundaries. Her ability to think outside limits is part of her genius—and it's the genius of many women I met. The eighteenth-century philosopher Immanuel Kant said a genius creates something original rather than copying what exists. He wasn't a great fan of women, so it's nice to throw his words back at him and point out that women who are able to ignore gender expectations make themselves strong enough to ignore *all* limits. Geniuses by their very definition are outliers who think expansively. A woman who sees beyond gender boundaries is empowering herself to create something original. It's her first step to becoming a genius.

Most academics work in a narrow field, but Fei-Fei's PhD thesis daringly crossed disciplines. An intellectual juggler, she needed two advisors to work with her, and by the time she hit the real world, her perspective on AI went well beyond that of the standard computer scientist. She was a humanist and a cognitive neuroscientist and a physicist. No way she would see AI as just a tool for driverless cars. In the latest incarnation of her work, she is contemplating how to use AI to change health care and hospitals and promote equality. You don't usher in the Fourth Industrial Revolution (as AI is being called) by being timid.

Fei-Fei told me about a conversation she'd had with Elon Musk, the self-made billionaire who founded and helped start PayPal and Tesla and SpaceX. Discussing the potential doom that could come with AI, he expressed surprise that she seemed to be optimistic about its future. She explained that she would do everything she could to make this a positive technology.

"He asked me why I cared and I said, 'I'm a mother.' He laughed because he understood. This is about the future. It's not just about being geeky."

I wondered briefly if that is one more reason that we need women scientists—because they are often the ones looking at the humanistic side of discoveries. But I don't like patting ourselves on the back for what women do better—because like every other blanket statement about men and women, it falls apart when you get down to individuals. The lines between humanist and scientist are often blurred. Men are fathers—they also have an investment in the future—and there is no obvious reason that women should think about health care and education and equality more seriously than men do. In fact, Fei-Fei told me she had been inspired by the great physicists of the twentieth century, like Albert Einstein and Erwin Schrödinger, who started drifting away from equations in the latter part of their lives and asking bigger questions. "I started to follow that beacon of light and realize that I'm more interested in life than atoms," she said.

Fei-Fei is likely to help create that positive future she envisions because she is an original, thinking in different ways, taking everything she knows and combining it in new directions. She lives outside stereotypes and expectations. She is not defined by being a woman or a man. She is Me. Fei-Fei Li. Nobody else is like her.

———

Let me make it clear that the Men, Women, and Me formulation has nothing to do with sexuality or whom you sleep with—it is about your perception of your own abilities and possibilities. It is about not seeing limits. Fei-Fei is married to a fellow AI scientist she met during graduate school. After many years at different schools (what academics call "the two-body problem"), they are now both at Stanford, working in similar areas of AI, and parenting their two little children.

I had a conversation about the Men, Women, and Me concept with a wonderful older woman who had been active as a second-wave feminist, the bold women of the late 1960s who formed consciousness-raising groups and marched and protested for women's equality. In her view, women being able to see themselves outside of the socially decreed stereotype is only to the good.

"In the sixties, you might have wanted to create your own definition of self, that *Me* you talk about, but you had to struggle against a lot of restrictions," she told me.

It's hard to be original and creative and free when everything in the society is forcing you into a restrictive corner. Some of the rights women were denied at the time are almost inconceivable now. A woman needed a husband to cosign for a bank account. She couldn't get a credit card in her own name. The concept of marital rape didn't exist. In many states, birth control pills were available only to married women.[2]

Or perhaps those limitations are not so inconceivable. There are still societies that keep women restricted and submissive—and there

---

2 In New York, unmarried women would sometimes put on a gold band and bring a male friend to the hospital with them to qualify for a "therapeutic" abortion. It does make you wonder how many laws relating to abortion and birth control are really just about punishing women and keeping their bodies under men's control.

are plenty of structures in our society right now that are fairly appalling. We admire the United States Constitution as a great document—and yet the word "women" never appears in it. The Equal Rights Amendment never passed. America has thousands of laws, but not one of them helps men and women integrate their lives at home and at work. America remains virtually the only country in the industrialized world—yes, the whole *world*—that does not require new parents to get paid time off.[3] Every couple or single parent is left to figure it out on their own.

It's not an accident that America chooses to be a backward-looking outlier in this matter. America ended employment discrimination only in 1964—and that *was* an accident. Legislators trying to kill Title VII of the Civil Rights Act, which banned discrimination for race or religion or national origin, threw in "sex" at the last minute. They hoped that saying women had to be treated equally in the workplace would finally extinguish any chance of passing the bill. It didn't. Okay, if you can't get rid of a woman because she's pregnant or has a family, you can at least make it hard for her. Very hard. And that's what American policies (or lack of them for parental leave) continue to do.

But back to my second-wave feminist friend. She asked me not to use her name because she thought her comments might be too controversial—and at age eighty or so, who wants to be a target on social media?

Her question was this: If we could truly achieve a place where gender restrictions had been eased and stereotypes erased, would so many students now be announcing themselves as nonbinary? Would people need to describe themselves as gender fluid if their birth

---

3   According to a study of the 193 countries in the United Nations, only the United States, Papua New Guinea, and Suriname have no national paid-leave policies. There may be a few island countries in the Pacific Ocean that also don't have paid parental leave. But they do have nice scenery.

gender allowed them to do anything? Wasn't the very need for a non-binary designation a reflection of an unforgiving and sexist society? I didn't have an answer, and she mentioned that questions like these have been a feminist flashpoint on both sides of the Atlantic. She wasn't trying to get involved in the political debate. But after years of fighting for equality, it struck her as both stunning and sad that, in her words, nonbinary becomes its own category, rather than how we understand the diversity and range of all people.

"If we were truly free to be you and me, then I like to think everyone could just accept themselves as they are," she said.

I smiled at her reference. Marlo Thomas's 1972 album *Free to Be . . . You and Me* remains in the top one hundred albums of all time, and several generations have now grown up listening and singing along. But I'm not sure how much effect it has had. The football player Rosey Grier crooned that it's okay to cry ("crying gets the sad out"), and a boy named William who doesn't like sports gets a doll—his grandmother pointing out that it's a good thing since he'll learn how to be a dad. Two babies don't know if each is a boy or a girl—she wants to be a firefighter and he wants to be a cocktail waitress, and he's afraid of mice and she's not. Does that mean anything? "You can't judge a book by its cover," she says. In the next song, the baby girl asks if she'll be pretty when she's bigger and if he'll be tall. She finally decides it doesn't matter: "Well, I don't care if I'm pretty at all, and I don't care if you never get tall . . . we don't have to change at all."

The great comic Mel Brooks sang the part of the baby boy, but even the director of *Blazing Saddles* and *Young Frankenstein* couldn't convince us to give up our gender stereotypes. We not only continue to judge a book by its cover; we put the pages in a completely different category if they're written by a woman. Hearing the cheerful, optimistic songs now is bittersweet. To Marlo Thomas and her celebrity friends at the time (including Alan Alda, Carol Channing, and Diana

Ross), the need for equality was obvious and important, and they felt themselves at a breakthrough moment of change. They must have felt in that hopeful era that all they had to do was send the message in humorous, catchy songs and we'd all get it.

All of the genius women I interviewed got it. Fitting into old-fashioned stereotypes was not a path to success, and they shook them off, making themselves free to be . . . astrophysicists, engineers, Nobel laureates. If society at large wouldn't listen to Rosey Grier and Mel Brooks and give up the strict lines of Woman and Man, they would step outside those lines and do it themselves. They were free to be Me.

A very smart lawyer I know who is a partner at a major firm teaches one class every year at NYU School of Law. She loves the students and enjoys sharing her knowledge and experience—but recently the school issued some new guidelines. Students were to be asked at the start of the semester what pronoun they preferred, and if someone in the class wanted to be outside the traditional "he" and "she," the teachers were urged to consider using "ze" for everyone. "The first time I used it in class—'Ze is correct'—I felt like I was faking an old Russian accent," she told me with a laugh. It's easy to dismiss this as pure silliness and political correctness run amok, and other friends of mine teaching adjunct courses at schools around the country have had similar experiences. But thinking about it later, I wondered if "ze," or whatever equivalent gets chosen, is this generation's Marlo Thomas moment. The students want to be free to flourish outside gender expectations and stereotypes. Though gender inclusiveness has somehow been twisted to be more about bathroom choices on college campuses than life choices, it's really the latter that matters. Women coined "Ms." in the 1960s to say that your identification shouldn't be based on whether you are married or not—and while Richard Nixon and other fusty men at the time publicly ridiculed it, the idea made sense. It caught on. I can be single or happily married, but that's not the main way to think about me—and frankly, it's not really your business.

When talking about the challenges of smart women trying to make a mark, we could fall back on the Nietzsche-inspired adage that what doesn't kill you makes you stronger. The problem is that bias *does* kill the nerve of a lot of talented women. They run off to try something that fits better with what the world expects. No matter who you are, it's harder than anyone might think to shine as Me in a Men-Women world.

Not long ago, I went with my husband to a fancy shop on Madison Avenue where he bought an expensive suit that the salesperson accessorized with an ice-blue tie and a very classy blue-and-purple pocket square. He looked very handsome. (He *is* very handsome.) A couple of weeks later as we were getting dressed for a friend's wedding, he put on the new outfit—and then put the square in and took it out of his pocket half a dozen times. Ron is never indecisive, so I finally asked him what was wrong.

"I just don't know if I'm the purple pocket square kind of guy," he said.

"You mean it's not manly?" I asked.

He nodded glumly.

We have been married a long time, and while I don't mean to brag on his behalf, there is absolutely nothing to question about his manhood. He knows that, and so do I. He is also one of the least sexist people I know—he was the perfect co-parent, always eager to do more than 50 percent as we raised our children. He understood about William's doll, he cared about my career as much as his own, and he makes pancakes on Sunday mornings a lot better than I do. But here he was, suffering from the faux divisions we create about what's appropriate for men and women.

The incident made me feel a little sorry for men, too—though not *that* sorry. It's easier to deal with the potential bias against wearing a purple pocket square than with the bias that keeps you from fulfilling your dreams as a genius astrophysicist, artist, or philosopher. But the general point is the same. When we separate, we diminish rather than expand.

The English poet and philosopher Samuel Taylor Coleridge told us 150 years ago that, "the truth is, a great mind must be androgynous." And Carolyn Gold Heilbrun, a celebrated professor at Columbia University and the first female professor to get tenure in the English department, argued in the early 1970s that we need to "free ourselves from the prison of gender." Genius and creativity flow when we aren't wedded to strict gender expectations and limits, or to the corrosive definitions of "masculine" and "feminine."

Here is what I know: My husband looks great in a pocket square—but not every man does. Fei-Fei Li is a brilliant star in her field—but not every woman could match her. We all do our best when we ignore expectations, figure out our talents, and do everything possible to enhance them. You can't be a genius, an original, if you are bound by hoary ideas that define Woman and Man and don't let you explore and create. All of the genius women I met had shaken free of irrational boundaries and were delightfully free to be Me.

CHAPTER 8

===

The Astrophysicist Who Does Not Need Tom Cruise

I'm a sucker for romantic comedies. I don't apologize, since you can be a strong and powerful woman, a true genius in your field, and still want love and romance. One day recently, I put on the now-classic rom-com *Jerry Maguire* while I worked out on a treadmill. I figured its charms would keep me going. Instead, it brought me to a dead stop. The movie, which got nominated for five Academy Awards, stars Tom Cruise as a sports agent, and it's famous for one of his football-playing clients repeatedly shouting—"Show me the money!" It's also famous for the speech Cruise's character makes to his wife, played by Renée Zellweger, after they've broken up and he realizes that he wants her back.

"I'm not letting you get rid of me, how about that," he says, eyes blazing, as he barges into her living room. "I love you. You complete me."

You complete me. In 1996, we all sighed happily at that line.

But as I watched this time, I had a different reaction. I stopped running on the treadmill for a moment and hit the rewind button. *You complete me?* I suddenly wished Zellweger had looked at him with her moony eyes and said, "Well, that sounds good for you. But what do I get out of it?"

Cruise is appealingly passionate in his speech, and he's also puppy-dog cute. It might be hard to turn him down, no matter what he said. But the "you complete me" idea kept nagging at me. It made me think of another much-repeated line in the annals of romantic serenades, when Jack Nicholson's character in *As Good As It Gets* tells Helen Hunt, "You make me want to be a better man." As far as romantic murmurings go, it's as narcissistic as the Cruise mantra. The underlying message is that a woman's job is to make the man better, more successful, and happier. *You complete me. You make me better.* Shouldn't love be about the other person, and not just you? And is it any surprise that both those movies were written by men?

Throughout history, men have been happy to find a woman who completes them—and it's not just romance they have in mind. The great composer Felix Mendelssohn turned to his older sister, Fanny, to complete him—or at least to complete his musical oeuvre. She was extraordinarily gifted and focused on her music, and he published many of her compositions under his name. He claimed to be doing her a favor. An upscale girl in the nineteenth century shouldn't be flaunting her talents in public, because who would marry her? As often happens when men are "protecting" women, it worked out rather well for him, too. He got all the credit for Fanny's music, and some of it was notably better than his. Fanny was particularly talented at the German songs, or *Lieder,* and Felix published at least six of her songs under his name. Queen Victoria once invited Felix to Buckingham Palace and thanked him for writing one of her favorite songs. What could the man say? Fanny had written it.

Growing up in a wealthy family in Germany, Fanny was prodigiously talented, and she and Felix shared tutors and music teachers. She was brilliant on the piano, and her first public performance, at age twelve, was said to be breathtaking.[1] But, despite the triumph, she had only one chance to appear (much later) in public again—because instead of being proud of her extraordinary talent, her parents were worried. A girl needed to hide her genius under a well-tempered clavier to fit into society and marry well. When Fanny was fourteen, her father, Abraham Mendelssohn, sent her a letter explaining that while Felix could go on and have a career in music, "for you it can and must only be an ornament, never the root of your being and doing."

It never occurred to either Abraham or Felix that music *was* the root of her being. Or if they did understand it, they didn't care. I find that letter, and others her father wrote, almost painfully sad to read. It is reminiscent of the anguish faced by Mozart's sister. A woman with a genius for composing was told that she had to give it up, as her father wrote her, for "the only calling of a young woman—I mean the state of a housewife." The line gives me chills. Imagine telling a genius man that his talents as a child prodigy were all well and good, but now it was time to suppress the talent and be a dad. He might turn to you and say, *Are you kidding? Why can't I do both?*

Fanny had a powerful drive to write music, and despite the pressure to abandon her talent and what made her happy, she composed some five hundred pieces, including songs and choral works. Like genius women before and after, Fanny had to figure out how to get her ideas and music heard. When the world doesn't want to listen to a girl—and you're a girl—what do you do? Fanny came up with the very clever idea of holding Sunday afternoon musical salons at her home. Though considered private parties, they were more like concerts than tea parties. She would invite two hundred or more people and have a planned program, but since the music was in her home

---

1   She played twenty-four preludes of Bach's "The Well-Tempered Clavier" from memory.

and not on an officially public stage, it was deemed acceptable in society. Now, that's genius.

Of course, we don't have to do things like that anymore, right? Except we do. Women of genius still have trouble being heard. They aren't specifically told to go home and have babies, but they are left on their own to figure out how to combine family and genius and private and public. It's not as obvious as in Fanny's day, but the pressures are just as real. All the political and social systems are neatly set against them.

Fanny's salons got wide attention, and her music was much admired and discussed in upper-class Berlin society. But after a while, that wasn't enough. Even a girl genius can long for public acclaim—and she finally got up her nerve, thumbed her nose at convention, and published some pieces under her own name. And surprise! Nobody collapsed in horror because a woman did great work. Instead, she got terrific reviews, and the brief period of acclaim that followed was, she said, the happiest time of her life. Sadly, in an ending that Tolstoy might have written, she died soon after.

Fanny's work is getting new attention now, and I think it's time to rethink brother Felix, too. I've read critics who say that his motivation in publishing Fanny's work under his name was to honor and recognize her in a time when she couldn't get that notice on her own. He knew she was great—and what greater honor than saying her works were worthy of his name?

Okay, sure—but I don't buy it. I agree that Felix knew she was a terrific composer, and maybe better than him. He had relied on her for advice on his music since he was eleven and a teacher asked him to write a short opera—and she did it for him. He might have felt guilty that her work wasn't known to a larger circle, but he certainly didn't want her getting too much attention on her own, either. What better way to avoid competition from your talented sister than to pretend you're a nice guy—and appropriate everything she writes?

If there is a lesson to be learned from the Fanny and Felix story, I think it is this. Beware of men who ask you to complete them.

I sometimes imagine a dinner party where I could bring together women across the centuries to drink wine and share their stories. Lying in bed at night, I plan the seating chart. Next to Fanny Mendelssohn, I think I would place Elizebeth Friedman. It might take them a while to figure out what they have in common. Unlike the upper-class Fanny, Elizebeth grew up on a farm in Indiana in the early 1900s. She didn't write music—she broke codes.

Friedman was a genius at solving complicated puzzles and seeing patterns that nobody else recognized. She got some fame in the 1930s when she worked as a cryptanalyst for the US Coast Guard and decoded messages that stopped gangsters and smugglers. Then during World War II, she hunted Nazi spies and broke their spy codes. Her husband, William, also a cryptographer, got a lot of the credit for her achievements—but (unlike Felix) he tried to deflect the praise. He often said that she was smarter than he was. They seemed to have a close and happy marriage, sending each other coded love letters that only the other one could understand.

Friedman's work essentially changed intelligence gathering in the twentieth century. Her brilliance in figuring out codes brought information that changed the war. Friedman dismantled three different Enigma machines, the complicated rotor-cipher machines that the Germans used to send military information. To understand the cleverly constructed machines, imagine a simple code where you substitute the next letter in the alphabet for every letter in a word.

GENIUS becomes HFOJVT—and a woman HFOJVT like Fried-man would be able to see a page written in that code and figure it out very quickly. The Enigma was an electrical machine designed so that every time you put in one substitution, the rotors turned, and a com-pletely different encryption appeared for the next letter. G might be-come H . . . but then the rotors turned so E became (perhaps) Y and N corresponded to (say) T. There were four or more rotors ever turn-ing and giving different positions for the letters, plus various other complexities adding to the permutations. If you had a machine on the other end, you could set it to unravel the complex pattern. If you didn't, the letters that appeared had no discernable pattern and looked like gibberish. There were literally *quintillions* (that's eighteen zeros) of possible solutions. Amazingly, Friedman conquered the problem. It was a stunning triumph, almost beyond belief. Her team decoded four thousand Nazi messages, which helped smash spy networks and save lives.

Friedman's husband might have been supportive and eager to give her credit, but not so for her über-boss—FBI director J. Edgar Hoover. Professionally, there's often a guy around who can use a brilliant woman to complete him—or at least add to his image. After Fried-man's war triumphs, Hoover twisted the story to get the accolades for himself. He blatantly wrote her out of the annals of the war and took the kudos. She did all the impressive work in code breaking for na-tional security, and then he fashioned himself as the hero. Friedman was a woman genius who wanted to help the world. Hoover was a powerful man with no morals. Guess who wins in that battle? Writ-ing a woman out of history was probably not even among the ten most egregious things he did in a day.

Hoover would never have had either the brainpower or the perse-verance to perform the genius feats of cryptanalysis that Friedman achieved. What's irksome is how easily he understood a different code—the one that dominates how women and men are perceived. That a genius woman code breaker had been one of the great heroes of the war, destroying Nazi networks with her technical brilliance, would have surprised people. That a man had been the hero fit the normative story. As long as nobody believes in women's achievements, it's easy for men to be self-congratulatory and take all the credit.

I hope Fanny and Elizebeth have a nice time talking to each other at my imaginary dinner party. They'll have a lot to discuss.

For my fantasy dinner party, I would send an engraved invitation to Meg Urry to join my historical guests—though I could invite her to a real dinner party, too. As a genius physicist studying distant galaxies with supermassive black holes at their center, Urry continues to advance science while trying also to advance women. Sitting with Fanny Mendelssohn and Elizebeth Friedman, she could discuss the difficulties women in the twenty-first century still have admitting to their own genius and pushing it forward in the world.

I first met Urry about fifteen years ago when she talked to a few Yale alums over lunch about her work. I didn't just admire her—I wanted to *be* her. Imagine understanding the universe in the way that she does! We are roughly the same age, but it occurred to me that if I were back at Yale as a student, I would want nothing more than to study physics with her. She is the kind of role model who opens possibilities that you never dreamed about before.

Urry's own credentials are beyond brilliant. She was a senior leader at the institute running the Hubble Space Telescope for NASA before Yale lured her to become the first (of course!) tenured woman professor in the physics department. With her sterling work and matching demeanor, she quickly became the head of the department (first woman to chair the physics department, etc.) and remains one of the most highly cited experts in her field.

I was eager to catch up with her again, and working around her busy schedule (she lectures all around the world), we finally met at her large office in a white-pillared mansion on one of the prettiest streets in New Haven. We hugged and chatted about children and jobs, and Urry laughed at my idealized image of her. She made it clear that all had not been as easy and straightforward as her glorious résumé and confident style would suggest. She'd had many years of dealing with men who wanted to undermine her for no reason other than her gender. "It's not like anyone is saying we don't want women," she said. "But there's this subtle discrimination because we just don't have it in our heads that women can be leaders in science or elsewhere."

It's not just the men who have that notion in their heads. At an event once that included some of the foremost women professors at Yale, the meeting organizer asked everyone to introduce herself and describe the field where she was an expert. Urry was stunned when almost every woman demurred. Instead of pronouncing her strengths, each made a comment like, "I wouldn't say I'm an expert, but I know a lot about . . ." or "I'm very good in . . ." These were all tenured faculty at Yale. "The standard of tenure is that you are the world expert in your field, and the currency at a university is the ability to state your own authority," Urry told me. What was going on? Maybe it's a kind of post-traumatic stress disorder, the aftershocks left from generations of women forced to hide their talents under a scrim of modesty. We become successful, the absolute experts in our fields, but we are either too modest to say so (*Don't brag!* girls are told) or don't fully believe in our talents. "Many driven women look only at what they haven't accomplished," she told me. "Men, on the other hand, usually think they are exceeding expectations."

I nodded—because we've all seen it happen. Some years ago, I asked Urry to write a cover story on her amazing work for the big magazine where I was editor in chief. Urry told me that after the cover story appeared, she got two types of emails. One was from women all over the world who thanked her for being an inspiration to them. The other was from men whose position was generally *You don't understand dark energy. Let me explain it to you.* When she got one of those emails from a ten-year-old boy, Urry kindly wrote back, urging him to continue studying math and physics so he could some-day contribute to the understanding of these big concepts. He sent an irritated reply: "But what about the theory I already told you?"

Urry shook her head when she told me the story. "It struck me as an exclusively male response," she said.

I knew exactly what she meant, because sometime after the piece ran, a new CEO came to our magazine and looked over some of my earlier issues. He paused at Urry's cover story.

"You know that there's no such thing as black holes," he said with a patronizing smile. "It's just what astronomers call anything they don't understand."

"Why do you say that?" I asked carefully.

"I know a lot about science," he said dismissively.

He was completely wrong. He was a guy who was lucky enough to stumble into being made CEO, but he had no clue about black holes or dark energy or the recent insights into astrophysics. There was no reason he would. Still, he had all the confidence of a powerful man who believed that his unsubstantiated opinion held more valid-ity than anything a genius woman could prove through research, dis-covery, and (dare we say) facts. He was a guy! His gut instinct would be right! Only it wasn't. Not at all.

———

Urry became a strong advocate for women from very early in her career. Many of the genius women I interviewed, like Fei-Fei Li and Jo Dunkley, had blinders about bias as they rose in the ranks and only started fighting for women when they had achieved their own success. But Urry got in the trenches early. Working on Hubble, she realized how badly the few (very few) women on the team were treated. Although the women wrote more papers, got more grants, and were generally more successful, they were being paid less. When she raised the issue, the men didn't really see that there was any problem. "It was an awakening," she told me. "I wanted to say, 'Are you crazy? We have two women out of sixty PhDs that you hired in the last five years. That's not a problem?'"

She organized a national conference for women in astronomy in 1992, and after two days of presentations and discussions, their magna carta emerged—a charter of rights for women that they presented to colleges and universities. While the conference was a huge success and led to several others, the recommendations for change didn't get quite the enthusiasm that Urry hoped. How revolutionary were the ideas? One position held that there should be some effort to include women on the short list when looking for new professors. That's not revolutionary—it's bland and obvious. And yet the reply from virtually all of the colleges came back—

Nope, won't do it! Totally inappropriate!

Forget writing women *out* of history; a lot of men didn't want to write them *in*. The opposition also included the women at many universities who said they didn't want any special treatment.

"What I think we need to make clear to women is that you're already getting special treatment," Urry told me. "It's called special negative treatment and the men are getting special positive treatment. You have to correct for that—otherwise you're dipping lower in the talent pool to get these less-qualified white men."

It's an interesting concept, right? Men like to claim that hiring women is a dangerous affirmative action that lowers standards. Urry says it's exactly the opposite. Let's say you have ten candidates for two spots and a man is the clear number one. You hire him. All good. Now for the next choice. If women candidates are objectively in positions number two and number three but unconscious bias doesn't let you see that, your next hire is the man who is actually number four. As Urry said, you're dipping lower in the talent pool because you are blinded by the supposed strengths of men.

Urry told me that when astronomers survey the sky, they naturally make adjustments to be sure there's no bias in what they're seeing. Is that bright star more powerful than the faint one, or is it just more obvious because it's closer? When it comes to seeing the relative brightness of male and female stars, though, scientists ignore the data and bend to their unconscious biases. Male graduate students, those bright stars, get prizes and recognition all the time and are regularly hailed for doing original work. Women grad students are assumed to be doing what they're told and are just hardworking cogs in their advisor's wheel. (*She completes him.*)

Now that Urry has rank and status, you'd think she'd be okay. Nobody can doubt that she's the top dog, the lead author, the head honcho. A chaired professor, she's also the director of the Yale Center for Astronomy and Astrophysics, and the idea-generating brainiac who leads a dozen or so researchers every year doing intergalactic explorations. Maybe when she was a graduate student, people attributed her successes to her male advisor, as happens so often to talented young women. But not now, right? Yes, now. It doesn't matter that the woman is leading the lab—she's still a woman. In a flip of the script so misogynistic it's almost hard to believe, when a top woman in science has a big success, the daggers and disbelievers still come out. Urry has heard the whisperings even about herself—that there must be a smart male student in the lab who did the work and deserves the credit. *She's lucky to have him.*

I burst out laughing when Urry told me that—but she didn't look like she found it very funny. Ludicrous, maybe. But also hurtful and dispiriting. It should be hard to erase a widely respected woman genius when she runs the show and keeps producing great work. So the deviousness of suggesting that a male undergraduate working for her must be the real genius is . . . crazy. Dangerous. Scary. It's easy to imagine that if one of those students goes on to be an important physicist—as is likely to happen coming from a top-flight lab run by a genius woman at a major university—then it becomes even easier in retrospect to suggest that the male brain and testosterone were the secret all along. Writing the woman out of the story takes a bizarre twist. Some men will do anything to stay on as the heroes of the story.

I don't mean to make too much of this, because Urry is highly respected for her breakthrough work and she knows that she has the scientific cred that allows her to speak up about women's issues. Her students adore her, and young women scientists idolize her. She has single-handedly changed attitudes, and when she gives talks around the country, there is almost always a young woman who rushes up to say that having Meg as a role model allowed her to continue her career in science. When she first got to Yale, women students who weren't even in her department would come to her for career advice and inspiration. "I don't know who they spoke to before I arrived," Urry admits. She has such a magnetic personality and easy but confident style that, like me, young women didn't just want to talk to her—they wanted to become just like her.

Changing the world is nice, but it's also tiring. Urry has spent a lot of years fighting off all the slings and arrows of outraged men. She has spent a lot of energy creating a science-fiction-like force field around herself to deflect attacks. When I met her in the past, Urry always seemed to have more energy than anyone I'd met. Everything was possible, and she had a take-no-prisoners approach to life. But when we talked this time, I realized that holding on to that force field takes both stamina and moxie. After a while it's exhausting. One reason women geniuses get written out of history is because they give up, worn down by the constant need to explain and defend and cope with insatiable male egos.

Urry isn't worn down, but she is more realistic than when she was young and just ignored all the obstacles in her way. Like so many of the women geniuses I met, she started out with unmitigated optimism—which is a help rather than a hindrance early in a career. "I always had a sense that the path was open and I could do any-thing," Urry told me. When you think you can do anything, you go ahead and do it—as I had seen already with Susan Wollenberg and Shirley Tilghman and Fei-Fei Li and so many others. If you have to worry that your work is going to be ignored, erased, or undermined, then it's harder to push forward.

Urry told me that when she was young and realized that there weren't any women doing what she wanted to do, "I figured that it must be because nobody else had ever wanted to." It took her some time to realize "that was baloney. Of course other women had wanted all this, but the path was not open."

Is the path open now? We like to think so. But it's still strewn with rocks. Her first year teaching at Yale, Urry was walking back from a meeting with a male colleague who invited her to get a cup of coffee. She wanted to join him and continue their conversation, but she had to get back and prepare for her class—she told him that the kids were so smart, she had to be ready for everything. He laughed. "I don't pre-pare for my classes," he told her. "If they ask a question I don't know, I just make something up and they believe me." Urry looked at him in shock. She had the opposite experience. "I told him, 'Even when I know exactly what I'm talking about, they still don't believe me!'"

Women sometimes help men write them out of history by writing *themselves* out of the story. They replace their female self with an im-age more likely to get acclaim or be treated seriously. It's not unrea-sonable. You can want structural change, but you're living and trying to succeed in the world as it exists right now. Sometimes the best ap-proach is covert resistance—and it continues to happen.

Not too long ago a struggling mom named Joanne wrote a nice book on wizards that was rejected by a dozen publishers. She finally found one who paid her a tiny advance and planned to print a thou-sand copies. Wanting the book to appeal to boys, the publisher sug-gested that she dump her first name and use her initials. She became J. K. Rowling, and the Harry Potter series became one of the most popular in history. The newly initialed author went on to be one of the richest people around.

Would Jo Rowling have done as well if her readers knew she was a woman? We can only guess—but apparently Rowling didn't think so. After the success of the Harry Potter books, she started writing crime novels for adults and chose the pseudonym Robert Galbraith. If people think you're a guy, you're more likely to get read. In a nice twist, Robert's first book had scant sales—and became a bestseller only when word leaked that it was by our girl Jo.

Great women writers have often hidden behind men's names. George Sand, the most popular writer in early-nineteenth-century Europe, was actually a noblewoman named Aurore Dupin. She wore men's clothes to give her the freedom she wanted as she moved around Paris, and she had a glamorous personal life with a husband, children, and many romantic affairs. Mary Ann Evans chose the pseudonym George Eliot for the seven novels she wrote in the mid-1800s, in part because she figured that a novel by a woman would be dismissed as light and frivolous. You'd be hard-pressed to describe *Middlemarch* or *Silas Marner* or *The Mill on the Floss* as either light or frivolous, and one of my favorite modern English writers, Julian Barnes, has called *Middlemarch* the best novel in the English language. But Evans was very aware that stereotypes affect how we perceive any work, and her heroines had to grapple with the limitations of their circumstances, too. At the beginning of *Middlemarch,* Dorothea Brooke is a young woman who wants to be different and special and change the world. At the end, she is married and spends her time giving "wifely help." She completes him, you might say. Her friends think it's a shame that "so substantive and rare a creature should have been absorbed into the life of another." Was it in her power to become anything more or different? It's more puzzlement than tragedy.

Two centuries later, it's still a puzzlement for women. Can you emerge as someone special, a genius, when all the social structures are against you? George Eliot gives the question a twist at the end by concluding that sometimes it is "we insignificant people with our daily words and acts" who make the world a better place, and she gives a nod to those "who lived faithfully a hidden life, and rest in unvisited tombs." It's not very encouraging that women who want to be special and noticed end up being told that "insignificant" isn't bad, either. Yet it's the very struggle that George Eliot faced in her daily life. As a character in another of her novels, *Daniel Deronda,* says, "You may try—but you can never imagine what it is to have a man's force of genius in you and to suffer the slavery of being a girl."

Whether a genius writer is George or Mary Ann, Joanne or J. K., changes how we think about the book in front of us. In fact, it's stunning to realize that gender influences how we see everything—including the moon and the sun. I learned that from Lera Boroditsky, a cognitive scientist at the University of California San Diego who has done breakthrough work on how language changes the ways we think about the world. She points out that many languages assign a gender to otherwise neutral nouns. For example, in French, a chair is feminine—*la chaise*. I once asked for partial credit on a vocabulary test in my junior high school French class since I had the word *chaise* correct and what difference did it make if I got the gender wrong? A chair is a chair. There are not girl and boy chairs. My teacher, Madame G., looked at me scornfully and explained that the feminine article *la* was part of the *chaise*. I got no credit at all.[2]

Professor Boroditsky has found that people who grow up having the gender of nouns ingrained see the actual objects differently. The word for "bridge" is feminine in German (*die Brücke*) and masculine in Spanish (*el puente*). You wouldn't think that would do much other than confuse anyone working through an online Babbel class. But, says Professor Boroditsky, German speakers are more likely to describe bridges with stereotypical feminine words like "beautiful" or "elegant." Spanish speakers take a masculine perspective, using words like "strong" or "long" to describe the very same picture of the very same bridge.

As for changing how we see the universe—in German, the sun is feminine and the moon is masculine, and darn it if Germans don't see the sun as softly sending light while the moon sits powerfully in the sky. Before you think there may be any astronomical validity

2 Even the word "the" changes so that you use *le* for masculine nouns and *la* for feminine ones. All the adjectives have to match by gender, too. Fortunately, the plural is always *les,* so you can stick with *les croissants* and be done with it.

to that, Boroditsky notes that in Spanish, it's exactly the reverse: masculine sun and feminine moon. The adjectives people use to describe them get reversed, too. The Spaniards look in the sky and see a strong sun and a sweetly whimsical moon.

That's startling, isn't it? The random assignment of gender to an otherwise neutered object changes how we view it. Recognizing that words can be powerful, hundreds of academics in France recently signed a manifesto to change the language and make it less sexist. They particularly objected to the French position that *"le masculin l'emporte sur le féminin"*—which means that "the masculine prevails over the feminine." Whether true or not empirically, it is definitely the case linguistically. A troop of graceful female dancers in toe shoes and flowing skirts are together called by the feminine plural, *danseuses.* But if there's one guy in tights among them, the prevalence of romantic tutus doesn't matter and they are referred to by the masculine plural, *danseurs.* The same rule applies for professors, tennis players, politicians, and doctors. From a feminist perspective, it's like the story of one cockroach in a bowl of cherries—it spoils the whole thing. This is a lot more than a grammatical quibble. The words we use determine how we see the world—and most languages are set up to be perceived from a distinctly masculine perspective.

But in neither language nor movies nor astrophysics do we really need a male voice to complete the sentence. When genius women find their own voice, it can stand alone—powerful and complete. There are many reasons that we have missed out on the talents of women geniuses. Sometimes we don't believe they are geniuses, despite the evidence. Sometimes they don't believe it themselves. And sometimes, we just aren't listening. But what's clear is that a genius woman will never need Tom Cruise—or anyone else—to complete her.

CHAPTER 9

Broadway's Tina Landau
Contains Multitudes

The first time I encountered theater director Tina Landau, she was sitting with actress, writer, and all-around brilliant person Tina Fey and three other famously creative women on a panel discussing women in the arts. I loved that she was smart and bold and articulate—and sported sparkling high-top sneakers. Cool footwear is not necessarily a sign of genius, but her wearing them wasn't a coincidence, either. Nothing was going to slow her down.

The panelists shared stories about the challenges of being a female leader—how you often can't get people to take you seriously and what it feels like when men refuse to look at you during a meeting and only talk to your male counterparts. While the other women described the difficult situations they'd confronted, the two Tinas didn't offer any complaints about being a woman among men. They had found approaches that worked and allowed their own talents to shine.

"I'm not a yeller. You can lead in a different way," said Fey, who was the first woman head writer on *Saturday Night Live* and has since created and starred in shows like TV's *30 Rock* and the movie

Mean Girls. She admitted that the chemistry in the room often changed when a woman entered. That was okay. You just had to know what to do with it.

"Often being a leader is listening in a compassionate and nurturing way," Landau said. "It's not a weakness—it's a way I can be powerful and strong."

I was struck by the confidence they each displayed and their sense of having found a style that was real to them. They didn't have to fall into the stereotype of a tough-talking man or a passionately powerful woman. Each could just be herself, sui generis, a Tina whose unique talent ruled a room.[1]

Someone mentioned that Landau was the only woman directing a show on Broadway that season. Landau seemed mystified by her singularity, but she also had something to clarify.

"I'm not a female director—I'm a director and I'm also female," she said.

I kept thinking about the distinction—and a few weeks later, I met up with Landau at an office a couple of blocks from where her Broadway musical was playing. Now a few words about that show. It was called *SpongeBob SquarePants: The Musical,* and I understand if you're a little skeptical about a Nickelodeon cartoon being transformed into a work of genius. I had press tickets to a matinee, and I couldn't get my husband or a single friend to join me. A toddler TV show turned Broadway extravaganza? *I'm so sorry, I have to walk my dog that afternoon.*

But what I saw onstage was sheer genius—the kind of creative wizardry that leaves you slightly breathless. The soul and heart and brain of the production was genius director Landau, who turned all

---

1 Tina Fey was also wearing flat shoes. In fact, every one of the panelists was in flats. Draw what conclusions you like.

expectations upside down. When she had first been approached to create a musical from the TV show, she was dubious—but she eventually decided to take it on as a creative challenge. Several people involved with the production—including the star, a young actor and excellent sponge named Ethan Slater—told me that the biggest thrill in developing the show was just being in the same room as Tina Landau.

The day we got together to talk, Landau was wearing another pair of high-tops, though not quite as sparkly as the previous set. She had just been nominated for a Tony Award for directing, and her show had received twelve Tony nominations—the most of any show that season. She told me that her plan to get through the awards season was to "have fun, buy cool clothes, and expand my sneaker collection."

Fun and cool seemed to describe her well, along with thoughtful and extremely smart. As a director, her originality and willingness to see the world slightly differently have set her apart. I asked her why she drew the distinction between being a woman director and a woman who directs.

"Labels are constricting," she said. "To say 'I'm a woman who directs' acknowledges my womanhood—but it's also saying that my gender identity does not limit who I am or define what I can do as a director."

How refreshing! How true! You can acknowledge (and enjoy) being a woman. You can also acknowledge being a professional or a standout in your field. But what do they have to do with each other? It's like that old logic problem where you try to figure out the connection between three statements. Imagine something like this:

1. I broke my leg.
2. I ate ice cream.
3. I got better.

All the statements are true, but numbers 1 and 2 don't lead to number 3. You can get distracted and think they're connected (*The ice cream made me better!*), but they're not. The three statements could be described as true, true, and unrelated. Similarly, Landau is a woman and she is a director, but whatever third statement you are about to make probably doesn't spring from a connection between the others. They are independent facts, true and unrelated.

Landau remembers being shocked the first time someone asked her about being a woman director. She had never thought of her career that way.

"In general, I like to think, as Walt Whitman said, that 'I contain multitudes,'" she told me, sitting back in her chair with a small smile. "Or I contain everything and its opposite, too."

The mingling of those multitudes may be what creates genius. When you give yourself an ability to be many things at once and to see many things without limits, then you can bring an originality and freshness to whatever enterprise you undertake. If you constrain yourself by labels, restrict yourself to coloring inside the lines, then you can never create a new picture. As Whitman said in that same poem, "Do I contradict myself? / Very well then I contradict myself."

Landau knew she wanted to direct from age six. Unlike many women who are producers and directors, she never felt like an outsider. Her parents were film producers and "I always felt kind of entitled to be here, in a humble way," she said. But as a woman, she *was* an outsider—and that came with its own advantages. She looked at productions with a fresh eye and an unjaded perspective. Instead of taking an authoritarian approach—telling people where to go and how to speak and what to think or feel, as most directors do—Landau invited her teams of actors and lighting designers and musicians to be part of the process. She wasn't interested in control and power. To her, the beauty of theater was "trusting that there's something that's not about my own ego or desire, but that will come from some mysterious confluence beyond me."

That openness to the unexpected allowed her to take chances that nobody else would ever consider. In creating *SpongeBob,* she spent months bringing writers, designers, acrobats, dancers, clowns, puppeteers, and pool toys into a rehearsal room and encouraging magic to happen. She believed in looking for a fresh view, working with passion and abandon and without inhibition. Landau understood that containing multitudes also meant knowing when it was time "to become the captain and grab the handles and steer the ship." She joked that as an opening night comes closer, her alter ego appears—she has nicknamed her Thelma—and begins demanding, "Faster, louder, funnier." By that time, it is a very large ship.

When she was an undergraduate at Yale, Landau became close friends with her classmate (and already famous actress) Jodie Foster, and she directed her in several productions. They have remained connected. "A few years after college, I remember Jodie saying to me, 'I used to see you as a black hole of despair, and now I see you as a blossoming sunflower,'" Landau said. She laughed as she told that story. She agrees that she was intense and serious when young, focused on her dark and searching side. But at some point, she decided that she wanted to focus on being openhearted and work out of love.

The ability to blossom as a sunflower in a challenging world may be part of Landau's genius. Many stories romanticize the mad genius who slugs alcohol in misery or cuts off his ear in despair (à la Ernest Hemingway or Vincent van Gogh), but even at the far reaches of talent, genius flourishes amidst positivity and hope. You have to believe that you can make something wonderful happen before it does.

Landau once thought that if she didn't go into theater, she would become an oceanographer. Being underwater for her was an exciting journey away from the everyday waking world to one where things look and sound and feel very different. Now she uses creativity in a similar way, as if she had put on scuba gear and entered an alternate realm. Sometimes what she creates is full-on fantasy, and other times sunny images about how the world could be. Her genius is in letting us experience them, too.

Landau and I kept talking as we left the office and strolled up Broadway to the theater where her show was playing, dodging the crowds and discussing some of the projects that were coming up for her. Creativity is always a risk, but Landau has learned that genius demands being true to your own vision. She tries not to care about the paycheck and the critics and to care only about the art. "You really tip the scale when you can ignore the internal demons that talk to you the whole time about 'will they like that or not?'" she said.

After I left her at the stage door with a good-bye hug, I stood for a long time in front of the theater. When a woman is successful, people always try to tease out what distinctively female traits she brought to the enterprise. Landau's approach as a director is overtly collaborative—she brings people together, makes them feel comfortable and safe, and empowers them to experience their own possibilities. She gives them the freedom to explore and try things. Not everything has to work out. It's okay. Trying and playing and maybe even failing are part of the process. It's one of the reasons that actors love to work with her.

You might say, *Aha! Collaborative! Isn't that the hallmark of a "woman director"?* Landau may want to eschew labels, but sometimes they fit, right? Women are more empathetic and cooperative; they work together with less ego and a bigger vision for the greater good. Maybe we need to recognize collaboration as an element of genius, one that is distinctive to women.

Only I can't make myself believe that the formula holds on any grand scale. Once again, generalizations just don't feel right. Some men are collaborative and inclusive, and some women like to go it alone. Whenever I hear that women are so good at working together, I wonder if I should check my DNA. I was fine working with big teams, or even leading them, when I was a TV producer and magazine editor—but there's a reason I'm a writer now. I'm much better at handling things on my own.

The problem with gender generalizations is that they are a bit like astrological forecasts. Told that you fit into a particular category, you believe what you hear—and then you twist your future to make sure it's accurate. Women are good collaborators? Well, I did write several popular books with a coauthor. I liked having someone to talk to and work with through the process. I guess I do collaborate well! But that was one part of my work, not all of it.

Thinking about how we twist generalizations to make them true for ourselves—and perhaps change our ambitions to make them fit the predictions—I Googled my horoscope on a popular site when I got home.

The times of being scared and worried about chasing your dreams are over, it read. *Dare to be bold and brilliant and the fruits of your labor will be truly amazing.*

I read it over a couple of times in surprise, and then I paused, thinking how appropriate it was to the work I was doing. Maybe I shouldn't make fun of horoscopes because that really did seem on target. I would be bold and amazing! And then I realized that I had accidentally clicked on Pisces instead of Capricorn.

Whoops.

I found the Capricorn prediction.

You will be completely focused on succeeding and completing your life goals, but it's also important to let loose and learn to have fun.

Hey, bingo! That really got it, too. I was focused on writing books but needed to break away and continue experiencing the world. Horoscopes work and inspire because we all find ourselves in the descriptions that we think apply. But the downside of forecasts or predictions or gender expectations is that we assert a subtle and unconscious force to make them turn out true.

We all contain multitudes. We have bits of Pisces and Capricorn, male and female, earth and fire. We can collaborate sometimes or go it alone, and choose which one feels like the best fit for us in both the short and long term.

Landau's genius is not that she is a woman and so knows how to collaborate—but that she takes collaboration to a different height, invests it with her own magic and insight, and then uses it with an unmatched degree of originality. That she is a Woman or a Gemini is close to irrelevant when compared to how she has taken her baseline talent and worked and focused and made it unique, exciting, and her own.

Some years ago when I was working at a company owned by Rupert Murdoch, I was asked to create a stand-alone magazine[2] based on the then extremely popular book by John Gray *Men Are from Mars, Women Are from Venus*. I blanched because I loathed everything about the book, including its ridiculous premise that men and women started out on different planets where they had different tasks to attend, and then they all moved to Earth and forgot from whence they came. I suppose it made sense that Gray fantasized this origin story since he didn't have any academic credentials that would support a

---

2 Those were the years when people still read magazines and bought them on a newsstand. Quaint, right?

more reasoned explanation. His conceit about the different ways men and women communicate wouldn't stand up to rigorous academic research, anyway.[3]

But I was willing to be open-minded (and needed the job), so I went to visit Gray in laid-back Marin County, California, where his huge mountaintop house proved that you can amass millions making stuff up. He had started out as the personal assistant to a popular yogi, so he had learned from the best, and now he had the attractive, pleasant, anodyne style that helps in securing your very own guru status. We had a nice day together, and my bosses were thrilled that Gray liked me and wanted us to work together. I wasn't good at challenging (male) power in those days, so I agreed to produce the magazine. It was beautiful and romantically sexy and sold well, and I did everything I could to twist the message inside to suggest that we *all* need to learn to communicate better.

What I really should have insisted on saying was that when we divide to conquer, we really only exacerbate the divides and let men continue to conquer. Gray wasn't really trying to bridge the gap between men and women—he wanted to make sure that each believed they had a set place in the world that they shouldn't challenge. He gave the game away a few years later when he publicly complained that feminism leads to divorce because it "promotes independence in women." Well, yes, it does. And if Gray's idea of Venus is a place where women have to be submissive and subordinate, then I wish he'd go back to his own planet and leave the rest of us to flourish in independence on ours.

John Gray could be dismissed as one more crank trying to pre-

---

3 Gray got his PhD degree through a correspondence course at the unaccredited Columbia Pacific University, which was shut down a few years later. The school was cited, among many other problems, for failing to meet valid academic standards for issuing a PhD.

serve male dominance, but he sold millions of books and his Mars-Venus vernacular became known around the world. Popular messages like his, however silly, can have real consequences. If you sound authoritative when you preach about male-female differences that you have essentially made up, a lot of people are going to believe you—and then it takes a while for everyone to unlearn the calumny. Pop psychology and faux brain science have given cover to blatant discrimination, including at some public elementary schools in Florida, Texas, and other states that began separating boys and girls in classrooms. Administrators claimed it would help them learn better. It doesn't. It just amplifies minor difference into major ones.

"There is no different formatting of boys' and girls' brains, and setting up educational programs on that false premise is just wrong," neuroscientist Lise Eliot told me the day we talked in Chicago.

The pseudoscientific claims are just a sneaky way to exacerbate any differences and make them seem immutable. Let's say that on average, boys are better with spatial tasks and girls with language. Okay, so what? In any classroom, some boy may have the natural language skills that will turn him into the next Robert Frost. If you insist that he focus on math, you have lost a future talent. Sometimes it's important to take the road less traveled.

Eliot has argued ardently against single-sex classrooms or any kind of divided learning. The evidence that boys and girls inherently learn differently is just too minimal to turn into policy. Remember all those women in the Mediterranean countries who grow up good in math and physics? Possibly the best way to encourage every child to grow as an individual would be to team a boy and a girl on every school project. Let them work together as equals. Let them discover each other's talents and admire each other's skills. Eliot points out that if we want women and men to be able to work together as adults, they have to grow up comfortable with each other. Exaggerating the differences between them makes that harder.

Some women I know who have attended single-sex schools are passionate about the opportunities they had to flourish, take leadership positions, and grow their confidence without worrying about guys getting in the way. They weren't afraid to raise their hands. But there's not much evidence that any of that helps as they step into careers where they have to talk and negotiate with men. Single-sex schools are a leftover from the days when women weren't allowed into the more prestigious men's prep schools and colleges and so created their own. However good an individual school may be, the Supreme Court was surely right when it ruled in a different circumstance that "separate but equal is inherently unequal."

In terms of bigger social change, single-sex schools may be detrimental—pushing people apart and suggesting men and women just can't get along on a daily basis. In her wonderful movie *When Harry Met Sally,* Nora Ephron wondered whether men and women can just be friends. I'd like to settle that right now. Yes, they can. I had a lot of male friends throughout high school and college, and I still do. I'm convinced that the ability to ignore gender and connect to people on some common ground has been the single most helpful element in my career.

My junior year in college, I lived in an ornate stone building with an ivy-covered entryway that had just two rooms on each floor, with a bathroom in between. My roommate Anna and I shared the floor with two seniors, Steve and Bill. The four of us became close friends who talked about everything, and after a while, we gave up worrying about who was in the bathroom at the same time. When I hear the hysteria now about bathroom protocols, I always want to ask—don't your stalls have doors? Ours did, and so did the shower. (It's also possible to survive a chance glimpse of a towel-clad friend.) Far more important was that after Steve and his girlfriend broke up, Anna and I took turns taking him out for ice cream and going for walks to make sure he was okay. When I was heading into New York by train for a job interview in those pre-GPS days, Bill drew a map for me on a napkin to show how to navigate from Grand Central Terminal to the office building I needed to find. The ease of our connection was a model I used with bosses and colleagues going forward. I liked being one of the guys, and it never mattered if the guys were women or men.

Eliot goes a step further and urges colleges to integrate sororities and fraternities—a movement that is gaining attention on some campuses. Ironically, getting men and women to be closer may be a way to decrease sexual harassment. "If your pledged 'siblings' include both brothers and sisters, chances are greater you won't objectify and molest each other," Eliot advised. Chances are also greater that sexism and misogyny, the hallmarks of many fraternities, won't flourish if girls are across the hall as neighbors and friends, rather than exotic creatures to be pursued at wild parties. And you know how sorority girls tend to finish every sentence on an up note, as if it's a question? Eliot points out that there's nothing intrinsic to being female about that inflection. Maybe if men and women are encouraged to influence each other more, some of the reinforced bad habits and behaviors of both sides will disappear. With an equal playing field, there will be a better chance for the stars of both genders to support and inspire each other—and to shine equally.

Curious about how others may feel about that, I went to see Sian Beilock, the president of Barnard College, one of the few schools that hasn't given up its focus as a college for women. She had been at the school for only a year when we met, and before coming to Barnard, she was a chaired professor of psychology at the University of Chicago, where she got interested in the question of why people choke under pressure, whether they're playing soccer or taking a math exam.

She realized that there was a lot of research looking at how we become good at what we do, but not as much asking why we sometimes don't live up to our potential. "The basic tenet of my research is it's not just what you know that matters but how you feel," she told me. Your environment and the situations you create for yourself "can have a big impact on whether you thrive to your potential or not."

Beilock told me seeing so many women professors at Barnard probably helped a lot of students gain confidence and see their way forward. "But I don't think there is a magic formula for education," she said. Barnard students also share classes with the men and women at Columbia University, which is literally across the street (or at least across the wide avenue of Broadway), so they are not abandoned to a single-gendered island.

The day we met, Beilock was trying to juggle a raft of responsibilities. She was giving her convocation address to the incoming first years the next day, which is always a big deal—and even bigger because she was so new in her job. Some minor kerfuffle on campus meant assistants kept coming into her office with drafts of a press release they wanted to put out. Beilock apologized for our interrupted conversation.

"Should I come back another day?" I asked.

"No, I'm fine," she said. She took a deep breath, and we started talking about methods for relieving stress. One of the personal tips she'd taken from her research on choking ("I like to do some me-search, too") was that it's important to be able to reframe a situation. If anxiety leads to physical symptoms like sweaty palms and a beating heart, tell yourself that those aren't signs you're about to fail. Instead, they mean you're ready and charged to do your best, your brain and body set to focus.

She told me about one night when she was an undergraduate

majoring in cognitive science and pulled an all-nighter at the computer lab, trying to figure out how to program in a new language. All the guys acted like they knew everything, and she remembered crying and thinking, *There is no way I am ever going to be able to do this.* But she hung in and mastered it. Now when she's facing something scary, she thinks back to that night and tells herself, *You thought you couldn't do that, but you did. Now you're here. You'll conquer this, too.*

Other women I interviewed had told me similar stories about overcoming something when young that encouraged them later on. Having faced one tough situation, they had the confidence to believe they could master the next problem that came up. This is more unusual than it sounds. Girls are often protected from challenging situations or told not to worry if they can't do something. I had read about one lab experiment where researchers invited moms of eleven-month-olds to set up a ramp for their babies to crawl down—making it as steep as they thought the baby could handle. The girls' mothers made it much shallower than the boys' mothers did—consistently underestimating what the girls could do. (The moms of boys overestimated.) The researchers said that the gender bias had absolutely no basis in fact. When they tested the babies later, the girls and boys had identical motor skills.

Coddling girls and not encouraging them to challenge themselves—or even meet their abilities—has repercussions. If your parents don't think you can navigate a crawling ramp because you're a girl, they'll probably continue—quite unwittingly—to send don't-try messages as you grow up. *You're having trouble with computer class, sweetie? Why don't you drop it and sign up for drama.* Boys are told to push through and not give up. Maybe it's why the SHE PERSISTED T-shirts caught on after a snotty old male senator used the phrase in describing what happened when he tried to stop Senator

Elizabeth Warren from speaking on the Senate floor. Women don't always persist—but we know we should, and we're happy to wear a T-shirt celebrating the ambition.

Beilock told me that at every step in her career, up through and including her new position at Barnard, she jumped on opportunities she wasn't sure she could handle and was scared every step of the way. But she made herself do it. One thing that helped was knowing that she contained multitudes.

"There is a lot of research in psychology showing that it's important to have multiple selves," she said. Not in a *Three Faces of Eve* way—nobody is advocating for split personality—but in the kind of multifaceted experience that so many women have learned to embrace. Beilock has a mom self and a president self, a researcher self and a friend self. "What's really nice is that if you screw up in one, you have these other selves as a buffer," she said. When she gets stuck in traffic and misses a school play and feels like the worst mom in the world, she can remind herself that she is still doing important academic research. She's also not the worst mom in the world because no matter how disappointed her daughter may be at the moment, in the long run, she has mom-the-college-president as a role model.

The old idea of work-life balance has come to seem less meaningful in this age where everyone is on constant call. Beilock is aware that college president and mom are both twenty-four-hour-a-day jobs, so it is okay for the lives to collide. The previous spring when Beilock was preparing for her first commencement as college president, she had lunch with Rhea Suh, an alum who ran one of the nation's biggest environmental groups. Suh was being honored with a Barnard Medal, but she told Beilock that she didn't think she could make it to the medalists dinner that night. She was a single mom and didn't have a babysitter for her seven-year-old.

Impulsively, Beilock told Suh to bring her daughter to the dinner. "I'll bring my seven-year-old too, so they'll have each other," she said.

Both girls got dressed up for the occasion, and they sat next to each other at the head table. Every time I think of those seven-year-olds in their very best dresses listening to their moms giving speeches and being honored at an important event, I get slightly misty-eyed. All the students and faculty at the dinner that night saw that passion takes many forms and lives are richer when many parts are seamlessly blended. They could look at the head table for proof of a deeply important lesson.

We contain multitudes.

CHAPTER 10

===

RBG and the Genius of Being a Cuddly Goat

Whenever I asked people for recommendations on genius women I should include, the most frequent name I heard was Ruth Bader Ginsburg. I'm a big fan of the Supreme Court justice and the early court battles she fought on behalf of women's equality, but I wondered why nobody mentioned Elena Kagan or Sonia Sotomayor, who are also on the Supreme Court. Smart and intense and strong, they are decades younger than Ginsburg. Does our fascination with Ginsburg—or RBG, as she has come to be known—say something about how we want our women geniuses to behave?

I met RBG once at the Glimmerglass Opera Festival in upstate New York at a performance of the short opera about her called *Scalia/Ginsburg*. It is at best a trivial piece of music, but fans had gathered because RBG was speaking afterward. The theater was sold out, and additional crowds watched on video from a nearby room.

Like most everyone else there, I came because I admire RBG— her intellectual power, her fierceness in becoming a lawyer when there were barely a handful of women in her Harvard Law School class, her fights for women's equality. She was a genius with a home life, too. She left Harvard to finish at Columbia when her husband got a job in New York. They had two children and were devoted and happy together until his death in 2010.

RBG is a force, and it was a thrill simply to be in her presence and listen to her talk. This is the woman who oversaw groundbreaking gender discrimination cases in the 1970s, arguing six of them in front of the Supreme Court. Her hard-fought cases changed the course of women's rights.

But she doesn't look like a fighter. She is tiny and frail, and even when she was younger, she looked like you could toss her into the air with one hand. Her appearance has allowed us to make her into an affectionate doll. Her birdlike body gets more attention than her bullish brain. She has been made cute and sweet and accessible. At Glimmerglass, you could buy T-shirts with her image and cartoons and coloring books. I read later that three grazing goats purchased by the capital city of Vermont are named Ruth, Bader, and Ginsburg. She is our cuddly goat, the genius as stuffed animal. Could it be that we love RBG because we have defanged her and made her a lovable icon rather than a fire-breathing woman?

When RBG was starting out, it was a reasonable strategy for a genius woman to make herself unthreatening and hide her talents under a cloak of domesticity. When the dean of Harvard Law School asked her why she wanted to attend and take a place from a man, she explained that it was so she could understand her husband's work and be a better wife. Hearing that now kind of makes you want to throw up, right? The true answer was probably *Because I'm better than any man,* but that wouldn't have endeared her to anyone. She understood that she couldn't just attend Harvard Law School—she had to justify her very existence there in a way the doubting men could understand.

After graduating from Columbia tied for first in her class, she couldn't get a job with a major law firm because they didn't want women. She tried to get a clerkship with Supreme Court Justice Felix Frankfurter, and though he had been the first in the court to hire an African American intern, he also didn't want women. The story might have ended there, but a well-known Columbia professor was sufficiently outraged that this genius woman was being ignored that he told a judge in the Southern District of New York that if he didn't hire RBG, he would never offer him another clerk from Columbia. Ever. The judge relented.

Nothing came easily, and how many other women would have just given up? There had been exactly one female federal appellate judge before her, and women represented less than 3 percent of the legal profession when she entered law school. But it wasn't just the total lack of role models that stood in her way. Her older sister died at age six, her mom died a couple of days before RBG's high school graduation, and her husband, Marty, got cancer when they were both young. RBG went to all his Harvard Law School classes to take notes for him while he was going through surgeries and radiation. Oh, and she had baby Jane at home to care for, too.

Genius or not, how do you keep going? RBG often quotes the advice her mother-in-law gave her on her wedding day, that in any marriage "it helps to be a little deaf." When something nasty or wrong is said, don't hear it and don't respond. RBG has said that she took that advice to every job she had, too—ignoring attacks and challenges and doubters. Occasionally, it must have been hard. In the late 1970s, she argued to the Supreme Court that jury duty, which was then voluntary for women, should be mandatory. Rights and responsibilities go together. Being on a jury is part of being a full citizen, so you can't exclude women. It was another example of how "protecting" women is really undermining them. It was also a brilliant position and part of RBG's long-held strategy of seeing gender equality from many perspectives. The nine male justices listened, and at the end of the arguments, Justice William Rehnquist turned patronizing.

"You won't settle for putting Susan B. Anthony on the new dollar, then?" he asked with a chuckle.

How cute. How charming. How revolting. Ginsburg probably wanted to throw a shoe at him—and when you hear the tape now, you kind of wish she did. She has said that she thought of telling him, *We won't settle for tokens.* But she didn't say anything.

So is that what you have to do if you're a woman genius? Shut up and be unthreatening? Speak softly and carry a big brain? RBG is known for the pretty lace collars she wears over her Supreme Court robes, adding a touch of feminine elegance to the outfit. How dangerous can a woman in lace be?

The irony of all the RBG dolls and coloring books, of the mainstreaming of her image on a tote bag that reads YOU CAN'T SPELL TRUTH WITHOUT RUTH, is that RBG was one of the great disrupters of her time. She wouldn't be pigeonholed. She could fight for radical ideas of overthrowing gender norms and making equality more than a theoretical concept, and still be a conventional wife and mother. In a recent popular movie about her called *On the Basis of Sex,* RBG is portrayed by the lovely actress Felicity Jones, and her husband, Marty, is the hunky Armie Hammer. When asked about the movie's marital sex scene, the real RBG smiled. "Marty would have loved it," she said.

Maybe the genius of RBG has been playing the game and knowing what is required so that you can turn around and use your talents the way you want. She lets people see her as a stuffed animal or a face on a T-shirt or a cute little action figure doll if that's what makes them comfortable. But she also speaks up and fights and thinks about women's issues and strategy differently than anyone else. The genius of many women has been to suss out their surroundings, understand the times, and find a way to triumph within the boundaries that have been set. If, like RBG, you do it right, those boundaries keep moving.

Women geniuses are always disrupters. They challenge a way of looking at the world or they dislodge an accepted truth or they overturn a standard approach to law or art or science. One reason we have trouble thinking of women as geniuses is that the gender norms— the very ones RBG fought—put women in a bucket of being social and friendly and nonconfrontational, which doesn't sound like being disruptive at all. But not all women fit into that bucket. Even if they do, it's irrelevant to their ability to turn the world upside down. As RBG has proven, you don't have to look like a disrupter to be one.

Cynthia Breazeal doesn't look like a disrupter, either—but she is one of the country's biggest stars in the groundbreaking world of robotics. The day we met at her office at the MIT Media Lab happened to be a school holiday, and when she rushed over to meet me, she looked like a schoolkid herself, wearing slim athletic pants and a bulky sweater. She chatted comfortably for much of the afternoon, taking a couple of calls along the way from her teenage sons to discuss dinner plans and who was driving where and their complicated after-school schedules. Just your everyday mom. Watching her from a perch on her desk, though, was a little robot called Jibo, which she had created and marketed through a company she founded. Outside her office were shelves of more robots, created by the Personal Robots Group at MIT, which she started and leads. She was more proof that you can be conventional in one part of your life and an innovative genius breaking new ground in another.

Breazeal's genius has had a profound impact on a field that is in itself disruptive—robotics. She works at the MIT Media Lab, a place that has been famous for the last thirty or so years for its huge influence in turning ideas upside down. No standard thinkers from already established fields need apply. The Media Lab welcomes only the brightest of bright people who don't fit into existing disciplines because they are creating their own way of thinking. Breazeal is one of those unusual thinkers. She remembers watching *Star Wars* as a kid and falling in love with the robots, R2-D2 and C-3PO. Instead of begging her parents for *Star Wars* figurines like other kids might do, she started to imagine what it would be like for robots to have rich relationships with people. After college, she thought she might want to be an astronaut, and she applied to get a PhD in space robotics. (At some point she also thought she might want to be a professional tennis player, and she still has the confidence and ease of a professional athlete.) She landed in the lab of MIT professor Rodney Brooks, who was innovating with planetary micro-rovers—small robots that would be able to explore the solar system and traverse the rough terrain of distant planets.

The point of view in the mid-1990s was that autonomous robots would save people from doing monotonous or risky tasks—things that were dull, dirty, or dangerous. Efforts at the time were focused on building machines that could navigate around rooms or pick up objects. But as robots were sent off into oceans and volcanoes and space, Breazeal had an epiphany. "I remember thinking, 'Why aren't they in our living rooms and interacting with us?'" Her colleagues were focused on building robots that could move objects in a warehouse or vacuum a room. She wanted one that could be as friendly as her socially and emotionally intelligent pals from *Star Wars*.

Breazeal decided to drop what she had been doing and move away from practical applications. She was pretty far along on her

PhD, but she went into Rodney Brooks's office and told him that she wanted to change everything and start again. She wanted to design robots that could be part of everyday people's lives. She wanted people to be able to interact face-to-face with robots that were socially and emotionally responsive.

"It was a radical shift," she admitted.

Going in a completely new and original direction is never easy. Her colleagues were focused on practical utility and solving problems, and what was the practical utility of a robot that could smile? "The father of robotics thought it was stupid and the father of AI also very publicly said, 'We think it's stupid,'" she told me.

Breazeal went ahead anyway and created a robot she named Kismet. It is now in the MIT Museum and hailed as one of the first-ever social robots. When you look back and tell the story after other advances in tech, it doesn't seem so amazing. But think about it. She was a young woman in the midst of getting her PhD, surrounded mostly by men, and willing to tell everyone that she could lead the charge to a different approach to robots. She believed in her original idea enough to gamble her career on it. Like Fei-Fei Li, who took a similarly disruptive and equally doubted position on teaching computers how to see, Breazeal was quietly bold. Each of them was willing to call on her own instincts and experiences to go in an original direction.

Maybe in that way, being a woman helped Breazeal on her path of genius. She had been an athlete and a popular kid, and she is warm and outgoing. What better person to come up with the idea of a robot that can talk to and interact with you? Her robots even tell jokes now and then. Kismet could learn things and respond and express appropriate emotions when Breazeal spoke to it. The mechanical but lovable face could arch its eyebrows and move its lips and twitch its ears, and its responses weren't preprogrammed—they were actual responses to the stimuli in front of it. In the mid-1990s, it was an extraordinary breakthrough and made Breazeal instantly famous in the world of robotics.

What the doubters didn't understand, Breazeal told me, was that the goal wasn't solitary intelligence but "building machines that could actually work in partnership with people." Her cute Kismet is credited with launching a new era of social robots. The implications go far beyond a smart machine that can do simple tasks like announcing the weather or ordering your groceries. Breazeal did one experiment where she tested whether people did better sticking to a weight-loss diet if they had reminders from a robot, prompts from a computer program, or a call from a nurse. The robots were the most effective. People liked having them around so much that they often dressed up the robots and treated them like a friend. When the researchers came to pick up the robots at the end of the test, people would rush out to say good-bye and give them a kiss as they drove off. (To clarify: They were kissing the robots, not the researchers.)

Most fields tend to focus on problems that need to be solved. If you're building robots, the big question at the time might be how they'll move—and for a while everybody writes papers on robot navigation. That was the state of the robot-development world when Breazeal was coming up with her idea. To break free of that siloed thinking and go in a distinctive direction is risky. She had to make her robot move, but she also wanted to consider what the machine looked like and how it expressed itself. She delved deeply into psychology to understand human intelligence and behavior and create a robot that seemed familiar to people—"otherwise it would be like working with an alien."

Being shunted outside of the mainstream for so long has been a dark cloud for women—but my ever-optimistic side likes to look for silver linings, so I wonder if that outsider status now gives some women an advantage in the genius wars. They aren't stuck on standard thinking. They have a different perspective. I don't believe that all women are naturally strong when it comes to emotional intelligence and social abilities, but given social expectations, they have developed those traits. And since those skills are both more complicated and more important than most men realize, they also give women an advantage in certain fields. "In AI, the things that are hardest for robots to do are the ones that are easiest for people—like social interactions and emotional understanding," Breazeal said. At a conference she attended on humanoid robots, a guy came up to her afterward and expressed surprise that she was so concerned about how her robots interacted with people.

"Yes, of course I'm interested in that," she told him.

"But why?" he asked. "People are so messy."

Breazeal shook her head when she told me that story. From that guy's perspective, robotics was about mathematics, and people just messed up the equations. Breazeal saw robotics as a way to *help* people. She was interested in the technical challenge of making the robots but also the psychological complexities of using robots to promote human flourishing. She wants robots that can model perseverance and a positive mind-set for children or help adults with the challenges of aging. Perhaps it's coincidence or expectation—but her lab now has many women working on robots that can solve social issues.

After Kismet, Breazeal and her team made more and more robots, and she now has those showcases full of them around her lab. One of her favorites was Jibo, a little guy about a foot tall that could twist and turn. Its face-like screen recognized you when you came into a room and might start a conversation or tell a joke. He was the kind of guy you wouldn't mind having around. She introduced Jibo on a crowdsourcing site and quickly raised $3.5 million to start a company and introduce him to the world. It was heady stuff. Investors gave her another $70 or so million, and *Time* magazine declared Jibo one of the best inventions of the year.

"Jibo is designed to convey a positive, optimistic belief about people. Through what he says and how he expresses himself, he 'knows' he's a robot, and he has kind of a quirky sense of humor about it," Breazeal told me, her voice tinged with the affection usually reserved for describing a lovably precocious toddler. "He's funny. He's kind of innocent. His personality design is very different—he's extroverted and will start a conversation with you. People have a lot of emotional engagement and empathy with Jibo." He actually listens to you and remembers what you say. Tell him one morning that you didn't sleep well and the next morning when you come into the room he'll ask, "Did you sleep better last night?"

Just as Jibo was starting to win people over, Amazon came out with Alexa, and Google with Google Home—personal assistants that could turn on your music or turn off your lights. They didn't have Jibo's personality, but they had more functionality and lots of money behind them. Breazeal struggled, trying to fight the big guys—and she lost. The day we met, she had recently shut down the company and had come to an agreement with MIT to use Jibo for research. He would help her figure out what qualities people wanted in their AI buddies at home. I'm sure she was disappointed, but she kept her cool. Most start-ups don't work, she reminded me. Male MIT professors start companies all the time that close down, and they get more chances. She would, too.

I asked Breazeal several times about being a woman in robotics and a woman at MIT, but she didn't see anything that could stop her. "I'm able to do what I'm passionate about, and if I can make something happen, it happens!" she said.

There it was again—the blinders to bias, the optimism, the focus on work. I was starting to think of it as the refrain of genius women. In their presence, you do think everything is possible, because they've done it and what's the big deal? They contain multitudes. They put aside gender stereotypes and put themselves in that third category of . . . Me.

"When you talk about trying to be a tenured professor and an intellectual world-class scholar and raising a family with kids—well, you make it work. I think for a lot of women our attitude is *I'm just going to make this work*," Breazeal said.

Breazeal's sons love the fact that their mom builds robots. Being a genius disrupter has made her the coolest mom around. Working at a place where genius and daring and creativity are celebrated, she can keep trying new ideas that thrill her—and her kids. If she ever gets down or discouraged, she knows how to solve the problem. She can hug her boys—or ask one of her social robots to cheer her up.

Genius women who disrupt expectations can be strong and confident like Breazeal or unthreatening but brilliant like RBG. Or they can be the least likely person you might expect—like a Mormon mother of five who follows her husband from Utah to New Hampshire and becomes an unlikely feminist heroine.

I first heard about Laurel Thatcher Ulrich from one of her students—a whip-smart and engaging young woman named Cara who was getting her PhD at Harvard. Ulrich had been a chaired professor at Harvard since 1995, and she was one of Cara's advisors. "Students undervalue her because she's understated and unassuming and not bombastic like a lot of the male professors," Cara told me. "But she has one of the sharpest minds I've ever encountered." She has also changed how people think about history.

Perhaps because she is brilliant but undervalued, Ulrich began to see that throughout history, women have also been . . . undervalued. In an academic paper that she wrote in 1976 on (of all things) Puritan funerals, she described how so many of the women who were the stalwarts of their community were ignored and forgotten.

"Well-behaved women seldom make history," she wrote.

The line got picked up as a rallying cry for women across the country and the world. It became a slogan on T-shirts, tote bags, mugs, and bumper stickers. Ironically, the woman who said it was almost as forgotten as those she described. If you check online, the "well-behaved women" quote gets attributed to various celebrities, including Madonna and Marilyn Monroe, even though the line was never meant to suggest that you make history by feigning sex onstage or letting your skirt fly high. The woman who actually said it remained unnoticed for a while. Well-behaved academics seldom make headlines.

In 1991, Ulrich wrote a book called *A Midwife's Tale*, based on the diaries of a late-1700s Maine housewife and midwife, that shook the academic world when it won the Pulitzer Prize. Ulrich got a genius grant from the MacArthur Foundation the next year and the call from Harvard shortly after that. Historians credit her with making the contributions of unsung women a fair topic for academic study. She finally started getting credit for the popular slogan that was still circulating, too. Recognizing its popularity, she eventually wrote a book called *Well-Behaved Women Seldom Make History*—where she notes that nobody quotes the other one-liners from her work on funeral sermons. It's doubtful that anybody would get a kick out of wearing a button that reads THEY NEVER ASKED TO BE REMEMBERED ON EARTH. AND THEY HAVEN'T BEEN.

Ulrich recognizes that the appeal of the slogan isn't its historical accuracy but what it reminds women about their behavior right now. For many women, "well-behaved" still means being deferential or submissive, not expressing opinions too loudly, and certainly not being disruptive. We are allowed to be outrageous only in a sexual sense—Ulrich saw one button with the slogan printed next to a drawing of a leopard-print stiletto heel. But Ulrich's point wasn't that women should be sexually outrageous. She had a more historical view—that the women who have quiet but positive effects on society, the women who make things work every day, are overlooked. It's not that you should misbehave. It's not that bad girls have more fun (though maybe they do)—it's that we need to pay attention to those who *do* behave. Marie Curie, the one woman everyone can agree fits into the genius category, had an affair with a married collaborator. But Ulrich points out that "she isn't remembered today because she was bad but because she was very, very good" at what she did.

But even the most well behaved sometimes need to disrupt the status quo. We can't move forward, fight stereotypes, and let our talents shine without a reordering of expectations. Rosa Parks, who ignited the civil rights movement when she refused to move to the back of a segregated bus, is often portrayed as a simple seamstress who wanted to sit down because she worked hard and her feet were tired. The much-told story suggests that her achievement was accidental. But Ulrich points out that Parks had been working with the local NAACP and fighting for social justice long before that day on the bus. She was prepared. She wasn't being quiet.

Women geniuses change the world with their energy and new ideas. I'd like to think that by now we can all be bold and unafraid in our approach. We can build robots and make triumphant breakthroughs in artificial intelligence, all while challenging those who tell us our ideas will never work. But a full-court press is not the only way to disrupt the male-dominated game. The genius of Ruth Bader Ginsburg, Rosa Parks, and Lauren Thatcher Ulrich was to recognize the expectations of their time and place and then quietly move forward with what they wanted anyway. Cynthia Breazeal and Fei-Fei Li also triumphed within a system that might not have initially embraced them, but they remained politely dogged. Well-behaved geniuses can disrupt history, too.

CHAPTER 11

The Dark Lord Trying to Kill Off Women Scientists

Looking back over the centuries from our current vantage, we can see and be appalled at how even the most talented women were undermined and ignored and written out of history. The biases and barriers were so blatant that it's only somewhat consoling when the unfairness is recognized and there's an effort to make amends—as with the scientists who added meitnerium to the periodic table, atoning for Lise Meitner's being overlooked for a Nobel Prize. For all those forgotten women artists of the Renaissance, some museum stores now sell coffee mugs and books featuring the Greatest Women Artists— even if the museums themselves don't display much of their work. All the extraordinary women writers of the nineteenth century who were scorned? We extol their work and feel miserable for the bind that they were put in. Newly devoted young readers (and even some academics) send their love to Jane Austen and Charlotte Brontë and gush that Charles Dickens could have learned a thing or two from their prose!

When the events are happening directly in front of us, though, it's harder to recognize what is going on. Nobody ever blatantly says, "We're ignoring her because she's a woman." There's always a presumptive reason that the woman is being undermined or erased or told she's not as good as the guys. When it's your own talents or achievement in the crossfire, it's even harder to recognize the bias. Unless you have a very thick skin and a strong ego, at least some part of you believes that there is a reason for what is happening and that the men are right. You're just not quite as good.

So it has been eye-opening for me to watch the story of biochemist Jennifer Doudna unfold. I feel like I'm sitting in the grandstand of history, getting to watch as a narrative is written and rewritten in real time.

Working in her laboratory in Berkeley, California, Doudna essentially figured out a way to change genetic structures by snipping out one piece of DNA and replacing it with another. The technique, called CRISPR, has been called one of the greatest scientific breakthroughs of the century. Genes are the basic building blocks of life, so being able to change them and move pieces around is the holy grail of biology. Her technique could bring us everything from mosquitoes that don't spread malaria to babies who are free of genetic disease. If you can eventually turn your brown eyes blue (without contact lenses), you'll have Doudna to thank. The anxiety being expressed around the world about creating "designer babies" is also a result of Doudna's foundational research. Many, many people have been building on her basic breakthrough. That's the number one sign of genius—its effects reverberate.

Doudna has said that "there was definitely a eureka moment" when she realized what she could do—and where her breakthrough might lead.

Doudna worked in collaboration with a European colleague, Emmanuelle Charpentier. Two women changing the world. Two women who nobody could dispute are among the greatest scientists of the time. Two women geniuses.

What could be more thrilling?

In 2014, Doudna and Charpentier won the Breakthrough Prize, an award that had been launched only a couple of years earlier to celebrate the biggest achievements in science. Funded by a group of Silicon Valley billionaires, the Breakthrough Prize offers open nominations and an enormous pot—$3 million to each winner—and its medals in three different categories quickly became among the most coveted in science. The young tech savants behind the award seemed both eager and able to find geniuses much faster and with less old-boy politicking than the Nobel Committee. With a forward-looking perspective and a governing board that includes both men and women, they didn't have any problem recognizing women's genius.

In an effort to make science cool, the Breakthrough Prize ceremony is televised and includes lots of celebrities. Pundits (or maybe just science nerds) call it the Oscars of Science. The night they won, Doudna and Charpentier both wore elegant gowns and radiant smiles that would have translated to the actual Oscars. Doudna had the sophisticated bearing of a Hollywood actress starring in a Nancy Meyers rom-com. Charpentier, with jet-black hair and an air of French glamour, looked like she might fill in for actress Audrey Tautou in an update of her beloved movie *Amélie*.

When I watched the video later, I had the same ping of recognition that I'd felt in visiting astrophysicist Jo Dunkley: *This is what genius looks like. We've been ignoring genius women for so long, who would know?*

Before any of us get too flushed with you-go-girl pride, I am sorry to report that Doudna and Charpentier's triumph was soon undermined by a dumbfounding display of patriarchy and male entitlement. Almost immediately after Doudna and Charpentier made their breakthrough, some men swooshed in to rewrite the story. As has happened so often in history, they wanted to take most of the credit.

The conflict came from a discovery by the young and very impressive scientist Feng Zhang, who better fits our image of a genius. That is to say—he's a guy (possibly in a hoodie). He came to America from China when he was eleven and got degrees from Harvard and Stanford. Working at the well-financed Broad Institute in Cambridge, Massachusetts, he figured out a variant on what Doudna and Charpentier had done, using the process (called CRISPR-Cas9) on a particular kind of mammalian cell. Zhang applied for a patent on his work, even though Doudna and Charpentier had submitted their application seven months earlier. The savvy experts at Broad asked that Zhang's be fast-tracked. It was. He got the patent.

Scientific discoveries are complicated and so are patents, but could we imagine this story being told the opposite way? Two men make the discovery of the century. A woman takes it to the next step. Who do we think is going to get the patent then? The case ended up in a messy lawsuit, and experts say the patent Broad has fought to maintain could be worth billions of dollars.

I'm less concerned with the money (they'll all do fine) than with the effect all this will have on how the discovery gets described in years to come. History is not always as clear as we would like, and as we now know, sometimes the teller of a story is as important as the story being told. Right now, a classic game is being played out, with subtle and not-so-subtle maneuvers to drag the women off the field.

The effort to undermine Doudna and Charpentier occurred most blatantly in an article written by the head of the Broad Institute, Eric Lander. He's a respected scientist, but forgive me if I think of him in Harry Potter terms as Voldemort, the Dark Lord. His 2016 article purported to be a generous history of the people who contributed to CRISPR, but it clearly had one purpose—to champion his golden goose, Zhang, and minimize the women scientists. He barely mentioned them. The genial, collegial tone—*We're all in this together!*—made it all the more damning. It was as if he had written thousands of words and mentioned as many people as he could, just to be sure that Doudna and Charpentier didn't seem to be special in any way.

The article's bias was so blatantly offensive that social media exploded with an immediate tempest in a test tube—and when scientists get worked up on social media, you know something unusual is going on. The much-admired geneticist and Berkeley professor Michael Eisen called the piece "science propaganda at its most repellent." Eisen might be a Berkeley partisan, but Nathaniel Comfort, a well-known professor at Johns Hopkins University, which is unaffiliated with the controversy, was similarly miffed. Having written often about genetic research, he analyzed the article from an objective position and concluded that despite its avuncular tone and faux inclusiveness, its main purpose was to bury the women's achievements. He called it "Whig History"—taking the term from an old British essay and explaining that it is a way to use history as a political tool that "rationalizes the status quo, wins the allegiance of the establishment, justifies the dominance of those in power."

The Dark Lord is a classic example of a man in power. He understands how to manipulate the status quo to his advantage. His institute has a lot of money and power and good scientists, and he wants to make sure that nobody else gets any glory. Knocking women out of the story hardly takes any effort at all.

Dr. Comfort suggested that readers "note the gender dynamics of the story." He pointed out that "history by the winners still tends to end up being 'history by the men.'" A few women scientists rushed to defend Broad, saying that they have been well supported there. I don't doubt it. As the #MeToo movement has shown us, relationships between men and women can be complicated. Men who are in positions of power can be generous and thoughtful in some situations with women—and then turn into vicious, misogynist jerks when it can benefit them.

The Doudna-Charpentier story is distressing for its all-too-familiar ring, with echoes of Lise Meitner and Fanny Mendelssohn and Mileva

Marić and so many other women I had encountered, both now and through history. Each generation of men seems to find its own way to undermine brilliant women—and to appropriate some of their insights, too. Since I'm not a scientist and didn't want to jump to any unfair conclusions, I asked molecular biologist (and former Princeton president) Shirley Tilghman to help me out. I knew she was on the board of the Broad Institute, but given our open conversation about women and power and leadership, I also knew she was extremely fair-minded about everything, including men and women and gamesmanship. Could she explain to me the subtleties of the CRISPR discovery? Who had done what? Who deserved the credit? Her simple explanation was that Zhang took a system that was working well in a test tube (the Doudna-Charpentier discovery) and did what was necessary to make it work in a living cell.

"I'm stuck in the middle because I think what Jennifer and Emmanuelle did was simply groundbreaking and what Feng did was also groundbreaking," she said.

She likes and admires Eric Lander and told me that she had spoken to him many times about his outrageous position on the CRISPR controversy.

"Eric is one of the smartest people I know and way too smart to have written that article," she said.

"But he wrote the article," I said.

"Yes, he did," she said with a sigh, "and he knew exactly what he was doing."

She agreed that the crusade now was about who would win the Nobel Prize, and our Dark Lord was battling hard for his boy. As a board member, her fiduciary interest was in seeing Broad triumph. But as a woman in science who had seen these turf wars before, she had a more hopeful view.

"Jennifer is being clobbered, but the scientific community is rooting for her," she said. "For once, I don't think they're going to let a good woman be destroyed."

When women get destroyed, overlooked, or ignored, they often blame themselves or think there's a good reason for the slight. Jocelyn Bell discovered pulsars[1] back in 1967, which was one of the great break-throughs in astrophysics. So great, in fact, that it won the Nobel Prize in 1974—for her male advisor. Pictures of her from 1967 show a pretty girl with a nice smile and pointy-edged glasses. I bet the men in her lab called her "sweetheart" rather than "genius." At the time, Bell graciously said that since she was a postgraduate student when she made the enormous discovery, maybe it was fair that he got the award.

No, it wasn't fair. It was just one more example of the men in charge assuming that the woman's role must have been secondary. It was even more offensive because the advisor had initially scoffed at Bell's finding and said she must have made a mistake. She had to convince him that she was right. She was.

I can understand why she chose to be magnanimous—it's hard to go through life angry all the time. Much nicer to tell yourself that you know what you accomplished and who cares what anyone else thinks? You know that you were the first person on the planet to discover pulsars, and without your tenacity your advisor never would have understood what those signals meant. That should be enough, right? Plus you have to keep working with those men in power at

---

1   Pulsars are a type of neutron star that emits a beam of radiation. They are now used to map the universe and follow action light-years away. They have also been a key in testing Einstein's theory of general relativity.

your lab, and if you want to rise in various institutes and official societies, it's best if the men don't feel too threatened by you.

As time goes on, maybe your perspective changes. You lose some of the youthful insecurity (*I really did discover it!*) and realize that even though you scored on the achievement side of genius, you didn't get the celebrity. So outside of a small circle, nobody knows that the genius in this story was you. Nobody knows that women really can be the geniuses.

But now we all know—because in 2018, Professor Dame Jocelyn Bell Burnell (she'd added a name and some titles in fifty years) was awarded a special Breakthrough Prize in physics for that earlier discovery. We can have our questions about Silicon Valley billionaires, but they keep getting it right with their awards. They understood that when the young woman genius makes the discovery and the man she works for takes the credit, something needs to be fixed.

Then the story gets even better. Dame Burnell graciously accepted the acknowledgment and immediately announced that she was donating every penny of the $3 million in prize money to help advance women in physics. She explained that she wanted to help eliminate the unconscious bias that undermines women's advancement. It was a wonderful action, as magnanimous as her first gesture—and effectively flipping that one on its head.

Unconscious bias. That's what took fifty years to rectify in this case. Looking back, it's easy to see how the men exerted their power and undermined her achievement. I don't think they were being vicious or mean or even misogynist—it was just accepted that they would write a woman out of history and take the credit for themselves. There was nobody to stop them, and even Bell herself played the expected game of being the subservient girl. But it's just delicious when, fifty years later, a genius woman can use a $3 million award to politely thumb her nose at the men in power—and tell them that it's time to change.

Overlooking the genius women in science is a centuries-old game that men have played. But it's not limited to science. Women artists and writers and philosophers and archaeologists also regularly get dumped on the ash heap of history. In my research, I have been stunned to discover how many genius women made a mark in their time and then were forgotten. Though perhaps "forgotten" is too gentle a word, suggesting a natural dwindling of memory. What really happened was that the Dark Lords in every generation and every field used their powers to erase women. Fortunately, an army of Dumbledores (to continue the Potter metaphor) are trying to fight the dark forces and bring back some light.

One of them is Christia Mercer, who figured out that if history gets rewritten once, it can be rewritten again, this time putting women back in instead of leaving them out. That's what she's trying to do in the chronicles of philosophy, one of those subjects that is largely male and considered the stomping ground of natural geniuses. When I was a little girl and first heard about philosophers, I imagined them as people (okay, men) who conjured ideas by sitting alone on a wooden chair in an empty room, not talking to anyone. Perhaps I was confusing a philosophy department with solitary confinement? I'm not sure. When I went to meet Mercer, I got a very different view. Her office at Columbia University had couches and a big desk and lots of papers. She herself was so warm and friendly and engaging that I immediately wanted her as a friend who would meet me for a regular coffee and afternoon chat. With short gray hair and an easy laugh, she has a comfy style that fronts a fierce intellect. Mercer was the first woman (here we go again) to climb through the ranks of

Columbia's philosophy department and get tenure. A doorstopper of a book she wrote on the influential seventeenth-century German philosopher Gottfried Leibniz gave her great credibility—and she has used it to challenge traditional thinking about philosophy.

Mercer has been responsible for resurrecting some of the forgotten women's voices in philosophy, many from centuries back. She launched a book series on new narratives in philosophy and began to question standard philosophy's all-male canon. She told me that she got away with challenging the long-established edicts of the field because she had proven her chops with the Leibniz book—and has been around a long time.

"I tell people who want to be taken seriously—never dye your hair. Keep it gray," she said with a laugh.

It's probably a good idea to keep a light touch and a sense of humor when you're trying to overthrow an entire field, since the men trying to preserve the status quo don't feel quite so threatened. But Mercer ruffled some traditional feathers when she wrote a paper suggesting that the great Descartes ("I think, therefore I am") wasn't quite as original as he gets credit for. She pointed out that many of his smart ideas were stated much earlier by the mystic Teresa of Ávila. A nun in the sixteenth century, Teresa was a darling of the Jesuits, and her fame grew as the church moved to canonize her in the seventeenth century. Ideas often develop in different times and places independently, so I asked Mercer if there was any evidence that Descartes had read Teresa of Ávila.

"Teresa was the Beyoncé of the seventeenth century," Mercer told me, smiling at her own analogy. "You could not ignore her. You might not like her or you might think she was out there, but everyone knew of her." Since Descartes went to a Jesuit school, he certainly would have known a lot about her works.

If everyone knew of her then, what happened later? I took a couple of philosophy courses in college, and I'm pretty sure her name never came up—either on her own or as an influence on Descartes. Neither did the dozens of other women who were central to seventeenth- and eighteenth-century philosophy. Sophie de Grouchy, Anne Conway, Elisabeth of Bohemia? Sorry, they don't ring a bell. Mercer told me about her philosophy colleague Eileen O'Neill, who was among the first professors to try resurrecting these women's voices.

In a wonderful academic paper that I read later called "Disappearing Ink," O'Neill spent page after page after page describing these women philosophers and dozens of others whose work was influential, both in its own right and in affecting people who came afterward. I got overwhelmed reading about them and trying to keep them all straight—and I bet that was exactly O'Neill's intent. By letting us see the extraordinary depth of women's contributions, she hoped to make it clear that their absence in the canon now was, as she wrote, "pressing, mind-boggling, possibly scandalous."

The scandal of women being scrubbed from the philosophy map had many causes, but perhaps most striking is what O'Neill called the "oxymoron problem." An oxymoron describes two words that seem to contradict each other—like sweet sorrow or jumbo shrimp. Putting them together can be funny or poetic—or simply jarringly wrong. If I tell you to bring me some hot ice, you'll explain that there is no such thing. And so it was that starting in the nineteenth century, if you asked about a woman philosopher, the men who controlled the academic spheres would explain that there is no such thing. Samuel Johnson famously explained that a woman preaching or philosophizing was like a dog walking on its hind legs—"It is not done well but you're surprised to see it done at all." Ha ha. Very funny. All these years later, that nasty, cutting line gets repeated as a joke all the time. But the work of the women philosophers whom it was meant to undermine? Forgotten.

Sadly, O'Neill died young, in 2017, at what should have been the peak of her career, but colleagues like Mercer have continued carrying the flag. Rather than just finding "cool women who got left out and should be remembered," Mercer told me that O'Neill's groundbreaking genius was to show the women's powerful philosophical worth.

Mercer has brought attention back to Anne Conway, who lived in the seventeenth century and wrote an extraordinary book called *The Principles of the Most Ancient and Modern Philosophy* that challenged the thinking of the big boys in philosophy like Descartes and Hobbes and Spinoza. For much of her life, Conway corresponded with the great English philosopher Henry More, starting out as his admiring student and getting to the point where she challenged positions in his work. According to Mercer, everybody thought Lady Anne was really smart and a great critic of their philosophical theories, but they never imagined that she had her own ideas until the very end, when she dared to write her own book.

Can you imagine how hard it would be to have the whole world telling you to behave as a proper lady when you wanted to see yourself as an intellectual and a great philosopher? How do you let the genius side of yourself get through when everything in society is demanding that it be repressed? In the seventeenth century, women weren't allowed in universities and couldn't get an education, and writing was considered a manly task.[2] Mercer found it both fascinating and depressing to read some of the letters written by genius women like Anne Conway and Princess Elisabeth of Bohemia to the great male philosophers of the time. They wanted to engage in intellectual exchanges with the philosophers, but they had to be careful. They knew to present themselves as modest and self-effacing—so

---

2 Any number of women novelists will tell you that men are still considered the "real" writers and they are "women writers." But that's another story.

their letters are full of phrases suggesting some version of "I'm just a young maiden, what do I know?" or "I probably don't understand all you've written, but here's my question . . ."

The women philosophers were savvy enough to be deferential and charming in their correspondence to appeal to the men. But then, said Mercer, they would unleash the most cutting question or insight that the men had ever heard. "As a woman, you couldn't just say, 'I think you're wrong for the following five reasons'—you had to be patient and develop your views without letting on. We all talk now about 'mansplaining'—can you imagine how annoying it would be to live your whole life having men tell you things that you already understand?"

The women geniuses of an earlier day tended to be wealthy women, the aristocrats and royalty of their time. It's not a surprise. With regular education banned for women, only those who could afford private tutors got any training in writing and ideas. Like the women artists of the time, they needed both money and a sponsor—usually a father or spouse who supported their desire to learn. When you think how hard these advantaged women still had to struggle to be heard, it makes you mournful for those with fewer resources. History doesn't pay attention to women who spend their days in the kitchen or laundry room. Whatever genius those women possessed, they had no way of letting their talents develop or be heard.

Wealthy or aristocratic women had the advantage of hobnobbing with the intellectuals who were happy to be invited to their expansive estates and talk ideas over expensive sherry. Genius doesn't develop in a vacuum (despite my childhood image of the solitary philosopher), and women had to find a way to be part of the exchange of ideas. Émilie du Châtelet, a brilliant philosopher, physicist, and mathematician in the early 1700s, was famously tossed out of a café in Paris where the mathematicians of the day hung out when she tried to join in their conversation. Thrown out of a café! Forget universities—women weren't even welcome to discuss big subjects over a cappuccino. Legend has it that she changed into men's clothes and came back to the Café Gradot to rejoin the conversation. I don't know that it's true, but I certainly hope so.

Du Châtelet's father was a minor nobleman, and she was lucky—he recognized her talents early and brought in tutors for her. She was married off to another nobleman at eighteen and quickly had three children—but by age twenty-six, she was back to studying and got some of the great mathematicians of the day to teach her. She had met the outspoken writer Voltaire at her father's house when she was younger, and they eventually renewed their friendship. Why not? How else is a woman going to learn anything? She invited Voltaire to stay at her country estate in the north of France, near Champagne, and they became intimate partners—intellectual and otherwise—for sixteen years or so. Her husband continued to live at the house, too. (You have to love the French.)

The fact that du Châtelet and Voltaire were lovers has made good gossip for centuries. But they also collaborated and encouraged each other—and du Châtelet produced works of unquestioned genius. Her four-hundred-page book on physics was translated into many languages and became one of the most important science books of the time. Her translation and commentary on Isaac Newton is used to this day. Mercer told me that all of the citations in the big encyclopedia of the time that had to do with time, space, and physics were direct citations from her. Anyone studying science at the time learned it from du Châtelet. She was admired and respected and quoted by everyone. The topics of time and space and causation being studied in physics and philosophy were very similar, so she was considered one of the great philosophers of the day, too.

How is it possible that she was written out—and you and I and most of our friends have never heard of her? As I've said, there are Dark Lords in every age and era. According to Mercer, the famed German philosophers like Kant, Hegel, and Schopenhauer "were all deeply misogynistic and couldn't bring themselves to include women in their story." A later famous German philosopher—we'll leave him nameless for a bit of spite—wrote a big book on the history of physics and intellectual history, and guess what? He didn't mention du Châtelet at all.

Mercer shuddered as she told me that story and said that just thinking about it gave her goose bumps. "This was not like pulling out a weed that is okay to ignore," Mercer said. "Her roots, the roots of her ideas, run through all the others who followed. They made a conscious decision to take her out of the picture."

A few weeks after I met Christia Mercer, I had a few friends over for dinner and told them the story of Émilie du Châtelet. Both the men and the women at the table shook their heads at the egregious unfairness and then offered comforting assurances that "things have changed." I told them next about Jennifer Doudna and CRISPR.

I doubt that Doudna would take any comfort in seeing herself as the Émilie du Châtelet of our day. But the echoes of the stories are so strong that they are hard to ignore. A genius woman changes our view of the world. She is admired and revered. Then the men do whatever they can to make her contribution seem unimportant. It's all very subtle. Things have changed, yes. Only not really.

One of the men at my dinner party politely asked if I might be overvaluing Doudna's contribution. Just a few days earlier, a Chinese scientist announced that he had used CRISPR to create the first gene-edited babies. Didn't that have greater consequence than what Doudna had done?

"The gene editing couldn't have happened without Doudna's original breakthrough," I reminded him. He nodded and didn't challenge me further. He's a sensitive guy who would never want to be accused of bias. And neither of us wanted to get into an argument over a dessert of peach tart with cinnamon ice cream.

As I thought about it later, I realized that science (like most subjects) moves in stumbles and bumps and leaps. People build on each other's work. We have moved so far in our understanding of physics and motion and force that we can send rockets to Mars and travel above the earth in airplanes without being the slightest bit uncomfortable (except if you have a middle seat). But that doesn't make Sir Isaac Newton's discovery of gravity and planetary motion any less remarkable. We will tell the story of his seeing the apple fall from the tree forever, with pride and admiration. When it's a woman who makes the initial discovery, though, our memory is shorter and we aren't quite so impressed. Maybe people expect women to be mothers, so our giving birth to ideas also seems unexceptional. Women send their (real) children into the world to be independent and, instead of taking credit for their achievements, just feel pride when they flourish. When it's great ideas that they bear and send into the world, though, the genius women behind them deserve awe, respect, and a share in history.

We can't sit in the grandstand any longer watching history being rewritten without women's contributions included. Christia Mercer is a great model for how women can take control of their own stories and those of our foremothers. So, Jennifer and Émilie and Jocelyn, this is for you—writing the new history, the real history, is what I'm trying to do right now.

PART THREE

How Women Geniuses Fight . . . and Win

I would like today to ask that we begin to dream about and plan
for a different world. A fairer world. A world of happier men
and happier women who are truer to themselves.

—CHIMAMANDA NGOZI ADICHIE

One person plus one typewriter constitutes a movement.

—PAULI MURRAY

CHAPTER 12

Battling the Ariel-Cinderella Complex

Through my months of research into women and genius, I had many moments of incredulity and outrage. *So much systemic bias holding women back!* But I also found myself happily inspired by the wide-ranging strategies used by women geniuses of the past. In a fair world, they wouldn't have had to be quite so clever to get their talents heard. But when you face a brick wall, you don't win by running into it—you figure out how to get around or over it. At a time when women had no political rights, Madame de Staël became a famed activist of the French Revolution by sharing her genius ideas with intellectuals in her own home. Told that a proper nineteenth-century woman couldn't play her instruments and compositions in public, Fanny Mendelssohn created music salons in her private living room and invited hundreds of people to attend. Eager for outlets for their music and art, Hildegard of Bingen and Plautilla Nelli did their creative work in the protective walls of a convent. With women mostly unwelcome in science labs, Lise Meitner and Jocelyn Bell worked wherever they could and didn't worry about who noticed.

The current women geniuses I met had less blatant obstacles—universities were open to them, and they often had a role model or two who had ventured into the field first. But still they had to be both clever and tenacious. Ruth Bader Ginsburg fought for women's rights by bringing lawsuits that seemed to advantage men. Fei-Fei Li and Cynthia Breazeal and Meg Urry did their own twist on "fake it until you make it"—they pretended that there were no obstacles in their path until they had pushed so many aside that the path really did seem clear.

Many of the challenges women face now are subtle but insidious, starting with the images received endlessly in popular culture. You think you're being entertained—and all of a sudden you realize that the underlying misogyny isn't entertaining at all. The whole culture is sending you a message that rejects the idea of women being smart or strong or powerful. And whether you're a genius woman or just admire those who are, you have to fight back.

When I first saw the Disney movie *The Little Mermaid* many years ago, I stormed out of the theater at the end in a total rage. My husband claims that I ranted so vociferously that people on the street turned to stare at me. Well, good, since I was protesting the message of the movie—that a woman didn't need to be heard.

"I can't believe that the mermaid wasn't allowed to speak!" I roared to my then brand-new husband.

"It was a Disney fairy tale—it's supposed to be frivolous," he said calmly.

"It's not just frivolous—it's dangerous!" I said.

In case you've forgotten, redheaded mermaid Ariel needs to get the "kiss of true love" from Prince Eric in order to live on land. She makes a deal to give up her voice so she can woo and win him. She can't sing. She can't talk. All she can do is look beautiful to get her prince. Could there be any more blatant way of telling girls to shut up and look beautiful?

The movie was hugely successful, and Disney built a whole franchise of games and videos and music around Ariel, and then launched a Disney Princess line to further commodify all the ways little girls could be taught to focus on things that will never help them fulfill any potential. My fury over *The Little Mermaid* made such an impression on my husband that he still mentions it from time to time. It has become part of our family legend.

When I met up recently with my friend Shana to talk about women and genius, I told her that I was starting to wonder what effect the Disney Princesses had on girls' expectations for themselves. Shana, a savvy and energetic entrepreneur who now runs her own fitness company, is usually sunny and upbeat. But suddenly a look of mortification crossed her face.

"Did I ever tell you what happened to me with *The Little Mermaid?*" she asked in a whisper.

I shook my head no. I'd never told Shana my story of movie rage—so what was her experience?

"Go for it," I said.

She bit her lip as if she were about to confess to a jewelry heist, but from her expression, this was considerably worse than being part of *Ocean's 8*.

Shana told me that she was about ten when the Disney movie came out, and she became totally obsessed with Ariel, the heroine mermaid princess. She collected every Ariel doll, action figure, and poster. She carried an Ariel lunch box to school every day. McDonald's was doing a *Little Mermaid* promotion, so she went on a Happy Meal spree to get all the figurines. Cleaning some drawers recently, she had found her long-saved treasure trove of Ariel idolatry—and was horrified.

"I stared at them, and it finally occurred to me that Ariel is an appalling role model," Shana said, her eyes wide. "She wasn't allowed to speak! Can you believe it? A mute mermaid was my idol!"

I sympathized. Being older, I had skipped the idolatry and gone right to the fury. But I could understand how vexing it was to look back at the palimpsest of a younger self and see it scribbled with bad influences.

"You seem to have emerged okay," I said.

Shana sighed. "Thanks, but I looked at the figurines in that treasure box and I wondered, *What was I thinking?*"

Shana wasn't the only girl to put the beautiful but dumb (as in mute and speechless) mermaid on a pedestal. (Can a mermaid even stand on a pedestal?) And the veneration continues. The movie is still popular, streaming on a channel near you, with another generation watching. When I went home and checked the Walmart website, I found dozens of Ariel dolls—some of them with feet, and some of them with the webbed tail of a mermaid. Way to hobble a girl. Can't walk and can't talk.

A couple of days later, Shana emailed me that we weren't alone—she had found other warriors in the battle against Ariel. The very talented actress Keira Knightley, who has starred in movies from *Bend It Like Beckham* to *Pirates of the Caribbean,* had taken a stand, announcing in an extensively retweeted interview that as much as she liked *The Little Mermaid,* she wouldn't let her three-year-old daughter watch it. "I mean, the songs are great, but do not give your voice up for a man!" she said on a very popular talk show. *Cinderella* was also on her no-go list, because why care about a princess who "waits around for a rich guy to rescue her"? The comic actress Mindy Kaling also joined the anti-Ariel squadron, explaining that if her daughter wanted to watch the movie when she got bigger, Mom would be there with a running commentary from the other side of the feminist fence. "You don't have to be mute to attract a man and get all your dreams to come true," she said.

Surely some women can get through childhoods sprinkled with sexist fairy tales and still grow up to be doctors and lawyers and astronauts and actresses and . . . geniuses. On the other hand, why make it so hard? I thought speaking out against Ariel and Cinderella was notably brave of Keira Knightley—who is gorgeous and as thin as a reed but showed a steel backbone when she reaffirmed her comments as she strolled down the red carpet at a movie premiere. What made it so courageous? The new movie everyone was coming to celebrate starred Knightley—and was produced by Disney.

Are Keira and Mindy and Shana and I being excessively picky here, undermining a Disney flick with terrific animation and wonderful songs because of a quibble with the plot? I suppose it's always dangerous to undercut a pop culture icon that has lots of fans, but it's also too easy to give excuses and explanations for why in this particular case, the fatuous depiction of a woman is okay. Women step back from speaking out because we don't want to be accused of sounding shrill or demanding or (a big one for me) ungrateful. But in this case, it's a mistake to say that the fairy-tale plot doesn't matter. Overlook it if you want—but when you buy that Ariel doll for your daughter, realize that you're telling her it's okay to be dumb.

Disney has heard the complaints of sexism for so long that some of their more recent animated movies try to give the female characters more agency—and they get definite kudos for the 2016 *Moana.* The hugely popular *Frozen,* released a few years earlier, was the first to be codirected by a woman—and Jennifer Lee helped give the story a more girl-friendly focus than it had in earlier stages of development. (As long as the women can all speak, we've come a long way.) The kiss of true love that saves the day isn't from the man (who turns out to be the villain) but from the sisters Elsa and Anna, saving each other. Nice. The movie became the highest-grossing animated film of all time, but Disney still had a little hesitancy about a woman's powers. The princess Elsa has a superpower—but instead of it letting her leap over tall buildings or kill the bad guys, she turns things to ice. Her power hurts people, including her sister, and she has to hide it. The day I saw the new musical based on the movie, I started scribbling some troubling lines on the back of my *Playbill*.

"We must keep her powers hidden from everyone," Elsa's mother says.

"I'm afraid of my powers," Elsa says at one point. "They look at me and see a monster," she says at another. And then the mantra that both she and her parents repeat:

"Conceal it, don't feel it, don't let it show."

If you're a woman with power or strength, you can't let anyone know about it. You have to cover it up. The wildly popular song "Let It Go," sung by Idina Menzel in the animated movie, is meant to be the turning point where Elsa stops worrying about hiding and finds her own power. It's a great song and Menzel is terrific, but the result isn't quite as inspiring as you may hope. Elsa undoes the problems her power has caused, but does it make her heroic? Not really.

One of the biggest sellers at the lobby concession stand were the blue gloves that Princess Elsa wore to keep her powers from hurting anyone. When two little girls sitting near me came back from intermission proudly wearing the gloves, I glared at their mother. Didn't she get it? The message of the gloves was that a powerful woman needs to cover her strengths and hide her magic. I might have said something, but my husband caught my look and grabbed my hand, no doubt remembering my *Little Mermaid* tirade.

"Shh . . . let them enjoy the show," he whispered.

I nodded and kept quiet. But the problem is that it's always easier to keep quiet than to stand up and fight a social norm that can be wrong and damaging. A lawyer I know named Amanda lives in a fancy section of Los Angeles and sends her four-year-old to an expensive preschool that prides itself on being forward-thinking and enlightened. When the teacher sent home a note announcing a "Superheroes and Princesses" dress-up day the following week, she was stunned and called to complain. The teacher explained that most of the girls were already obsessed with princess costumes—so what was the harm? The harm, of course, was in reinforcing a stereotype that lets boys fantasize about having strength and superpowers while girls wallow in tulle and tiaras.

"What was I going to do?" Amanda asked when we talked about the problem. "Keep her home from school? Tell her that all her friends were victims of a sexist social order?" We want our kids to be happy and fit in, so we shut up and play along. Amanda got away with dressing her daughter as Wonder Woman—but she considers it a small battle in a bigger war. There are princess birthday parties yet to negotiate and playdates where preschoolers wave their wands at Cinderella. (Oh, that's a good plan for success—wait for your fairy godmother to find you.) You can tell a girl all you want that it's important to be smart and self-directed, but when the third-grade play is *Sleeping Beauty,* where the girl has to hang around waiting for the kiss of a prince to wake her up, what are you going to do?

The structural problems and #MeToo issues that can properly arouse fury don't appear from nowhere. There is a very real connection between bias in the workplace and the lack of parental leave in America and the damaging messages that we just shrug off. Many parents have told me that their little girl picks her own clothes—so it's not their fault if she only wants to wear a princess costume or tutu or purple frilly dress. I'd have to agree that it's not an individual par-ent's fault—it's *all* our fault. Toddlers don't come up with these ideas themselves, and our actions have consequences. Women are trained for their submissive role from an early age, and when they start to feel power and strength rising in themselves, they've been taught to put on blue gloves—and hope that it will pass.

How do women get the fortitude to fight the big business of the Ariel-Cinderella Complex? It all comes down to power—and a question of who sets the standards. Famed classicist and Cambridge professor Dame Mary Beard probably hasn't spent much time at Disney mov-ies, but she would be able to place Ariel in a tradition of silencing women that goes back to the ancient Greeks. A few years ago, she gave a very popular lecture at the British Museum (later shown on the BBC and turned into a book) that she called "Oh Do Shut Up Dear!" Taking the problem of women being denied the chance to speak back some three thousand years, she described how at the very beginning of Homer's *Odyssey,* the young son Telemachus tells his mother to go up to her room and not give orders in the palace because "speech will be the business of men, all men, and of me most of all." Beard delight-fully points out that there is "something faintly ridiculous about this wet-behind-the-ears lad shutting up the savvy, middle-aged Penel-ope." But it shows that from the very start of Western culture, young men grew up learning to silence women—even their own mothers.

In her mid-sixties now, Beard has appeared on many BBC shows, and with her long gray hair, unpretentious looks, and strong feminist positions, she has been a target for online trolls and public attacks. She always fights back. When one television critic viciously attacked her physical appearance, she responded with a tone-perfect newspa-per article. He was condescending about her looks? She could be similarly condescending about the fact that he wasn't well educated so "thinks that he can pass off insults as wit." She pointed out that throughout history, there have been men like him "who are frightened of smart women who speak their minds."

Beard knows that women are usually told not to engage with their attackers on Twitter or elsewhere. Let it pass rather than blowing it up even bigger. Beard won't let anything pass—and her courage and audacity always make me want to stand up and cheer. (I also wish that I had just a tiny percentage of that audacity.) Like so many other genius women, she made a name for herself by exceeding the standards set by men in a male-dominated field. Then she used that reputation to change the conversation and look at the odd impediments that have been in women's way.

Despite Angela Merkel and Hillary Clinton and Margaret Thatcher and the much-beleaguered Theresa May, Beard says that women are still viewed as being outsiders to real power and we have no actual template for women being *in* power. She jokes (at least I hope it's a joke) that when she herself closes her eyes and pictures a professor, she still can't even picture herself. The power structure continues to be coded as male, so when women try to achieve, they are "grabbing" power or "smashing" the glass ceiling—suggesting an attack on something they shouldn't have. Sure, things are slowly evolving, but Beard says she is not willing to wait patiently for things to change.

Her solution? We need to see power differently. Having more women in legislative bodies and top corporate positions would be a change, but it's also important to think about what we are trying to achieve beyond the numbers. Power for women has an individual connotation too, and while it would be nice to (finally) have a woman president, for each of us right now, Beard says that power means "the ability to be effective, to make a difference in the world, and the right to be taken seriously." The line struck me for its simple accuracy.

Even genius women who are brilliant and admired aren't always taken seriously. The ten-year-old boy who tried to explain dark energy to physicist Meg Urry didn't take her seriously. The men who tweet at Mary Beard about Roman history are treating her as an unserious woman, not one of the most esteemed professors at Cambridge. But I think it is these genius women like Beard who are our great hope for gaining power, or redefining it. She herself is formidable and smart and creative, and in speaking out with wit and wisdom, she gives each of us a power base and a way to perceive our personal power that is different from the silent princess image.

The Disney Princesses aren't the only female stereotype that can be soul depleting for a smart woman. One day when I was in the Bay Area, I met up with genius engineer Andrea Goldsmith, who has been an innovative star in advancing wireless communication. You know how easy it is for all the devices in your home to talk to each other now? Her techniques have been part of that dramatic change in our lives. Her ability to combine the practical with the theoretical has won her rafts of impressive awards, and she has started two companies and written texts that are now standards in engineering. A professor of electrical engineering at Stanford, she's one of only three tenured women in a faculty of some fifty-five people, but despite the depressing statistic, she is endlessly upbeat—effusive, energetic, fast-talking, and bold. The person who introduced us described her as a force of nature. When we met, Goldsmith was wearing a black sweater and pants with a bright red blazer, which seemed to parallel her curly black hair and bright-red lipstick.

"My favorite colors," she said, when I complimented her style.

Genius women find ways to create something original in life, to avoid the stereotypes and restrictions and discover the power they need to thrive. For Goldsmith, gaining her own power required getting away from the San Fernando Valley in California, where she grew up. It turns out that Valley girls are more than the stuff of movies and legend—they packed the corridors of her high school and "were all about clothes and cars and superficial stuff. I was independent and interested in history and politics. I definitely didn't fit in." Afraid that if she stayed around, she would start hating school, she took an equivalency exam to get her degree and left. She ventured to Europe and became friends with a girl her age who was singing in the *bouzoukia*, the old-fashioned Greek nightclubs. She suggested Andrea might try it, too.

"I never sang. I didn't speak any Greek. But why not? I'm seventeen years old, so I said yes." She spent the next six months traveling through Greece, learning the language, and singing in nightclubs in small villages. "It was an amazing experience not to follow a straight and narrow path," she said.

Avoiding the straight and narrow might be an essential part of developing genius talents. If you conform to a Valley girl style—or any other code of female behavior—you erase your own originality. "You need to listen to your own voice and tune out other voices," Goldsmith told me. Taking risks and being your own person can pay off royally, but it's never comfortable to shake up the status quo. She jokes that friends try to keep their teenagers from asking her for advice—because who knows what unconventional approach she'll recommend for them. We laughed about that, but I loved Goldsmith's tale of dropping out of high school and singing in Greece. Should we all try it? Absolutely not. But it's a great example of how taking a quixotic direction can inspire a woman to flex her own power muscles. Genius women don't heed stereotypes, accept standard roles, or conform to expectations. They are willing to try the unexpected, and they develop their own strength by refusing to play the role of Cinderella. The shoe doesn't have to fit. Nobody needs to find them or define them.

Goldsmith came to Stanford as a professor when she had a one-and-a-half-year-old son and was pregnant with her daughter. "I didn't know how to tell people, so I figured I wouldn't say anything and they'd just figure it out," she said. Weirdly enough, nobody ever said a word to her. Right after she delivered, Goldsmith came into her office to pick up some things, holding her three-day-old baby in her arms. An older male colleague came in and said, "Andrea, you had a baby! Why didn't you tell us you were pregnant?"

"He had the office next door to me and I walked by him every single day!" Goldsmith said, laughing. "He was a lovely man, but I guess he just never noticed." Her dean had also never said a word. Afterward, he explained that he wasn't sure if she was just stressed and eating a lot.

Goldsmith found these experiences amusing—which may be the best way to approach any situation. She's also aware that the singularity of being a woman among men means that you develop a way to get around barriers more adeptly. Figuring out how to deal with the challenges, with the implicit bias and the explicit bias, requires drawing on different skill sets.

"I agree that you can't say men are better at one thing and women are better at another, because there's a lot of overlap," Goldsmith said. "But maybe women become better at collaborative projects or big-vision ideas because of our own experiences rising in a male-dominated profession."

Both of her children are now undergrads at Stanford, and while we were talking, her daughter knocked on the office door. Goldsmith invited her in and introduced me, explaining that I was writing a book on the genius of women.

"Oh, Mom, you're perfect for that," her daughter said, giving her a big hug.

"Is she a good mom?" I asked.

"The best!" said her daughter, keeping her arm around her mother.

We all talked for a while, and when her daughter left, Goldsmith grinned. "We didn't even set that up," she said.

Her daughter is thinking of majoring in engineering—and it's not a surprise. She knows she can do it because she has seen a woman— her mom—do it before her. She won't be intimidated. Goldsmith told me that change happens when a woman gets in a position where she can mentor five or ten people who are junior to her and make them successful, and then they do the same for the next generation. "It gets better over time," Goldsmith said. I thought of other genius women like Jo Dunkley and Fei-Fei Li and Cynthia Breazeal and Meg Urry, all working energetically to bring along a next generation of strong and smart women. I started to have the glimmer of hope that maybe Goldsmith was right—and with the determination and influence of these genius role models, things *would* get better over time.

One of the companies Goldsmith started went public in 2016, and though she had left by then, she was invited back to ring the opening bell of the NASDAQ. Amidst the flying confetti, some of the early employees told stories about the positive culture she had created. One remembered a day everyone at the company was worriedly waiting to find out if the first chip they had produced actually worked. For a start-up, the success (or not) of a first chip is hard to overstate since the next round of funding and the very future of the company depend on it. But Goldsmith came in with champagne and cake and announced,

"Whatever happens, this is a milestone for the company. We're going to celebrate. If it doesn't work, we'll figure out what to do next." Ten years later at the bell ringing, people talked about how much her positive spirit had meant.

Goldsmith's ability to rally a team, to motivate people and make them feel good, didn't come just from being a woman. There are many male CEOs who do the same. Genius comes when you take the experiences you've had, good and bad, and figure out how to move forward with them. What does singing in Greece have to do with wireless technology? Probably not a lot. But in her travels, Goldsmith learned about interacting with people and honed her ability to think creatively and broadly. She brought that perspective to her research—and now has a stack of patents to show for her inventiveness and fresh takes. She credits her broad experiences with allowing her to think in new ways so she could ignore restrictive thinking and find her own voice.

I think Goldsmith is correct that her voice never could have been so original and strong if she had hung out too much longer with the Valley girls. Like my friend Shana discovered, it's easy to get hooked by seductive social norms that suck at your soul—and it can take a long time to break free of them. If everyone around you loves Ariel, you may not immediately realize that her dreams (*shut up and get kissed*) aren't necessarily the best for you. Similarly, if you're a smart and independent young woman in a school where most (Valley) girls are dedicated to clothes and ditzy expressions, you need the temerity to find another dream for yourself. You need to be bold enough to find an original path that lets you become the genius ideal that others can then copy.

Goldsmith was able to do that herself—but not everyone can. I said earlier that a fish doesn't know it lives in water, and the same is true when you're swimming with mermaids. You don't always see a way to navigate yourself to land and stand on your own two feet (tails be damned). Perhaps an adventurous woman singing her way through Greece and then helping to imagine the next generation of wireless technology could be a new Disney movie. Why not? There's a lot of power in not being a princess.

CHAPTER 13

Why Oprah Wanted
to Be a Beauty Queen

If you're a genius woman and you win a Nobel Prize, sell your paintings to the Louvre, or discover the cure for the common cold, you can pretty much bet that someone, somewhere will tweet about the size of your butt and the dimensions of your breasts. Among the genius women I interviewed, there seemed to be two approaches.

1. Pay no attention . . . you shouldn't be judged on how you look.
2. Pay attention . . . you're *always* judged on how you look.

As in so many areas of their lives, genius women have to figure out for themselves what works and what doesn't in the beauty-versus-brains—or perhaps beauty-*and*-brains—sweepstakes. No matter how talented you are, it's easy to get caught up in the social standards of how a woman should look—and to start to think of that as perfectly reasonable. Even the strongest and most confident women often start out by playing the smile-and-be-pretty game, and who can blame them? It's easier to try to win with the preset (men's) rules than to stand up and say you're going to be an original. You want to be a genius? Well, okay. But first the patriarchy says you might want to focus on the superficial—and be a beauty queen.

Just how powerful is the pressure to be deemed beautiful? Consider Oprah Winfrey. We now know that she is a charismatic genius whose skills at empathizing, communicating, and touching an audience are almost unparalleled. She is one of the most successful talk-show hosts in history, a sui generis genius with honorary doctorate degrees from Harvard and Duke, and the first black woman billionaire in history. She has inspired millions of women to be themselves and find their own center of power. But at age seventeen, she needed the judgment of others—and she was thrilled to be crowned Miss Black Tennessee.

Many decades later, Winfrey looked back at herself when young and realized how hard she worked to please other people and become the image they wanted. Writing a letter to that younger self, she started it: "Dear beautiful brown-skinned girl." She knew that her younger self was dating someone named Bubba (really, Bubba!) and trying hard to impress him. Like so many young women, she was seeing herself only through his eyes. "A lesson you will have to learn again and again: to see yourself with your own eyes, to love yourself from your own heart," she wrote. "Self-esteem comes from being able to define the world in your own terms and refusing to abide by the judgment of others." By the time she wrote that, she didn't need any pageant judge handing her a tiara—she would win life on her own terms. Whether she was curvy or thin, glamorous or in sweats, her aura of beauty came from her inner self-esteem and the power she had created for herself. That's the genius of one incredible woman.

Oprah wasn't the only smart woman who succumbed early to beauty-queen fever, perhaps (at that point) not seeing any other way to success. Bess Myerson wanted to be a pianist and was a star at New

York's High School of Music and Art—but how was a Jewish girl supposed to get wide attention right after World War II? Pretty was the entrée, so she entered the Miss America pageant. When she won, the announcer plopped the crown on her head and crooned, "Beauty and brains—that's Miss America of 1945!" Sycophantic or slimy? You choose. Either way, she used her winnings to continue studying music and later played at Carnegie Hall and with the New York Philharmonic. The fame of her beauty-pageant win gave her the leverage to let the "brains" part of her title get an airing too, and she served on presidential commissions under three different presidents and became well-known for championing consumer protection and social causes. Oprah eventually realized that she didn't need to be a beauty queen to be a winner. Myerson parlayed the attention her appearance brought to do the things she really wanted in the artistic and political realms. That's another kind of genius.

Need more? Diane Sawyer was one of the most successful news stars on ABC television, anchoring the evening news, primetime news shows, and *Good Morning America*. She started her career as a sharp-witted press aide for President Nixon and spent years at CBS television, too. But before all that, she was America's Junior Miss. And whatever you think of Sarah Palin, she was governor of Alaska and ran for vice president of the United States. But first she was Miss Wasilla (Alaska).

The danger of all this is that an extraordinary woman like Oprah can try molding herself into a socially accepted pretty-girl when young, only to challenge the whole concept of beauty standards later. But many women who get caught in the beauty trap never emerge. The writer Oscar Wilde once said that "no woman is a genius. Women are a decorative sex."[1] If you spend too much time worried

---

1   Wilde didn't have too much more respect for men, who he said "represent the triumph of mind over morals."

about being decorative, it could be that you prove Wilde right. It is hard to be original and creative and bold—all hallmarks of a genius—if you're busy conforming to a social expectation that all that really matters about you is the superficial.

While beauty pageants have (fortunately) dimmed in both luster and appeal over the years, smart women continue to look for affirmation that they are pretty and accepted and . . . well, *normal*. Social validation has become more democratic—or maybe just more ubiquitous. Instead of catwalking in a sash and bathing suit, anyone can now post a glamorous Instagram photo and wait for the likes to come in, or create a sexy YouTube video and count how many views it garners. The need for acceptance can seem never ending. And if it's not the area where you normally play? A woman who is focused on becoming a genius scientist or astronaut or CEO doesn't get let off the beauty hook—though it seems wildly unfair to be expected to wield mascara and a curling iron before presenting your breakthrough research in fundamental physics.

Smart men don't have to spend much time worrying about how they look or what they wear, but a woman genius can rarely toss on jeans and a lab coat and call it a day. Her wardrobe will be parsed as carefully as her equations. When I talked with roboticist Cynthia Breazeal at the MIT Media Lab, she told me that her colleagues often urge her to wear a hoodie and rough up her appearance a bit. She's a tech star—she should look like the guys in Silicon Valley. But that's not her style. She wants to dress the way she likes, and she doesn't see what being glamorous has to do with her skills, talents, or academic life. In college, Breazeal thought about becoming a professional tennis player, and she still has the body confidence of an athlete. She gave one widely seen talk wearing a very short skirt and over-the-knee black boots, and she thinks it sends the right message that a techie genius can also be an alluring woman. "Give the rest of the world the benefit of the doubt that my being a professor at MIT will outweigh what I'm wearing," she told me. "People should be able to look beyond my shoes to hear what I'm saying."

"Look beyond the shoes" is a great mantra. But not everyone does it, and beauty can be complicated. Psychologists say that attractive people benefit from a halo effect, since we unwittingly assume that someone who is strikingly good-looking has other advantages, too. The halo that comes with a nice body and fine features means that the Hugh Jackmans and Will Smiths of the world get credit for being kind, talented, smart, and trustworthy without doing a thing to prove it.[2] Various studies have found that attractive people earn 12 to 14 percent more than their average-looking colleagues, are treated better in the justice system, and are more likely to be considered competent when they apply for a job. For women, the halo effect also holds to some degree—but then it gets thorny. Unless you're trying to be an actress or a model, you get points for looking good—but can also *lose* points for the same reason. How seriously are you being taken as a genius intellectual if colleagues are busy commenting on your big blue eyes and Jimmy Choo shoes rather than your original theorems? Several studies show that the spillover effect for attractive men is that they seem smarter than they might really be. The spillover for attractive women is quite the opposite—they have to overcome the expectation that they are frivolous and superficial, and they are less likely to be seen as leaders and authorities.

Theoretical physicist Lisa Randall fits any definition of a genius woman. Her work is important and original and has a *Twilight Zone* appeal of looking at extra dimensions of space. A chaired professor at

---

2 Perhaps I chose bad examples, since as far as I know, Hugh Jackman and Will Smith really are kind, talented, smart, and trustworthy. But you can probably identify for yourself a couple of attractive people who aren't.

Harvard, she has written several popular books, been named to various magazines' lists of most influential people, and created theoretical models to explain dark matter. The fact that she is an extremely attractive blonde who dresses to show off her good looks gets her both praise and contempt. Producers of science shows are eager to put her on TV—and then people who watch those shows wonder if they can trust a scientist who is so darned attractive. Compare her to astrophysicist Neil deGrasse Tyson, a similarly excellent popularizer who appears on TV often. He lacks Randall's academic brilliance and original research—but he's tall and handsome with a commanding voice that somehow gives him an unearned authority. His attractiveness adds to his authority in the same way that hers detracts.

Trying to escape this double bind for a woman is tough enough when you're a chaired professor. It's almost impossible when you're just starting out. Do you join Cynthia Breazeal in saying (as she told me), *I'm gonna wear what I wanna wear?* Do you try to conform to a typical pretty-woman standard, hoping it will be easier for some people to accept you—while taking the risk that others will dismiss you for the same reason? Or do you say screw it, buy a pair of Birkenstocks, and bow out of the whole appearances game?

I suppose those are the choices the rest of us have, too. But it gets complicated. During a Republican presidential debate in 2015, moderator Megyn Kelly—a savvy journalist and former corporate lawyer—asked Donald Trump about the degrading comments he regularly made about women's physical appearance. "You've called women you don't like 'fat pigs,' 'dogs,' 'slobs,' and 'disgusting animals,'" she said. He interrupted with a sneering comment that got laughs and cheers from the audience. Kelly persisted, noting other disparaging remarks about women he'd made. He didn't have a good rejoinder then, so he struck back the next day with a vile, rabidly misogynistic comment about Kelly. But proving that Kelly's question had been fair and

accurate, he continued the attacks on women's appearance throughout
the campaign. He derided Carly Fiorina, the first female CEO of a
Fortune 20 company, and Mika Brzezinski, host of a popular morning
TV show. Needless to say, he chose to attack Hillary Clinton's looks,
too. She called him out for describing a former Miss Universe as "Miss
Piggy." But none of it mattered. He became president.

The 41 percent of women who voted for Trump somehow weren't
mortally offended by a man who calls women "pigs" and "dogs."
Perhaps they were so used to being judged on appearance in their
own lives that his comments sounded too familiar to be shocking.
If you get used to men talking in a certain offensively judgmental
way, you forget how wrong and demeaning it is. You unwittingly
adjust your own life (and buy some more makeup) in order to fit into
the inherently bad structure around you. However smart or creative
you may be, you accept on some level that men are still allowed to
judge you by standards that never apply to them. It all becomes part
of the daily male-female drumbeat. As Cornell philosopher Kate
Manne has explained, "Hostility toward women would simply be an
individual quirk . . . absent a system of patriarchal oppression in the
background." When a lumpy and overweight man feels comfortable slandering people much more attractive than he is, as long
as they are women, you once again understand the power of the
patriarchy.[3]

The game of Beauty and the Genius starts early—and the rules
aren't written anywhere. A young woman named Kara who runs an
impressive nonprofit in Boston visited our house in Connecticut

---

3   Trump even attacked indisputably gorgeous model Heidi Klum. Heidi Klum! She didn't have
much trouble laughing it off.

recently with her five-year-old daughter, Elise, an extraordinarily smart and articulate little child. It was fun to talk to her and watch her turn a box of colorful paper clips into a math game. As Kara and I were making breakfast one morning, I reported on a delightfully wise comment her daughter had shared with me. Kara laughed and agreed that her daughter sometimes sounded like a little professor. Knowing that the five-year-old was out of earshot, I added that Elise was also very beautiful—something that she must hear a lot.

"Yes, too much," Kara said with a sigh.

"One reason I didn't say it in front of her."

"I appreciate it," Kara said. "Usually when people say it directly to her, I say, 'Yes, Elise, you are beautiful. You're also a renegade and smart and creative and good at math!'"

I loved the idea of telling a smart and very beautiful five-year-old that she's a renegade. It seemed a good path toward genius. A willingness to be original and not necessarily care about outside expectations lets you become the person who does something groundbreaking and cutting edge. Kara was right to try to protect her daughter from the social pressures to be just like everyone else. But those pressures can be powerful. Another little girl I know, Belle, also struck me as unusually gifted and intellectually precocious when she was very young—but then she started spending a lot of time focused on how pretty she could be. (Perhaps her name was an influence?) She got manicures at age four, had her ears pierced at age five, and had a spa birthday party at age six with experts to do hair and makeup. In the photos her mom posted on social media, Belle regularly posed with a hand on one hip and a leg thrust forward, as if she were channeling Taylor Swift on the red carpet. The come-hither seductiveness made me cringe. For a first-day-of-school picture when she was eight, she wore heart-shaped sunglasses, a tiny miniskirt, and lace-up sandals. Lolita couldn't have done it better.

I mentioned Belle the day I met with Sarah-Jane Leslie, the Princeton dean and researcher who found that once they hit age six, girls who are told a story about someone who is "very, very smart" assume that the person is a guy. As she elaborated on her research, I wondered out loud if girls stop thinking of themselves as smart when they become focused instead on being pretty. From my own vantage, I would have described Belle as "very, very smart" early on, but with all the girlish trappings she insisted on now, I had a different view. It was hard to think of her as a potential genius.

Instead of nodding her agreement, as I'd expected, Leslie bristled. If she were a porcupine, the quills would have shot across the room at me. "Go apologize to that little girl right now," she said sharply.

Startled, I pointed out (defensively!) that I had never said anything to Belle about my concerns. Leslie reminded me that children pick up everything, no matter what you do or don't say. That's why the social messages that circulate in the air have such impact.

Okay, fine. But . . . why would I be apologizing, anyway?

"Because you're putting an unfair pressure on her by asking her to choose one socially rewarded activity over another," Leslie said. "You're saying that she can't care about being pretty and also be an intellectual—when really they are orthogonal dimensions."

"They're what?" I asked. I didn't even know the word.

"Orthogonal. They're not related to each other. They don't predict each other. Making a girl give up a way of being in the world that is itself rewarded is one more way we oppress women."

I gulped. Here I was, trying to save Belle from the tyranny of beauty so her brilliance could shine—and instead, I was oppressing her. Who knew?

Leslie sat up a little straighter, and I realized that she was wearing a Tory Burch dress with a neatly cinched belt at the waist and pretty high heels. Behind her desk, I spotted a designer handbag.

"I've been utterly unapologetic my whole life about being a girly girl—and able to do other things, too," she said, catching my look.

Clearly I'd picked the wrong person to complain to about spa birthday parties. Or maybe the right person—because Leslie had an important perspective. She didn't feel her affection for pretty clothes and traditionally feminine style undermined her power to be taken seriously as a researcher, academic, and dean. Her own multifaceted identity was why she felt so strongly about Belle. In her view, society pressures girls to be pretty and sociable—and rewards them for conforming to a girlish ideal. Some (like me) might object to that pressure and think we need to work (hard) to change it—but right now, it's undeniably true. Asking a girl to choose between that social side of life and the intellectual, ambitious, career side of things is a lose-lose proposition.

"For a six- or seven-year-old, being part of a social group that conforms to certain social expectations is just a way of having fun. It's not taking a stand on whether she's an intellectual or will achieve something important in life," Leslie said.

Thinking about it later, I realized that Leslie was right about the unwinnable contradiction we create for women. A genius woman like Dame Mary Beard who doesn't use Botox and is perfectly happy to look her age is attacked for not being sufficiently glamorous when she goes on TV. Rampaging men resent a woman who doesn't seem to be trying hard enough to appeal to them. But a woman who conforms to societal expectations and makes sure that her hair is glossy and her clothes appealing is attacked for not being serious enough. I had even done that to an eight-year-old. Women geniuses and CEOs and politicians get analyzed for their clothes and style, and we generally conclude that they are all some version of Goldilocks—this one does too little and this one does too much. It's almost impossible for a woman to be told that she's just right.

———

Having learned about orthogonal dimensions—things that exist independently and don't affect each other—I realized that we don't blink if a male genius or CEO or politician likes to spend weekends playing golf or going to football games. We would never worry that one activity distracts from the other. (Well, maybe there can be too much golf.) So why should something a woman finds entertaining be considered frivolous—whether it's a manicure, a new lipstick, or a shopping spree for sexy shoes?

The problem may be how a focus on beauty affects a woman's general sense of herself. Watching a football game on television may be a waste of time, but it rarely ruins anyone's self-confidence. On the other hand, lots of studies have shown that the cognitive effort that goes into worrying about whether your hips are too big, your lipstick is even, and you should (or shouldn't) get Botox takes away from other efforts.

The psychologist Barbara Fredrickson, now a chaired professor at the University of North Carolina at Chapel Hill, did a fascinating study with several colleagues early in her career in which she found that women do worse on a math test if they take it after trying on a bikini. They weren't *wearing* the bikini to take the test (an excessively frightening image for any woman)—they had just tried it on. Women who tried on a sweater before the test didn't see their math scores go down.

My first thought after reading that study was—*That's crazy!* But I guess it's not crazy at all, because all I have to do is think of myself staring into a mirror as I try on a bathing suit and it's not just my math score that would be ruined. It would be my whole day. Frederickson pinpointed the problem in the clever title of her research paper: "That Swimsuit Becomes You." Our identity and sense of confidence get tied into how we look. For a woman, appearance isn't just part of who we are—it can become all of us. If a guy gains a little weight, he might decide that he needs to lose it. A woman might decide that she's now an unworthy human being who shouldn't step out of the house (and definitely shouldn't shop for clothes).

Social expectations about a woman's appearance are rigid and often cruel, and they are extremely difficult to escape. When Cambridge professor Mary Beard was attacked for not fitting into the norm of a pretty, trying-to-please woman, she wasn't exactly trying to crash a Victoria's Secret fashion show. One of her TV shows was about the Roman Empire, and there's no more formidably brilliant and charming expert on the subject than Dame Beard. It's hard to imagine an academic man on television for his knowledge and insights being treated with similar malevolence.

Women understand the beauty game that is being played, and most (with wonderful exceptions like Mary Beard) feel helpless to escape—which gets us back to why trying on a bikini makes you do lousy in math. Women fall into a pattern of what Fredrickson calls "self-objectification," which means we are always looking at ourselves as we think outsiders would, and doing that "consumes attentional resources, which is manifested in diminished mental performance." It takes cognitive effort (even if you're not conscious of it) to step outside of your body and then look back at yourself from the perspective of a no-doubt disapproving man or sorority sister. The part of your brain that is busy worrying about why you don't look like Gisele Bündchen can't be solving equations at the same time.

Fredrickson found that men didn't have the same problem with self-objectification—and their math scores were unaffected by what they wore or tried on. I have a friend who is a dapper Oxford don and always dresses in a Savile Row tweed jacket, crisp white shirt, and expensive cuff links. His face is smoothly shaven, and his well-combed hair doesn't bear any resemblance to Einstein's bushy mad-scientist mop. His careful grooming doesn't seem to have an effect on his very impressive intellect or his soaring reputation at Oxford. He can enjoy his clothes without getting consumed by them because society doesn't measure men by their physical appearance in quite the same way as it does women. Women are constantly being judged—everybody notices how we look, and then we notice the noticing (sorry to get meta here) and the destructive cycle is under way.

Sometime after that bikini study, Fredrickson shifted her research and began focusing on positive psychology. She has found that upbeat emotions make people more creative, open, and aware, to which I say—yes! When I spent a year living gratefully for my book *The Gratitude Diaries,* I discovered that being positive and grateful changes how you see the world. You have a greater sense of control over your experiences, and everything from your marriage to your career to your health seems better.

It may be that a switch from gender studies to positive psychology isn't all that dramatic. The relentlessly negative messages women get that they're not pretty enough or good enough or smart enough take a toll. It can be a fun, positive experience to dress up and feel attractive as long as it's self-motivated—but Frederickson's research on body image found that for women, it's almost always about being accepted by an outside gaze. The outward-looking focus on beauty risks making a woman less positive about life and so less creative and open. Less interested in being original—and less likely to be a genius.

The enormously talented writer, Harvard professor, journalist, and historian Jill Lepore recently wrote a nearly one-thousand-page one-volume history of America called *These Truths,* which has been praised as brilliant and revelatory. It has also been hailed as the first book of its kind written by a woman—which means that until this very moment, American history was quite literally written by men. Lepore has written books on all aspects of American life, from racism in eighteenth-century Manhattan to the story of Benjamin Franklin's sister Jane to the real-life (and fascinating) story of the creator of Wonder Woman. She is also a staff writer for *The New Yorker,* which for any of the rest of us would be a much-desired full-time job. For positive role models, you can't get much better.

But all the praise and respect she has garnered as both a genius academic and a popular writer haven't shielded her from being undermined by the male gaze. The lofty and usually staid *Chronicle of Higher Education* once published a cartoon of Lepore as Wonder Woman, complete with skimpy costume and red knee-high boots. I can understand what the editor was (perhaps) thinking—the accompanying article was by an author who had also written a book about Wonder Woman and was bemoaning his inability to compete with Lepore for sales or attention. She was powerful, like a superhero. He was just a shlubby guy without her credentials. But the cartoon was wildly inappropriate, and Lepore later called it "an incredible trivialization . . . to depict me dressed as a character I had identified as coming from the visual culture of pornography." The men seemed to be saying—*You're so great, Lepore? A serious academic of political and intellectual history? We can write you off as just a sexpot with a cinched waist* (and eyeglasses). She knew that women had to do much more than men to prove their intellectual authority, but it startled her to realize that even once earned, that authority "is stolen from them, it is undermined."

Being treated as a dress-up doll rather than an intellectual can (amazingly) have a positive side. Lepore says the offensive cartoon helped her decide to tackle her sweeping book on American history. If you're going to be belittled, take on the biggest project you can.

Make it harder for the doubters. Someone is going to mock you as Wonder Woman? Don't change what you wear or buy new eyeglasses. Write a book that weaves women's history into political history rather than separating them, as male historians have traditionally done. Show how women participated in American political culture even before getting the right to vote in 1920. Show the role women played in abolition and prohibition and realigning the political parties in the 1970s. Then go on TV to talk about it, having proven yourself one of the great historians of the generation.

Wonder woman? You're darned right. And it has nothing to do with the costume.

After all my interviews and research, I remain somewhat torn on the question of how beauty affects genius. I understand Cynthia Breazeal's adamance about looking great if she wants and Sarah-Jane Leslie's insistence that society rewards girls for looking pretty, so it's wrong to take that pleasure away from them. But. And there is a big "but" here. The excessive emphasis on women's appearance makes it harder to focus on anything else that they achieve. How many words were spilled analyzing Hillary Clinton's pantsuits? How many little girls worry about how they look rather than what they know?

Stanford law professor Deborah Rhode has decried the beauty injustices women face, noting that almost every state allows discrimination based on appearance. "The world would be a better place if women were judged more on competence and less on appearance," she said—but good luck with that happening. Women have been fired for being too heavy or not wearing enough makeup or looking too sexy in a pencil skirt. (Yes, all of those have happened.) Rhode is one of the most heralded and quoted law professors in the country, but her personal grouse involves women's stiletto-heeled, pointy-toed, open-backed shoes, which she describes as "the last acceptable haven for misogynists." When she headed an American Bar Association committee, she watched her male colleagues striding fast and purposefully while the women in their high heels "fell behind, each step an ordeal." I wear high heels (though not very high) whenever I give a speech or make an appearance because it's expected—and I want to please my audience. But then again, for centuries in China, women bound their feet as a sign of beauty and to please others. Toes were broken, feet distorted, and pain ever-present because the tiny steps women were forced to take on their heels were considered erotic. The practice continued until the early twentieth century. In a modified form, Manolo Blahnik continues it today.[4]

I wear less makeup than almost anyone I know—but my makeup bag is still full. Right now, my eyes are watering from the mascara I put on this afternoon for an interview. Being uncomfortable (and slightly allergic) doesn't stop me from wearing eye makeup on important occasions. Ridiculous, right? But Rhode has pointed out that we seem to have accepted the belief that "a woman's unadorned face is unattractive—and a man's isn't." A woman bartender in Nevada once sued because she had to wear makeup and nail polish while her male colleagues just had to show up. She lost the case. Which bartender made the better margarita or concocted the most original gin creation didn't seem to matter.

Whether you're a woman bartender or a lawyer, a politician or a physicist, you get caught in these dilemmas. It takes me thirty minutes longer to get ready in the morning than it takes my husband— which is at least three hours a week that I'm losing from doing something productive in my life. I'm not saying that I could solve the

---

4 Women who wear high heels always tell you that they are perfectly comfortable. I am here to tell you—they are lying.

great Theory of Everything problem in physics if only I had those three hours back. But maybe I could use that time to solve the Theory of Something.

The eighteenth-century women's rights advocate Mary Wollstonecraft thought that if women weren't taught from infancy to focus on their beauty, they could break free from social constraints and achieve a lot more with their minds. As she more poetically put it, "the mind shapes itself to the body, and, roaming round its gilt cage, only seeks to adorn its prison." I do worry about genius women whose talents are caught by their gilt cage. We think we are flying free until we slam against the (very pretty) bars.

Asking whether there is a connection between beauty and genius in men would seem laughable. But with women, whether the two are contradictory or compatible remains baffling. So one more story about beauty pageants. Shortly after I graduated college, I got a call out of the blue from an official of what was then the Miss Teenage America pageant, asking if I would be a judge. He knew about me because I'd garnered an early reputation as a sports reporter—a "woman sports reporter," I suppose people said, since at the time it was still surprising. He hoped I'd bring some attention to the pageant from a sports perspective, helping update the image of the teen event. It sounded interesting, but I had a problem. Even then, I loathed beauty pageants. I admired the women who tossed makeup and hair spray and corsets into a "Freedom Trash Can" on the boardwalk of the Miss America Pageant in Atlantic City way back in 1968, forever giving rise to the phrase "bra-burning feminist" (even though they never burned a thing). I agreed with the premise that keeping women as superficial baubles prevented them from soaring in more important areas. On the other hand, I was curious. I accepted the offer to be a judge and the plane ticket to Texas.

I admit that I had fun that week—it was exciting being at a pageant without having to be *in* a pageant. The contestants I met really were smart and athletic, and many saw the pageant as a way to get noticed and launch serious careers. I wrote a positive (and perky) article emphasizing the number of soccer players and volleyball champs and gymnasts among the contestants. Sounding like that 1945 announcer, I crowed how teenage girls could have beauty and brains and muscles, too!

When I came across that article recently when cleaning my basement, I felt a twinge of ambivalence all over again. I wonder what happened to those teen contestants. I hope some of them ended up parlaying their beauty-queen experience into other success, the way Oprah and Diane Sawyer and Bess Myerson and Sarah Palin did. But I equally worry that some of them got fully distracted by it, focusing on one socially approved aspect of being a woman at the expense of nurturing other aspects of potential genius. I have yet to be convinced that genius can best be advanced by swimsuit competitions or push-up bras.

So how should women play the beauty game? On this one topic, I couldn't determine a clear answer. After hearing both sides of the beauty-and-brains story from various genius women, my sense is that caring deeply about being pretty and caring deeply about being smart can indeed be orthogonal traits. But sometimes they're not. Because even for genius women, it too often happens that the bathing suit becomes you.

CHAPTER 14

Geena Davis and the Problem of Being Nice

One recent evening during the Tucson Festival of Books, I was one of ten authors invited to a fancy country club to talk about our books and writing styles. After drinks and dinner, we sat in a row in the front of the room, passing a mic back and forth, as the moderator asked clever questions that got everyone relaxed and laughing. When he invited audience questions, a woman asked how each of us had done in school. The first writer, a man who had won a Pulitzer Prize, reflected that he used to get As in English but Cs in math. The next couple of writers, also men, offered a similar report card. Then it was my turn.

"I'm a girl. I worked hard. I got all As!" I said.

There was a knowing roar of laughter and applause from the audience.

The next few guys reverted to the story of "mostly Cs but an A in English." When the mic finally went to the only other woman on the panel, a young writer who had recently graduated Oxford, she said shyly, "Same as Janice. I'm a girl and worked hard and got As!" She got another round of applause.

In summation, the eight male writers had spent their school years focused on the subject they loved and were content to get floundering grades elsewhere. The two women writers were resolute and purposeful and determined not to give an inch. Who is really the hero here? We got the applause, but there's a downside to all those As. My young writer friend and I probably worked so hard in school (at least in part) because we intuited the cultural double standard. Maybe we couldn't express it in high school, but we knew we had to be better than everyone else to get noticed. We didn't have the liberty to screw up.

Perfectionism is a great ingredient for mainstream success—but not so good for genius. Being too much of a stickler for conventional recognition tamps out any intellectual risk taking. Genius requires boldness and a bit of audacity. You have to be intrepid. Once you believe deep in your heart that you can get a C and still survive, that you can fail and then have another chance, you are more willing to try the unexpected. Demanding a lot of yourself is good—but demanding too much, as women may do, isn't a sign of confidence. It's a sign of fear.

Geniuses have to be able to throw over conventional thinking and venture in new directions. A few weeks earlier, I'd met up with Daphne Koller, who made a huge success (and the potential for bundles of money) creating an online education site called Coursera. Starting the company wasn't an obvious move. She was a wunderkind professor of computer science at Stanford, known for her exciting breakthroughs in machine learning. By her early thirties, she had won a MacArthur Genius Award. Her career path seemed set. But Koller was a restless genius.

"I had this increasing urgency to have an impact in ways more direct than just writing papers and hoping that someone reads them," she told me.

One of Stanford's most popular courses at the time, taught by Koller's colleague Andrew Ng, regularly attracted four hundred students. When Stanford experimented with putting the class online for the general public, some one hundred thousand people enrolled. As Koller later joked, Ng would have to teach the class for 250 years to have that kind of impact—and he might get bored repeating himself.

Struck by the possibility to do something significant, Koller and Ng decided to see if they could take the classes from the best professors at top universities and offer them for free around the world. A big order, under any circumstances—and I pointed out to Koller that it had nothing at all to do with what she'd done in the rest of her career. She worked on data sets and machine learning and artificial intelligence, and she was getting praise and recognition for all that. What made her toss it all over for something that might not work? She shrugged and told me that she had spent a lot of time being successful by doing things that made her comfortable. She wanted to push herself further, try the truly big initiative. "You only succeed if you're willing to fail—and then pick yourself up and try again," she said.

So she tried—on a two-year leave of absence from Stanford. And when the company was still fragile after that time, she quit her secure tenured position at Stanford to continue nurturing it. "If it failed, it could have been a spectacular failure," she said. Instead, it was a spectacular success. When it was finally soaring a few years later, Koller left to join an arm of Google working on computerization of biomedical issues. And then she ventured out again, to launch her own company focused on drugs and health care. Not a lot of other people are working at that intersection of biology and machine learning, and Koller's genius has been the ability to see "unexpected connections between things that don't normally go together—and then take those ideas and apply them in a new way." She didn't know a lot about biology when she started, but she didn't mind asking questions and not trying to impress anyone at first. The impressing came later.

Did she face discrimination? Sure. But you "learn to brush off the little things because you can't fight every battle. The big ones you do fight," she said. Growing up in Israel, she graduated college at age seventeen, got her master's at eighteen, and then decided to "pick myself up and go to the other side of the world" to get her PhD at Stanford. Talking to her, it struck me that to take the kinds of risks she did, both professionally and intellectually, you have to be willing to be an outlier. You can't be waiting for someone else to give you approval—or mark your report card with As. You decide that you will make your own marks.

Her advice to women is to take big risks and step outside your comfort zone. Look for places where you have leverage—because what you are doing is different. "If something can be done by a thousand other people, you can have only incremental impact. You really make a difference in areas where you can be unique." Most of us aren't unique—but if we have enough courage, we can find that little corner of ourselves that might be different and worth developing.

Wandering through an art fair one day, I saw a framed picture with the words I DON'T KNOW WHO YOU ARE, BUT I NEED YOUR APPROVAL. I stopped and laughed—and probably a lot of other women who walked by did the same. A few hours into the fair, the original piece by performance artist Lisa Levy already had a red dot, meaning it had been sold, and the gallery had made five thousand printouts of the image so everyone could take one. I hope that we were all taking it ironically. But maybe not. Women are taught early to judge themselves through other people's eyes, and when you do that, you can never make a Daphne Koller–like impact. We slip into ingratiating mode with lots of giggles and smiles and self-deprecating comments so as not to threaten the men in control. We want them to like us. A soft approach can seem like a good idea until you realize that it's not too far from the high school girls who play dumb to attract insecure boys. Nobody really benefits from that.

Actress Geena Davis has played knockout characters in movies like the feminist classic *Thelma & Louise,* and she is known for being equally gutsy in real life. She's about six feet tall and determined and looks like she could run the world. She once played the first female president on a TV show—and was completely believable. But when we chatted one morning, she told me that she had been raised to be extraordinarily polite and make sure that everybody liked her and she was never a bother. If she went to someone's house, she wasn't even allowed to accept a glass of water. Being thirsty was not an excuse for inconveniencing anyone. When she started in movies, she continued with the always-be-nice style that plagues so many women—requests become apologies (*I'm so sorry to bother you . . .*) and reasonable demands are twisted to be soft and nonthreatening (*If it's not too much trouble . . .*). Davis said she "tried to be very, very easy to work with and never have any needs." Complaining about her salary or asking for a script change was outside anything she would even consider. She was afraid to express her opinion about anything in her personal life, too. On dates with guys, she wouldn't even suggest which restaurant to go to.

Shooting *Thelma & Louise,* Davis watched her costar Susan Sarandon come to the set every day and say what she wanted without apologies. She was bold and fearless and fully comfortable in her own skin. "I thought, 'Wait a minute. Women can be like that?'" said Davis. She began copying her costar's off-screen courage and embraced the power of the movie characters too, who took charge of their lives and "never relinquished control of our fate to anybody else." Thelma and Louise may drive off a cliff at the end (must all strong women still die?), but Davis considered it a metaphor about making your own choices and keeping your freedom in a sexist world. "I think that's why women, or anybody who feels powerless, comes out of that movie excited and pumped and energized," she told me.

As she started being able to assert her own ideas and strength, Davis realized that our society is male-centric in both obvious and subtle ways. We consider male references to be the normal ones. She told the story of being in the park one day when her three children were toddlers and deciding to change the usual default. Pointing out a squirrel, Davis purposefully said, "She's so cute!"—but it was too late. Her twin boys turned to her in surprise and asked, "How do you know it's a girl?" She felt like she had already failed. The twins were four years old and already seeing the world—and all the dogs and squirrels in it—as male by default.

The male-centrism is everywhere. She started the Geena Davis Institute on Gender in Media because while watching shows with her children, she was "appalled to notice so many more male characters than female ones in preschool shows and little kids' movies." It seemed both obvious and wrong to her, but whenever she casually mentioned the problem to studio executives, they told her, "Oh no, no, that's not true anymore." She began collecting data and found that it was still completely true. In one study of family movies from 2006 to 2009, she found exactly zero female characters portraying doctors, lawyers, business leaders, or politicians. Over the next decade, the numbers improved and movies starring women actually did better at the box office. But male leads still outnumbered female leads by two to one. When she now meets with studio heads and network execs and producers, Davis explains that it's fine to be entertaining for kids, and she's not asking anyone to create shows to send a message. She'd just like them to take *out* the message that women aren't important.

When we chatted, Davis was warm and friendly and had a

wonderful laugh. But now her niceness comes from a core of strength, not weakness. She told me that when she started her institute, "my tactic was congeniality"—she didn't try to embarrass anyone publicly, and her approach was private and direct. It worked. People like collaborating with her, and after she showed up with solid data and a forceful pitch, projects got changed. Davis said that many producers tell her that when they hear a kids'-show pitch now, they think, *What would Geena do?* It's a great question to ask yourself, whether you're male or female.

The #MeToo movement has reminded us that men who may have only their own interests at heart still decide what gets recognized and admired. When the people who set the national agenda (and the TV schedules) see women as objects to be seduced rather than as colleagues and peers, they undermine women's power and genius at every turn. A terrific television series from Amazon Studios called *Good Girls Revolt* was based on the true story of the women at *Newsweek* magazine in the 1960s who fought to be treated equally. The series—smartly written and beautifully acted—got good reviews and was one of Amazon's most successful shows ever with female viewers. But it was cancelled after one season by a misogynist executive who proudly admitted that he had never watched an episode. You could practically hear him boasting—*I killed the show about female empowerment!* He was delighted to let the series' creator, Dana Calvo, know that she might have the talent—but he could wield his power and undermine it. He also passed on two other female-focused shows (*The Handmaid's Tale* and *Big Little Lies*) that went on to get big audiences and multiple Emmy Awards for other networks. It turned out that he didn't just undercut women—he reportedly lewdly propositioned them, too. He left Amazon amidst charges of sexual harassment.

When I chatted about *Good Girls Revolt* with Genevieve Angelson, one of its talented stars, she described the cancellation as "an undeniable example of systemic misogyny." The problem was more than theoretical to her. She had gone from having a very big paycheck to none. The breakout role that might have changed her life was yanked away. Her setback made me think of a comment by Charles Jones, the Cambridge professor who initially defined genius for me. He had warned that you can't just dig back in history and expect to find as many genius women as men—because too many women *never got a chance.* When he described the "social structures that constrained their development," it wasn't just highfalutin academic talk. It was as straightforward as a guy who cancels a show out of misogynist vitriol. Centuries ago, Fanny Mendelssohn Hensel suffered because of men in power who subverted her talent. This time it was Genevieve Angelson.

Women initially launched #MeToo as a way to talk about the sexual harassment they had experienced in the workplace. But, more broadly, it is now a cry to be noticed, recognized, and appreciated. *I have a right to be here, too!* About a year into the movement, some two hundred prominent men have lost their jobs from #MeToo charges, and 43 percent of their replacements are women. Jennifer Salke took over for the misogynist at Amazon and announced that she wanted "big, addictive shows for women." When women are making the structural decisions, they don't have to worry about being nice or placating. They understand the Geena Davis lesson that women need to be seen.

Carol Anderson, a chaired professor of African American studies at Emory University, told me that smart women are always protecting themselves against the expected male backlash that comes from being too strong and too smart. Should there even be such a thing as too strong and too smart? Does it exist for men? It's all part of what she called "the gendered language of deprecation"—which means that women dealing with men often undermine themselves so as to sound nonthreatening. "Women are always aware of the threat of male violence," she said, "and they worry about inciting it if they're not sufficiently deferential to the male patriarchy." To challenge social norms and question male dominance can literally be dangerous. "Women shield their intellect to protect their bodies," she said.

I met Professor Anderson one evening when we began talking at a party, and within five minutes, I thought she was the best cocktail party conversationalist I'd ever met. She was a stunningly original thinker, with brilliant insights that she mitigated with a warm smile and a big laugh. Instead of discussing the weather or the quality of the hors d'oeuvres, she talked about status threats and white men protecting their ground, about the anger they feel when women or minorities advance into their territory. I was surprised since I had never really thought about male anger and violence affecting the decisions that genius women make.

At some point, I mentioned that I didn't regularly confront male anger or aggressiveness—probably because I'm not particularly tough. She interrupted me immediately.

"Of course you're tough—you ran that big magazine," she said. "You just tried to make everyone feel good all the time to keep any anger at bay, right?"

Well, yes, right. I told her about the day one of my male editors handed me a story he wrote that struck me as mumbo jumbo, and I tried to find a nice way to say so.

"I may be our dumbest reader, but I don't really understand what you're trying to say," I told him.

Our dumbest reader? We had 72 million readers at the time. I was not the dumbest. But it was my instinct to offer criticism in a way that wouldn't ruffle any (male) feathers. My quick and tough-minded copy editor overheard the exchange and shook her head. When I didn't seem to understand what she wanted, she beckoned me into her office and closed the door. "I may get fired for saying this," she said, "but you're the editor in chief of the magazine. We look up to you. Would you please stop being so self-deprecating?"

I didn't fire her—I thanked her. She was smart enough to realize that sweet and charming is actually kind of nauseating, and one woman undermining herself has repercussions for all others. I had unwittingly used self-deprecation as a form of self-preservation. Women in all professions learn the art of being politely deferential to men who don't necessarily deserve their deference, protecting themselves against actual violence (which wasn't my concern) or against the undermining that can rain down when men feel threatened.

To one degree or another, we all hone our own style of expressing expertise and authority without pissing people off. The need to do so hasn't changed much. Maggie Gyllenhaal is two decades younger than Geena Davis, but she recently described how careful she tries to be when expressing her opinion to her producers. Like Davis, she's an amazingly brave actress and hardly a wilting flower, on-screen or in real life. She has advocated for human rights causes and spoken loudly for #TimesUp, the movement fighting sexual harassment. She is politically bold in public and a golden girl in private, married to one handsome actor (Peter Sarsgaard) and the sister of another (Jake Gyllenhaal). Yet Gyllenhaal said that when she watched a first cut of the HBO show in which she starred, she would spend hours trying to compose the perfect note to send the producers with her suggestions for creative changes. "I'd think, does my brother have to do this? Probably not—he'd just pop off an email," she said.

Gyllenhaal is savvy enough to know that popping off an email could backfire for her. Men still control Hollywood. Women aren't expected to be confrontational. Her need for caution is real. But it's also damaging to women to have to dance on eggshells. It makes me think of those early women philosophers who prefaced every comment with some version of "I'm just a maiden, so what do I know . . ." Saying that changes both what we can achieve and how we are seen.

For Professor Anderson, the need to be careful about her every step is even more dramatic. The evening we met, I downloaded her bestselling book *White Rage* (she has written many) and asked if we could connect again. When we sat down together the next afternoon, I told her that I'd stayed up way too late the previous night reading her amazing and powerful book.

"I also noticed that you had ten footnotes in the first two pages," I said.

She gave the warm and hearty laugh that I'd already come to identify as her trademark. "I'm a black woman so I need to make sure that everything is checked and double-checked and buttoned up and backed up. I'm not allowed any slipups," she said.

Well, of course. In addition to being the distinguished chair of the African American Studies Department at Emory, she has won numerous teaching awards and received grants and fellowships from the most respected organizations in the country, including the Ford Foundation. This year she has a Guggenheim Fellowship. If a genius sees the world from a different perspective and inspires us to see it that way too, she qualifies. But the titles and honors don't necessarily change people's dismissiveness. Teaching a class one day on the aftermath of World

War I in Italy and France, she was interrupted by a white male student in the second row, riled about her discussion of racial discrimination.

"Where'd you get that?" he called out rudely.

Taken aback, she thought of smacking him down (intellectually, of course) but decided to try a milder approach.

"What did you say?" she asked. She hoped her tone would make it clear that he had stepped over the line. But it didn't.

"Where'd you get that? I've been to Europe and the people there don't act like that," he said.

Ah yes, he'd been to Europe! As a sophomore in college, he surely had more experience and was better informed than any black woman could be. Professor Anderson decided to try humor. Leaning forward and putting her hands on her hips, she asked, "You were there in 1917?"

The other students laughed. The kid realized that his arrogance wasn't being admired or appreciated. The class could continue.

Professor Anderson smiled broadly as she told me the story, but I realized how dispiriting it must be to face derision and disrespect every day, even from your own students. Other women professors had told me about being doubted in the classroom, challenged and questioned in ways that would never be true for male professors. But for Anderson, the problem was multiplied manyfold. Her solution has been the daily version of footnotes—being better than anyone, never allowing herself a mistake, making sure everything she says is supported by original sources. It must be exhausting, I thought. Absolutely exhausting.

Many talented women drop out of careers in the face of male rebuffs. It's not fair to have to prove yourself over and over, they say—and of course they're right. But right now, what other choice do you have? The inbred bias is awful and needs to change. But until it does, if you want to get noticed, if you want to make a mark on the world, you have to be strong and clever enough to make a case for your own genius. Nobody else will do it for you.

"There's a moment in every woman's career when you have to decide—are you going to knuckle under or follow your own path?" said Professor Anderson.

She never knuckled under. But she hit one of those crucial turning points when she was trying to get tenure at her first job and had everything lined up, including a publishing contract for her first book. Academic publishers send manuscripts out for review, and she waited excitedly to get the first reviews back. And waited. And waited. Finally, she asked the publisher what was going on.

"I never sent the manuscript out," he said. "I didn't like your tone."

"My tone?" she asked.

"You were a little heavy in writing about the lynchings."

He had wanted a book about white saviors, and her research had found a different story. ("I'm not the one who *did* the lynchings!" she told me.) She decided to yank the manuscript from him. "You need to have confidence first in the quality of your work," she said. An even better publisher liked her work, and when the book came out and began winning awards, the first publisher told everyone that he'd had the manuscript first. "He made it sound like a good thing!" she said.

Professor Anderson knows that some people look at her successes and start hissing that she must have gotten some advantages from affirmative action. She is happy to discuss that. At lectures, she often brings up the "third rail of American life" and asks the audience who they think benefits the most from affirmative action in college admissions. Since she's African American, they know it's a trick question. It can't be African Americans or she wouldn't be asking. So it must be . . . white women! They are the lucky ones who get a push forward even if they aren't as talented!

Nope.

"I explain that the biggest beneficiaries of affirmative action have been white men," Professor Anderson told me. She has the evidence (of course) to prove it. Across the country, women do better than men in high school, getting higher grades and test scores and racking up more extracurricular honors. If colleges selected their classes strictly on merit, they would be about 65 percent women and 35 percent men. But they can't do that. Students would complain and the school's ranking would drop. So admissions offices adjust the standards for men—*lower* the standards—to make the classes closer to fifty-fifty.

"The narrative has been that women and minorities take the spots that white men deserve," Professor Anderson said. "But the truth is the opposite."

Men taking the places that women deserve! Who knew? But now that we do know, maybe the story can change.

Up to this point the narrative has been that men (white men, that is) have the talent and ability. Stanford sociologist Cecilia Ridgeway, the expert on status and gender, had explained to me that an assumption of male competence is deeply rooted in Western culture and that "a status framework is hard to shake." But it needs to be shaken because right now, it sets up an unreasonable double standard. You know the old line that women have to be twice as good to get half as much? It's not whining—it's fact. Since higher status is accorded to men, they can make even the most blatant blunders and still recover. *He's usually good—it was just a mistake!* He gets another chance. If a woman slips up, she's done. *I told you women can't do this job.* Our minds are excellent at doing the necessary somersaults to prove that what we already thought is correct. We do this every day, in every way, in matters big and small. If you're a fan of potato chips and get one that is too salty and burnt, you shrug it off and reach into the bag for another one. If you're already wary of potato chips when you get the bad one, you toss out the bag.

I find it shockingly wrong that we toss away talented women like so many overly salty potato chips. But Professor Anderson sees it even more expansively. Thinking about all the would-be math geniuses and computer scientists who never had a chance to develop, she points out that you don't build a powerful country by diminishing your work force and not letting talented people advance. "Racism and sexism and misogyny have cut off opportunities and potential and that has weakened the United States. It has hurt our ability to compete economically and destroyed lives."

Women geniuses could take us to Mars and back, alleviate cancer, build new cities. On a rational level, it doesn't make any sense to undermine them. Why continue to push aside the women and minorities who have talents that could save us? Professor Anderson looked at me meaningfully when I asked her that question. She didn't laugh this time. Instead, she raised an eyebrow and said, "You ever hear that expression about cutting off your nose to spite your face?" You can see why I adored this woman. She sees how outrageously biased the world has been against women and minorities, and with great calm, intelligence, and wit, she will keep trying to make all of us see it, too. Whenever a woman or minority gets a top job or impressive award, there's some underlying impression of compromise. But the real compromise comes when we ignore talented women. All of us are equally to blame when that happens. Men have rigged the system, but women can't ease up in the battle to change it.

Paradigms of strong and unstoppable women are important in the movies, as Geena Davis has insisted, and they are powerful in real life, too. When I met Daphne Koller for drinks, she had her phone on

the table to check texts from her two teenagers. She told me she had
to leave at 7 P.M. to get home and make dinner. As Koller took a final
sip of her nonalcoholic mojito and stood up to leave, it occurred to me
that for the two teenage daughters texting her their whereabouts,
Koller was an extraordinary role model. You want to keep girls from
falling into the too-nice, too-giggly, and too-nonthreatening trap and
let them know that it's okay to be a genius? Then let them see what
it means to not let anybody stop you. Koller has been unstoppable in
three different areas now—as a MacArthur fellow, as the founder of
Coursera, and now at her biomedical company. But what she's proud-
est of is her endless willingness to try—"and if you fail, then you go
and you learn some more and you try again, and you do better next
time," she said. You don't worry about being nice and nonthreatening; you just do the work. It's an approach simple enough to be the
moral of a children's storybook. But for women it can be complicated.
Those who manage to pull it off can be on the path to genius.

Koller's husband had been a successful entrepreneur and sold his
second company right after they had their first baby. Feeling slightly
overwhelmed, Koller insisted that his next gig needed to be "less intensive than being a start-up CEO and running all over the globe."
He moved into venture capital and continued his successful career
closer to home, where he could be an equal parent. Koller regularly
advises young women that it's vital to pick a partner who views your
career as being as important as his. "The joke now is that I'm the
intensive start-up CEO—though I'm not sure he finds that equally
funny," she said with a big smile.

Part of Koller's brilliance has been to synthesize new ideas and
take risks by moving in unexpected directions. She's bold; she's intrepid; she tries to have an impact on the world. What gives some
women the courage to go out on a limb and not worry about falling?
Most of the genius women I met had that kind of courage, and I

expect that the conundrum of women never getting a second chance rarely occurred to them. Maybe the world doesn't want to give women the benefit of the doubt, but genius women know you don't have to be nice and ask for a second chance, or even a third. You just take it for yourself.

CHAPTER 15

Frances Arnold Knew She Was Right (and Then She Won the Nobel Prize)

Talking to so many genius women across many fields, I started thinking about the traits they had in common. One thing stood out above all others. Beyond genes and chromosomes and DNA profiles, beyond parents and mentors and teachers, the secret to letting genius flourish seemed to be a powerful belief in your own ability. As a genius woman, you constantly encounter people who want to undermine your work and whose unconscious bias makes it twice (or three or four times) as hard for your achievements to be viewed fairly. The best way to fight back isn't necessarily lawsuits or Twitter feuds—it's standing tall with the kind of ardent surety that makes people finally take notice.

I encountered that confidence and belief with wondrous clarity the day I spoke to Dr. Frances Arnold, who won the 2018 Nobel Prize in chemistry. She had been on my list of genius women to talk to from the start of my research, and when I heard that she was being awarded the Nobel, I swaggered around as if I'd personally gotten the call from the Swedish Academy. After all the years of extraordinary women being overlooked and ignored, at least one amazing woman was being feted around the world.

Dr. Arnold ("Call me Frances," she insisted immediately when we spoke) looks a bit like the actress Robin Wright, with close-cropped blond hair, elegant features, and a calmly regal bearing. As a political powerhouse in the popular show *House of Cards,* Wright coolly manipulated people—and as a genius in real life, Dr. Arnold brilliantly manipulates the evolution of cells. Many years ago when she started the work that eventually won her the Nobel, it was unexpected and unusual, a completely new way of thinking about chemical reactions that upended the traditional approach going on in labs around the world. Needless to say, there were many doubters. How did she get the tenacity to forge ahead?

"I just knew I was right," she said. "I did not doubt myself."

Honestly, I think she deserves a Nobel Prize for that statement alone. The confidence isn't just in retrospect, either, because she went ahead with her revolutionary ideas from the beginning. Dr. Arnold says that she was inspired by nature, "the very best inventor and engineer of all time." Since evolution created everything in the natural world, perhaps it could also be used to design new and useful enzymes or proteins. She essentially moved the evolution of enzymes into the lab and speeded up the process, generating random mutations that eventually created an enzyme with the desired traits. Her startling insight into what came to be called "directed evolution" changed everything. As the Nobel Committee put it, she used genetic change and selection "to develop proteins that solve humankind's chemical problems."

Since nobody had invited me to Sweden, I watched Dr. Arnold's Nobel Prize acceptance speech on video. When we talked later, I pointed out that she had used the word "diversity" several times in her speech—mentioning the "diversity of transformations" in the natural world and describing evolution as "a remarkable diversity-generating machine." Was I reading too much into it to think that her eloquent presentation hid a bigger message about gender diversity in sciences—and the rest of the world?

"My message about diversity is very clear," she said firmly. "Without diversity, you go extinct."

Yes, very clear. She had mentioned diversity several times in different contexts because she sees its power—and women are very much a part of that force. As she explained it, if everyone has the same background and the same experiences and the same perspective, then they naturally trample along on the same much-used paths. "You leave out the possibility of really powerful new solutions—and that's a sure road to extinction," she said.

Like so many of the other genius women I met, Dr. Arnold went on her own path from an early age. If she sensed an obstacle in her way, she would just change direction and move around it. "That's what evolution is, by the way," she told me. Flexible and ready to adapt if something wasn't working out, she learned to take a sharp left turn if she didn't like what was ahead on the right. Doing that requires some fortitude, and the advice she gives young women is to stop being so afraid. "The more fearful you are, the more difficult it is to try something new," she said.

Dr. Arnold appears to be a golden girl, the genius who has done everything right, taken every correct turn, and been showered with praise and awards. But that glowing sheen reflects her attitude toward the world rather than the actual events of her life. Told in a different way, her life could be seen as a series of catastrophes rather than conquests—she has faced a roll call of tragedies and challenges that might have felled someone else. Her first husband, a hugely respected chemical engineer named James Bailey, died of cancer in 2001, leaving her as a single mom with one young son. A few years later, she was diagnosed with breast cancer and spent a year and a half in treatment. She remarried a much-admired astrophysicist—who died in 2010. They had two sons together, and one of them, William, died tragically in 2016, in an accident, at age twenty. Hearing the litany, one wonders how Dr. Arnold has remained standing, never mind flourishing as a chaired professor at the California Institute of Technology (Caltech), running a world-renowned research lab, and starting a company based on her innovations.

"I sit down and remind myself that I have two wonderful remaining sons. I have a great job. I have everything anybody could ever want," she said. Controlling how you respond to a negative situation can make the difference between endless misery and a glimpse at happiness. She has learned to reframe tough times and find the good. "I think it is super important to be grateful—but you know about that," she said, kindly referencing my book on gratitude. She calmly noted that instead of looking at all the things she has lost or doesn't have, she looks at all she *does* have.

Her ability to hold that perspective seems to me its own kind of genius, as important as the brilliant work she has done with enzymes and proteins. Anyone would have forgiven Dr. Arnold for bowing out of her career after her first husband's death or after her own scary diagnosis. Excuses for why you can't go on or have changed your priorities are easy in life. The genius comes in finding the fortitude to move on and not quit—to care enough about the work you are doing to see that it matters and will bring its own glimmer of happiness back.

I've read a lot lately about talented and educated women bowing out of demanding jobs for one reason or another. One woman didn't like putting up with a condescending boss and so gave up her career. Another said the family income would be higher if her husband worked sixty hours a week and she worked only twenty. Yet another felt awkward challenging the suburban norm of stay-at-home moms with a schedule that demanded frequent travel. All of these are understandable positions, and there is no glory in working if that's not what you want to do. But it's important for smart women to realize what they are giving up as well as what they are gaining. As Barnard president Sian Beilock pointed out to me, having many outlets brings a valuable balance. In that way, perhaps genius women have an advantage over others in creating a full and satisfying life. To love the work you do enough to pursue it under any circumstances is a gift to yourself—and ultimately to the many others who might benefit from it.

Dr. Arnold told me that not blaming other people for her misfortunes has helped make her a happier person. She worries about the bright young people she works with who don't have that perspective. They've gone to great schools and have potentially exciting careers ahead of them, and while "the obstacles they face are pretty minor in the scheme of things," they focus on them so much that they start to seem overwhelming. You won't hear her lamenting that she is the only American woman ever to become a Nobel laureate in chemistry since the prizes began in 1901 and only the fifth woman overall. That still beats the paltry three women who have won in physics and the one lone soul in economics. But that's me lamenting—not her.

Do men try to stop women from advancing in science? Some do, sure. But not all of them—and she considers that the more important point. Looking for the good applies to professional situations as well as personal ones. Since there were very few female role models for her in science when she was starting out, she made sure that she worked with men who were supportive of good science, no matter where it came from. She thinks it's a detriment to young women now that "they are surrounded by this constant negative view that men are out to get them—and it's not true. Some men are—but you just avoid them." Later in our conversation, Dr. Arnold came back to that comment to give some perspective. She knows that not everyone can avoid the most problematic guys, and some women are stuck working with them day to day. Once again you can quit or complain or shout that the world isn't fair. Or, as she had advised some disgruntled college women the previous day, "you can act like a kindergarten teacher, treat them with humor, and deflate them." America (and much of the world) needs to change the structures that continue to undervalue and trivialize women. But while fighting for change on a macro level, you can make sure your own life and work go ahead with all the vigor and energy you choose to bring to them. Don't get consumed with the hand-wringing about "Where are all the women?" to the point where you undermine your own ability to advance. If there aren't enough women in your field, then try—like Frances Arnold and Meg Urry and Shirley Tilghman—to be the person who advances enough in her own career to change that. It's lousy and it's hard and heaven knows we'd all be better off in a less misogynistic society. But realism and courage are both requirements of genius. "I would like to see women face the world in a powerful and positive way, not a negative and fearful one," Dr. Arnold said.

Dr. Arnold has sixty patents, many of them inventions that use her techniques for cleaner, safer technologies. She recently started a company that seeks to replace pesticides with an organic, nontoxic approach, using insect pheromones to disrupt mating. As she explains it, you spray "a little bit of their Chanel No. 5, let's call it," and the confused males fly around, looking for the female, but already outsmarted. Dr. Arnold often hears from young women who say that they won't go into engineering because they want a career that lets them take care of people. Being a wife and mother is one way to do that—but creating technologies that make a safer, more sustainable world also nurtures, with impact on a grander scale. As she sees it, bioengineering and sustainability chemistry are the most caring professions around. "When I explain it that way, most women get it," she said.

Dr. Arnold was a renegade from the time she was young—she didn't like school; she drove a cab; she moved out of her family's house when she was still a teenager. Is that kind of disruptive spirit one we should encourage if we want more geniuses?

"Oh gosh, I sure wouldn't want to have a kid like me," she said with a laugh. But she encouraged fearlessness and exploration in her own children, and she traveled around the world with them one year, living and exploring in Africa and Australia. "I watched their brains and their world open up in ways that no amount of schooling can do," she said. She wanted her children to see that the world is a cool place, without boundaries for men or women, a place where you can't control everything, but if you mix positivity and confidence and passion, you can overcome whatever life throws at you.

Honestly, being like her would not be such a terrible thing.

For weeks after I spoke to Dr. Arnold, I thought about her amazing ability to stay undaunted. Her personal life had rocky times. Her professional ideas were unconventional. She faced what she described as the "same stupid sexist behaviors" that all women in science confront, but she had the gift of looking away. She managed to reframe every problem in a positive light.

I had started my research with the insight that genius is the place where extraordinary ability meets celebrity. But I was starting to see a third element that defined genius. Fearlessness. To take the ability and get it noticed requires the kind of strength of conviction that I heard over and over from genius women. If you are fearful, you can't be powerful. You internalize criticism and let it knock you out, rather than taking the parts that seem useful and ignoring the rest. The more fearful you are, the more difficult it is to try something new and stand up to the forces arrayed against you. Those forces may be doubting male colleagues or regressive social structures or the blows that life and fate strike for reasons unknowable. For genius—for real success in life—you need an attitude that can defy all that.

Fear makes you conform to the standard path—and genius, almost by definition, can't be standardized. I don't have any reason to think that women are naturally more timid than men, but if you're not feeling powerful, you are less likely to take the risk of being unconventional and more likely to look for a pretested recipe for success. If you spend any time in the kitchen, you know that a recipe takes you only so far. Your own combination of spices and ingredients are what can make it a masterpiece. If you don't have the guts to add a little ginger to your banana bread, you're going to have the same bread as everyone else. It will probably be fine, and maybe "fine" is all you really want. But genius—whether in baking or chemistry—comes from that extra dash of originality. You need confidence to write your own recipe—and you can't worry if not everyone likes ginger.

While we're talking about food, it's worth noting that the great genius chef Alice Waters, who started the restaurant Chez Panisse back in 1971 and is credited with changing how the country (or at least some of it) eats, was always happy to create her own recipes, both literally and metaphorically. Her emphasis on fresh, local, and seasonal ingredients may not sound revolutionary now, but it upended the French-cooking creed of butter and cream and the American focus on packaged mac and cheese.

Waters was the first woman to win the Outstanding Chef award from the James Beard Foundation—which is odd, isn't it? Women are traditionally the cooks in the family. They develop recipes and techniques and style. So why is it that when people go out for dinner, they traditionally expect a man in the kitchen? The bias here is truly striking. There is absolutely nothing in either genetics or environment that would make a man better at whipping up a tarte tatin, and yet the Culinary Institute of America didn't start accepting women until 1970. The dominance of male chefs, now gratefully starting to decline, seems predicated on an odd twist of patriarchal logic that says women should make the pasta at home but need men to boil the water in the restaurant. It's just another example of how pointless our gender stereotypes can be.

True genius has an effect on future generations—and by that standard alone, Waters lands squarely in the genius category. Just like Dr. Arnold's directed evolution is now a standard for chemical engineers, Waters's approach has become the new definition of American cuisine. Every corner grocery store now carries organic food, and chefs who worked with her now have their own restaurants all over the country, advancing her methods. If your waiter tells you which local farm grew the lettuce on the menu, you have Waters to thank.

What inspired her to be different and provocative at a time when American restaurants were (at best) trying to copy everyone else? Living in Berkeley, California, back in the 1960s, the eventual site of Chez Panisse, she was part of the antiwar and free-speech movements of the time. Her activism affected her deeply, and in becoming a chef, she was inspired by the counterculture attitude that you can go in your own direction and never follow rules. She wanted to try things and figured if she made a mistake—well, so what? "If you burned the corn soup, you called it grilled corn soup," she once explained.

Genius evolves—you don't have to be born knowing what you want to do, and you don't have to be a prodigy from age four, either. Waters traveled extensively before going to Paris to learn about food. Dr. Arnold started off working in solar energy when she was just out of school and then changed direction. She wasn't afraid of picking up and trying something different. Once she had her plan, though, she was fearless. Obstacles and doubters? You treat them like a wilted piece of iceberg lettuce. Worth noting—but then you push it aside and replace it with something better for you.

Hearing about my interest in women and genius, several people told me that I had to speak to at least one of the sisters Wojcicki—Anne, Susan, or Janet. All are brainy and strong and ambitious, and they have achieved almost mythic status around Silicon Valley as examples of how you can raise fearless women. I finally caught up with Anne, the youngest of the three, after a few canceled meetings (she's a busy genius).

"Hey, thanks for being patient!" she said cheerfully when we connected.

Even among the nonconformists of the high-tech world, Anne is an original. The founder and CEO of a major company in Silicon Valley, she strides through her offices most days wearing sneakers and workout clothes. And why not? An exercise fiend, she bicycles to work and is always running somewhere, both literally and figuratively. She's fit, energetic, and in great shape—and nothing is going to hold her back.

Growing up in an intellectually rigorous family, Anne learned early that conformity is for other people and the rules do not (have to) apply. Her dad was a professor at Stanford, and Wojcicki's neighbors were "a lot of academic misfits with a celebratory sense of following your own passion and being unusual." I laughed when she said that because it was the first time I'd heard "misfit" being used as high praise. But she adored the eclectic community and took from it the powerful lesson that there was no single, definitive way to approach life. "I have no fear of failure because for me, there is no black-and-white version of success," she said.

The fearlessness helped when she launched the company 23andMe—named after the number of paired chromosomes in the human DNA. Wojcicki wanted (at least in part) to give people direct access to their genetic profiles. For a moderate fee, you're sent a kit, and after you spit into a plastic cup and return it, you get an analysis of your DNA. The report includes details about your ancestry (*You're 5 percent Irish and 22 percent Jamaican!*), your risk of getting certain diseases, and whether you are more likely to prefer chocolate ice cream or vanilla. *Time* magazine called the direct testing the "Invention of the Year" in 2008, two years after the company launched.

Wojcicki saw the company as a rebellion against the entrenched health-care industry and a way to put health care back into consumers' hands. If you have a genetic predisposition to Alzheimer's or Parkinson's disease, you have a right to know about it. The company began garnering customers, headlines, and lots of adulation—until the FDA ruled in 2013 that they could continue with the ancestry profiles but had to abandon the health reports. It might have sunk another CEO—and Wojcicki says she spent a couple of days in her pajamas, trying to figure out what to do. She remembered that when she was younger and had a problem, her mother would tell her to put her head down and deal with it. Very few things that life presents are insurmountable obstacles. "My sense was that if I stopped whining, I could get it done."

She got it done. The company eventually made peace with the FDA and got back on track with its medical profiling. Some 80 percent of people who send their DNA for testing agree to let the company use the sample for research, which is important to Wojcicki's larger goal of using big data to solve health issues. But after 23andMe also got major influxes of money from drug companies wanting access to their huge DNA database, critics raised questions about how they were using personal medical information. There will be other questions and criticisms ahead—Wojcicki is a woman doing something that hasn't really been done before, and (as we know) that results in many detractors. But she's calm about it. "I have my moments of being frustrated, but you try to capture opportunities and make the most of them," she said.

In Silicon Valley, Anne and her sister Susan are high-tech royalty—with (I'm guessing) fewer crowned jewels than real monarchs but more money. Google quite literally began in Susan's garage when founders Sergey Brin and Larry Page set up their first office there in 1998. Susan was an early star in marketing and advertising at Google and is now the energetic and inspiring CEO of YouTube, as well as the mother of five children. Along the way, Anne and Sergey connected, and they got married in a very private 2007 ceremony in the Bahamas, where they both wore bathing suits and swam out to a sandbar. (In their one bow to tradition, her swimsuit was reportedly white and his was black.) They had two children together before getting divorced in 2015, when Brin had a very public affair with another colleague. Anne had some bad days along the way—the affair and the FDA battle both broke into the spotlight at about the same time. But sounding like Nobel laureate Frances Arnold, she told me that she has a "rosy, optimistic" outlook and figures that "there's always a way to spin something in a positive way" that lets you keep plowing ahead.

When you're starting a company, it certainly helps to be linked to one of the richest men in the world—I get that. But it's also unfair to attribute Anne's talent and success to her marriage. She was spirited, determined, and creative before she met Brin—maybe it's what attracted him—and she remains that way now. Part of her genius is tapping into the zeitgeist and knowing what people want. Her company is based on real science, but she has also figured out that people like to be entertained, and if you make science fun, they'll stick with you.

Before my conversation with Wojcicki, my wonderful sister-in-law Chris sent me the report she received after sending 23andMe her saliva and $199 (down from the thousand bucks the company charged when it started in 2007). The first page showed that she didn't have any of the genetic variants that could contribute to more than a dozen different diseases. Good news. The following pages had even more compelling information—she probably preferred salty foods to sweet ones, had slightly higher odds of disliking cilantro, and was likely to wake up around 6:42 in the mornings. Oh, and she would get more mosquito bites than other people and was probably afraid of heights.

Looking at the report, I was astonished. Could there really be a gene for liking cilantro . . . or getting mosquito bites . . . or waking up at 6:42?

"More of it is true than you'd think," Chris told me with a laugh. "Though I have to say I'm not afraid of heights."

I asked Wojcicki about the somewhat wacky items on the genetic report, and she said that most of the correlations were from original research that her company had done. She saw it as part of making science interesting. Everyone likes party games when they're kids, and she thinks of questions like who has more Neanderthal in their genes as providing cocktail party conversation for adults. Wojcicki herself has always been proud of her strong teeth—she has no cavities—and recently she asked the research team to find out why that might be. "This is the fun stuff," she said.

Given that she has made a career out of figuring out who you are through your genes, I wondered if Wojcicki would be the one person to tell me that the differences between men and women are innate, engraved on our chromosomes, and immutable. But quite the opposite. Having grown up in what she described as a "gender-neutral environment," she always had close male friends and didn't distinguish between the talents of boys and those of girls. Her science study group in high school included three guys and three girls "and we were super competitive and toe-to-toe but always equal. There was no gender component at all. We all just blended." When she got to college and finally met someone who made a sexist comment to her about women's roles, she treated it with anthropological interest. "I remember thinking, 'Wow, you're a specimen to study—one of those people who think women are limited.'"

What she has learned is that genetic variants are interesting, but they don't determine an outcome. Genes are a lot like talent and genius—you may have a predisposition, but you need the right environment for them to flourish. Changing that environment can have dramatic results. For example, when Sergey Brin had a genetic profile done, he discovered that he has a gene mutation that predisposes him to Parkinson's disease, potentially giving him a fifty-fifty chance of getting the disease.[1] Being a numbers guy, Brin figured that you can always change the algorithm and fix the odds. Some research suggested that exercise and certain foods could lower the risk for Parkinson's for young men, so Brin exercises relentlessly and is careful about his diet. He estimates that effort will cut the risk in half—to 25 percent. Having made huge donations to Parkinson's research, he expects that advances in neuroscience will cut the risks in half again—to 13 percent. Even better.

---

1 His mother had Parkinson's, so it wasn't a complete surprise. DNA analysis can be a fancy way of talking about family history. His mutation on a gene called LRRK2 is believed to increase risk from 1 percent in the general population to 30 to 75 percent in those who have it. In talking about it, Brin generally splits the difference and calls it fifty-fifty.

Genius and talent can be perceived in a similar way. Maybe you have a genetic variant that will help you be a great pianist, a formidable physicist, or a stellar swimmer. But that says absolutely nothing about the odds that you will ultimately play in Carnegie Hall, fly to the moon, or win a medal at the Olympics. Your attitudes, your efforts, and the social pressures around you can all be transformative.

"The beauty of genetics is not that it determines who you are, but that it's a starting point," Wojcicki told me. "I believe in the power of your environment and the potential for change."

Wojcicki credits the community where she grew up for her confidence and boldness and smarts. Those misfit neighbors and friends regularly told her that she was unstoppable—and their belief that "you can do this" sunk in. So did the persistence that her mother, a journalism teacher, inspired. Whenever Anne had a paper to write for school, she gave it to her mother to edit—and got it back covered with red marks. Anne would rewrite, hand it to Mom again, and get it back with fewer red marks. And then do it again. "The real lesson was that life is a constant evolution and it's okay if you don't do well the first time you try," Anne said. "You need the opportunity to learn and grow."[2]

Wojcicki may naturally "sway on the more self-confident side," as she put it, but that confidence and strength had to be nurtured into genius. The genius to start a company. The genius to persist. The genius to change the way people think about their own genes. Her biggest discovery was that there is no single path to success.

"People aren't great every day," Wojcicki told me. "People are great over an average. You need a community that supports you on the bad days, too."

---

2 My children also had to deal with a mother who was a relentless editor. I have told them Anne's story, hoping that my red pen gets some (small bit of) credit for their resilience and genius.

Like Frances Arnold, Wojcicki has learned to get through the bad days, relying on optimism and personal resilience. She knows that you can fail and still bounce back. You can write a lousy first draft and then take all the teacher's (or your mother's) red marks and rewrite it so it's better. You can have a community that lets you see life as an opportunity to grow. Because once you have positivity and determination and fearlessness, you can be an unstoppable woman of genius.

CHAPTER 16

How to Succeed in Business by Wearing Elegant Scarves

Awell-funded project a few years ago sought to identify geniuses in obscure spots around the world. It struck me as a singularly ineffective approach—rather like hoping to find orchids growing in the Arctic, when you really should be building a hothouse to nurture them. So I was happy when I heard that the physicist Albert-László Barabási was studying the more relevant question of why some people get recognized as geniuses and others don't. Barabási is one of the world's great experts on complex networks—whether they involve people, technology, or nature. He has already found that success depends on a lot more than talent—it needs a network that spreads your ideas and gives you recognition. He defines success as "the rewards we earn from the communities we belong to," and he knows that women have often been blocked from those success-making communities.

When I gave him a call to talk about his work, he told me that world-changing success "is not just about your performance but about how people perceive what you do." I smiled when I heard that because it seemed another way of saying what I had discovered at the very beginning of my research—that genius is extraordinary talent paired with celebrity. The people we call geniuses aren't always the very top performers in their field. They just happen to be the ones who got the most recognition.

Barabási is using network theory along with big-data analysis to look at what distinguishes geniuses. One part of his project seeks to discover genius by analyzing data sets that reflect the careers and publications of scientists working since 1900. I asked him about the danger of falling into the same trap that bedeviled Francis Galton back in the 1800s. If you look at the people who have been successful, you are drawing conclusions only about whom the society has already nurtured and pushed to the foreground. You are showing the power of having power. He agreed, pointing out that the institutions that confer high-level recognition, like the Nobel Committee and the French Academy, are never fully objective and "show a generalized bias toward men." For every person they recognize, he thought you could find ten others, many of them women, "whose work and impact is indistinguishable."

No matter how big your network or how complex your data set, if it was created with bias, all that emerges is biased results. Barabási is trying to equalize the information in the databases because he knows that "the concept of genius is a societal construct" rather than an objective algorithm. "People bring such bias to the table that I often joke that machines would do much better at ignoring gender and finding genius," he told me.

"It doesn't sound like a joke," I said.

"You're right—it's true," he said with a laugh.

I was reminded just how complicated it is to get noticed in a world still relying on those old databases when I met up with Monica Mandelli, the managing director of a major investment firm. Her company's offices are in midtown Manhattan, and when I stepped into their sky-high reception area on the forty-second floor of an elegant office building, I was stunned by the floor-to-ceiling windows looking out over Central Park. It was one of the most spectacular views of the city I've ever seen. As I stood peering out those windows, I suddenly understood what it means to be on top of the world.

Mandelli is one of the few women who has reached the very highest heights of finance, emerging as a star in a male-dominated network. She wasn't the obvious person to reach the empyrean. She grew up in a small, conservative town outside Milan where none of the women went to college—not because they couldn't afford it but because they were expected to get married and have children and nothing more. The Southern Mediterranean expectation that women would be good in math, which I had learned from physicist Carla Molteni, didn't seem to apply in her northern Italy town. Mandelli was fine with the get-married-and-have-children part (she now has three), but she expected a lot more.

"Even as a child, I embraced change and was comfortable with being different. I always wanted a big life," she told me as we sat down together in a conference room (with similarly fabulous views). With clients all over the world, Mandelli was just back from a trip to Mexico and Brazil and was heading the next day to Berlin and Paris. She got the big life. Warm, vibrant, and smart, she has shown a genius ability to navigate over complicated (uphill) terrain. Growing up, she understood that it would be easier to conform and be like everybody else, but she had a "passionate desire to be myself and find my own voice."

When Mandelli talks about finding her own voice, it's more than a metaphor. When she first came to America, she was in her early twenties and worried that her Italian-tinged pronunciations wouldn't play well. She heard about a school that actors like Robert De Niro and Julia Roberts used to hone an accent for a part—and she signed up to *erase* her accent for real life. The teacher gave her sentences to practice that would Americanize her vowels. To this day, she remembers going home and repeating over and over, "Dorothy, please stand while they sing the national anthem."

If that story brings to mind Eliza Doolittle singing "the rain in Spain stays mainly in the plain," I think you've got it. Mandelli's husband couldn't figure out why she would stand in front of the mirror and talk about the national anthem. She persisted, though, until she encountered a coach at work who saw (and heard) her situation differently. His position was that in business, you want to be noticed. Americans have notoriously short attention spans, and studies showed that they listen longer to someone with a foreign accent.

"I think it was seven seconds longer—which is an eternity!" Mandelli told me. Not wanting to lose that edge, she quit the diction school and started thinking more broadly about what it meant to be nonconforming and original. Maybe a perceived liability could become a positive? Being different might also mean being memorable. "I'm warm. I'm passionate. I'm extroverted and naturally communicative. I'm from Milan so I have a sense of style and I can wear high heels and big jewelry and accessories," she said. "I decided to accept that whole persona and play to my strengths."

Genius in the business world isn't much different from genius in other fields—part of it is about being recognized and heard. If you have a dazzling idea at a meeting but nobody registers it until your male colleague repeats it, your genius doesn't matter. The day we met, Mandelli was wearing a gorgeously colorful and large silk scarf, tied with the elegant flair that only an Italian (or French) woman could muster. If genius is at the intersection of extraordinary ability and celebrity, then doing great work isn't enough. You need to grab people's attention and imagination. Mandelli told me that she advises young women never to be a fly on the wall. Speak up. Be seen. Wear an elegant scarf that demands to be noticed.

When I asked Mandelli how she had escaped the limited expectations of her childhood, she told me a story about going shopping one day when she was eight years old with her mother and her mother's best friend. The friend fell in love with a pair of red shoes, and after cooing over them for a while, she announced that she was going home to ask her husband for money and permission to buy them. "It was one of those pivotal moments that define who you are," Mandelli said. "I told myself that I was never, ever going to have to ask anybody for either the permission or the money to buy shoes."

Something sparked in Mandelli at that moment, just as it has in genius women over the centuries who realize that they are not content becoming the conventionally submissive woman society expects. She had a right to her own life and her own independence. She didn't know at that moment how she would achieve her goal—she was too young to know what job to pursue or what opportunities might be open to her—but she was confident that she would find her way. Many genius women had role models who gave them a sense of possibility, but you can also be animated by a *reverse* role model—a sense that what you see around you is not what you want or choose to become. Somehow, you will create your own future.

After attending the one university in Milan with a worldwide reputation, Mandelli launched a blue-chip career—Harvard Business School, McKinsey & Company, Goldman Sachs. Many professions are tough for women, and finance is among the more unforgiving. Mandelli started from the basic premise that "you have to be amazing at what you do; otherwise you're not going to survive." That, to repeat, is the starting point. Next comes the challenge of proving that you will not be daunted by endless travel, long hours, and certain alpha males trying to undermine you.

"I think there are unconscious biases that keep women from getting the right opportunities and the right stretch assignments," Mandelli said. A manager might not bring a woman to an important client meeting or put her on a career-making case. Beyond unconscious bias (could the woman really be the smartest one on his team?), the unstated fear is that she's just going to get married and have a kid and leave anyway. So why invest too much in her? That attitude could exist in any profession, but it seems notably strong in the male-dominated enclaves of finance.

Mandelli faced the problem directly, letting her bosses know that, yes, she was going to have a baby, but she was also returning because her career mattered. They could count on her. She had the same conversation a few years later, before delivering twins. She knew that as a woman, she was scrutinized all the time and held to different standards. Unfair? Welcome to the world. When she reached a position where she could do something about it, she would, but meantime she had to be at her best all the time. "Doing a great job is a necessary condition, but it's not enough. You have to turn up the volume on what makes you unique," she said. "I am who I am, and if they like me, great. If they don't, it's also going to be okay."

I expect that Mandelli would have become a managing director at Goldman Sachs (where she spent seventeen years) even without her colorful scarves. But they are a nice reminder that careers don't happen by serendipity and genius comes at least in part from relentlessness. As she fought her way through a tough and male-dominated business, she had the courageous spirit of the Little Engine That Could, bravely chugging *I think I can, I think I can* as she climbed her way to the top. Mandelli told me that she knows that "life beats you up a lot, and it gets harder and harder to stand back up after a fall." To continue on, you need some fundamental core of positivity and belief in yourself. As I discovered with Nobel laureate Frances Arnold and other genius women, it helps to know deep down that you are smart and capable—and that you're not going to let anybody make you doubt that. You have to keep chugging, no matter what anyone says.

Mandelli feels charged when she gives her all every day, but she knows that maintaining confidence isn't as natural for everyone else as it is for her. Younger female colleagues come to her for advice all the time, distraught that some guy took credit for an idea or that a boss ignored their contributions. Is the fight worth it—or should they just quit? She tries to imbue them with her excitement and sense of possibility. "I tell them, 'You're amazing and you can go so far. Life is full of endless opportunities. Don't let anyone discourage or diminish you—and don't let the situation drag you down.'"

It's good advice but hard to follow because daily situations do drag people down. Keep chugging? The poet Shel Silverstein once wrote a parody of *The Little Engine That Could* where the engine slides down the hill and gets smashed against the rocks. "If the track is tough and the hill is rough / THINKING you can just ain't enough!" he warned. The line always made me laugh, but Mandelli's approach is better. If you want to flourish as a genius, you can't be dragged down by rough hills or sexist circumstances—and you have to believe in your own success. Mandelli ignored slights early in her career and even found it mildly amusing that when she stepped into the first-class plane cabin on business trips, the man in 1A (invariably) asked her to hang up his coat. She would smile at his shock when she sat down next to him as the ticketed passenger in 1B—and then politely offer to find him an actual flight attendant. It doesn't happen anymore since many more executive women on expense accounts are filling the fancy seats. But at various new-client meetings, she does still get asked to pour the coffee.

Mandelli told me that she has regular family meetings with her children, now preteens, where they discuss a complicated topic—her goal being to help them think expansively, express opinions, find their voice. Recently the conversation focused on Greek myths and the choice Hercules faced between pleasure and duty. Going down one road would lead to a life of pleasure. The other road would be filled with incredible ordeals and obstacles, but he would be remembered forever with the gods on Mount Olympus. The children debated and discussed, and Mandelli was delighted with how they all (two boys and a girl) could articulate their arguments. She took great joy in helping her children realize that you always need to test yourself and give your all—and that you can take control of more things than you sometimes think.

After we finished our conversation and hugged good-bye (she's from Italy, after all), I spent some time thinking about how Mandelli herself would parse that particular Greek myth. It struck me that for her, Hercules's choice is not a conflict at all—because the pleasure *is* the duty. Her delight in overcoming obstacles, figuring out a path, and knowing the next step is part of her genius. And maybe it is what gets you to Mount Olympus.

That Monica Mandelli, from a small town outside Milan, became a global powerhouse makes you realize that women geniuses have a spark and a passion for achievement that no amount of bias or cultural conditioning can suppress. They make their own rules. But that indomitability is rare and amazing. It's the next level of women I worry about, those who have the spark—but whose fire gets doused more easily. Mandelli persisted and stayed positive and wouldn't be stopped. But for so many women in her field and others, constant negativity from their bosses and colleagues and society in general keeps them from reaching the heights they should.

Women through the ages have learned to be nice in the face of slights and often back away to keep everyone happy. But like Geena Davis, many women are tired of that now and looking for a new approach. A friend told me about a twenty-seven-year-old woman named Stef who was considered the rising genius at a major investment bank. After soaring for a couple of years as the star of the class, she was shocked when she got a mediocre review and a minimal (for banking) raise. Convinced that unconscious bias was at play, she found an article in a respected business journal that listed some of the red flags of sexism. She went through the review and highlighted in blue the exact words the article warned about—like saying a woman is too aggressive in meetings or has an abrasive style, phrases never used in a negative way for men. She brought the annotated review back to her boss and pointed out that if he took out all the phrases in blue—which was much of the review—what remained described her *actual* performance. It was all strong and positive and she had handled more deals than anyone else at her level. "On that basis you should promote me," she said firmly. He thanked her for the feedback and said he understood.

When I first heard this story, I was delighted. If you are brave enough to point out bias, you can beat it! But the boss never gave her the promotion. Six months later, Stef quit. I hope she goes on to become the star financial genius everyone expected her to be, and that she will use the story of the sexist review to remind other women to know their own worth and demand to be recognized. But last time I heard, she was still looking for a job. As Mandelli said, the more times you get beat up, the harder it is to stand. That some few women have managed to survive and thrive despite all the odds against them remains awe-inspiring. Most of the genius women I interviewed seemed to have emerged unscathed. But we have to change the odds so that more talented women can walk through an open door, rather than each one having to knock it down on her own. You shouldn't have to be bruised and bloodied before your genius is recognized.

Albert-László Barabási pointed out to me that we are better at praising women's talents in retrospect than in the moment. When he's not working on his networks and databases, he collects Hungarian art, including many works by women artists. One of his favorites, Dóra Maurer, recently had a solo show at the Tate in London—but he finds it bittersweet that accolades are coming only now that she is over eighty. "It's good that women artists are being put back into the canon, but part of your impact comes from having people follow you," he said. "We need women to be recognized as players throughout their careers. That's what we're still missing and what needs to change."

At a big charity dinner I attended recently, the keynote speaker was the woman CEO of a major company, who was charming, well-spoken, and smart. After the dinner, I began talking about genius women with a man sitting at my table.

"Can I give you an insight that will reflect very badly on me?" he asked.

When I nodded, he told me that during the CEO's talk, he began thinking about just how exceptional she must be—a true business genius—to have overcome all the male power and ingrained sexist bias at the company and land the very top spot. Or was the company trying to change its image—and it therefore helped that she was a woman?

"I'm embarrassed to admit the workings of my mind," he said.

"But you should understand that the first thing a guy like me notices about a successful woman is—*she's a woman.*"

I told him that I wasn't shocked at all. In fact, I was glad that he could see both possibilities—including that she might be so much better than anyone else. Because too often, the assumption is that if a woman has succeeded, there has been some compromise. She took the job from a man. And, yes, she did indeed. She got the job that a lot of other men and women no doubt wanted. But why would we ever think that a man has some greater natural claim on it than she does?

Just being aware of bias can start to change it. Shortly after that dinner, I spoke to Kristin Lauter, a mathematician who heads the Cryptography Group at Microsoft Research. Her breakthroughs into new and elegant ways to keep data private have changed the field, and she has a stack of patents to prove it. Her work is deeply complex and mathematically original—but you can think of it as a high-tech update on secret decoder rings. Remember Elizebeth Friedman, who broke codes to save us from the Nazis? Lauter creates codes to save us from hackers. When she first came to Microsoft from the academic world, Lauter was thrilled to discover that "instead of one or two people in the world reading my papers, top executives were having meetings wanting to understand what I'm talking about." Her work with elliptic curve cryptography (which I couldn't begin to explain) became part of Windows products as a way to protect the privacy of sensitive data. "I got so jazzed that the mathematics I knew would be useful for something in the public good," she said.

Doing things that matter was also her motivation for trying to change the implicit bias against women in math. Back in 2000, she turned down an invitation to speak at a math conference in Europe because she was about to give birth to her twin daughters. For the next several years, she didn't get invited to give any talks at all.

"Women get one chance, and if you miss an event, you don't get invited again," she said. "They essentially crossed me off the list."

Smart, persistent, and aware of what was happening, she got herself back into the mainstream. But the top conferences she attended often included only one or two women, and once in Japan it was "one hundred men and one woman, which can be scary." One day she sat down with a couple of colleagues and made a list of seventy-five women they thought should have been in attendance but hadn't been invited. Where were they, and why had nobody thought of them? You could call it the we-already-invited-one syndrome—a problem that women and minorities face in many fields. A couple of outstanding women get recognized, and tokenism gets confused with diversity. But the seamless integration of men and women? The recognition that extraordinary women are equal colleagues deserving of equal attention? Nope, not there yet.

Lauter became president of the Association for Women in Mathematics and started a research collaboration group for women. She called the group focused on number theory WIN, for "women in numbers."[1] It was so successful that she launched seventeen other networks for different areas of mathematics. "Women in Topology is WIT, but I still like WIN best," she told me with a laugh. I asked her if women-only math groups sent the wrong message—because isn't it better to be inclusive and get everyone working together? She agreed with the goal but pointed out since "the hierarchal structure that dominates the profession" was entirely male, she thought that nothing would change without "a proactive effort to get more women noticed."

Lauter graduated high school when she was fifteen and then got

---

1   Lauter started WIN with mathematicians Rachel Pries of Colorado State University and Renate Scheidler at the University of Calgary. Lauter's belief in the need for collaboration is real—she contacted me twice to be sure her collaborators would be mentioned.

her undergraduate, master's, and PhD degrees at the University of Chicago. By any definition, she was a mathematical prodigy, but she didn't fit the standard profile. "There is still the genius myth, and it's only men who get anointed as geniuses," she said. Both of her daughters are now also doing computer science at the University of Chicago, but when they were in second grade, one of the girls told her mom that the teacher had dropped both of them from the advanced math class. She looked back at her daughters' quizzes and saw they had all perfect scores. "I work on these issues of gender fairness and here we were, facing the stereotypes of a male math teacher," she said. "I was seriously angry. It's crazy to me that this was still happening." The teacher eventually apologized and put Lauter's daughters back in the class. But what if your parents don't take up the fight? What if you start to believe, at age seven or eight, that you really don't deserve to be with the smart kids?

When Lauter organized her math networks, she created a collaboration model, putting senior women mathematicians together with graduate students and postdocs, all solving problems together. Her idea was that there was power in role models and collaborative efforts. Math is more than just proving and solving, she explained. Math papers have to be read and appreciated, and more people together create more power. The networks of unnoticed women started to empower one another to be strong and get noticed.

As I thought later about my conversation with Lauter, her networks of women gaining power by banding together reminded me of *Swimmy* by Leo Lionni, one of my favorite books to read to my children when they were young. It starts when a whole school of small fish are eaten in one gulp by a bigger fish—and only one little fish is left. He goes off alone exploring the beautiful ocean, and when he encounters another school of fish, just like his own, they don't want to explore and see things because they are fearful of being devoured.

"But you can't just lie there!" says Swimmy. "We must THINK of something." He organizes the small fish to swim together—and as they take their places, their formation makes them look like the biggest fish in the sea. With that new power, they can swim happily and chase the big fish away.

To get your genius noticed, you can find your own distinctive voice and hope that it will be strong enough to overcome biases and get people to pay attention. Or you can join together with others just like you, form a network of talented women who might otherwise be devoured by their harsh and brutal environment. If it works, you can swim freely, safely supported by those around you, making it possible to enjoy the cool water and the midday sun.

CHAPTER 17

Why Sally Michel Was a Genius Painter and Mrs. Milton Avery Was Not

When actress Tina Fey interviewed for a writing position on *Saturday Night Live* in 1997, she knew the show was looking to diversify. She thought it would be a good opportunity for her—even though she realized how ridiculous it was, as she later explained, that "an obedient white girl from the suburbs counts as diversity." Fey became the first female head writer on the show, the second writer to be pregnant, and eventually the third woman to win the Mark Twain Prize for American Humor. In enumerating those milestones in a speech at the Kennedy Center, she added the hope that women could be "achieving at a rate these days that we can stop counting what number they are."

How nice if we could, indeed, stop counting. Or if we could at least start to realize just how crazy it is to see women as a distinct and homogenous group, standing in opposition to men. The English philosopher John Stuart Mill wrote a book in the 1860s called *The Subjection of Women* that argued ardently for the equality of men and women. The current system, he said, where women are treated as less capable, was old-fashioned and no longer valid in any practical or meaningful way. Men in power were happy to convince women that an essential part of sexual attractiveness was meekness and submissiveness. But that was just so much folderol. He pointed out that women were raised to believe that "their ideal of character is the very opposite to that of men"—and that it was time for such nonsense to end.

"I deny that anyone knows or can know, the nature of the two sexes . . . distorted as they have been," he wrote. "What is natural to the two sexes can only be found out by allowing both to develop and use their faculties freely."

I pause every time I read that because its truth is both so simple and so profound. Over the centuries and up until this moment, women have been held back and reined in, their intellectual abilities neither nurtured nor encouraged. What we think is "natural" to the two sexes is a distortion. Mills called the misjudgment of women's abilities "a relic of the past [that] is out of tune with the future and must necessarily disappear." He wrote that in the 1800s, and since then, the relic has not yet disappeared. We all fall into the old behaviors, even when we know how ridiculous they may be. Mill believed that it was impossible to know what women could really achieve if they hadn't been stuck in the old cycles and expectations. They—we—have never had a chance to show our true natures. He considered it "tiresome cant" that women have an inherent goodness and a natural willingness to sacrifice for their families. With a little more equality, a woman would have no reason to be so self-sacrificing—and guys might become a little more generous if they were no longer "taught to worship their own will as such a grand thing."

My favorite part of the Mill story is that he met a woman named Harriet Taylor in 1831, when she was a young mother with an early feminist bent. They began exchanging letters and ideas about equality and women's rights. Their friendship grew, and they lived and traveled together on and off for the next couple of decades, finally getting married after her husband died. In his autobiography, Mill took the rare step of saying that most of the books and essays he published had been joint works with Harriet. Only his name appeared on the title page, but he wanted it clear that they had developed the ideas together and the works were equally hers.

Well, bravo! Mill didn't just talk the talk. When he and Taylor were getting married, he wrote a long treatise saying that whatever legal rights that gave him (men had many in those days, women almost none), he wanted to make it very clear that she would have "the same absolute freedom of action, & freedom of disposal of herself . . . as if no such marriage had taken place." He said that he disapproved of all the rights given men during marriage and found the imbalance of power to be "odious."

I can't prove it, but I'd bet his was the only marriage proposal in history to have included the word "odious." In its own way, though, I also find it the most romantic one ever made. *I love you so much that I want to be with you forever, but I don't want to own you. I don't want you to be less than you are.* We don't know what a natural woman is yet because "until conditions of equality exist, no one can possibly assess the natural differences between women and men." The best you can do? Keep your own voice—and speak with it loudly.

Almost two hundred years after Mills, we continue to push forward and stumble back, and maybe we get closer to at least glimpsing our real possibilities. Tina Fey has opened doors for many women who have followed her in comedy, at least in part by showing that there is no overarching definition of "female comic." Funny women can have distinctive and original voices. Male comics have different styles, too. When Fey and Jimmy Fallon (now host of *The Tonight Show*) cohosted the popular "Weekend Update" news segment on *Saturday Night Live* for several years, Fallon was often the giggly and cute one while Fey was smart, arch, and all knowing. They avoided stereotypes and allowed themselves to be individual personalities with talents that broke boundaries and didn't need to be limited.

Fey managed to develop her own talent and genius despite what she called the "institutionalized gender nonsense" she faced when she started out. As part of the famed improv group Second City in Chicago, she was irked that the casts were always four men and two women. When someone suggested equalizing them (three men and three women), the producers and directors refused, insisting that there wouldn't be enough parts for the women. "This made no sense to me, probably because I speak English and have never had a head injury," said Fey. "We weren't doing *Death of a Salesman*. We were making up the show ourselves. How could there not be enough parts?"

Limiting the parts that women play in life is just as ridiculous as limiting them in improv—and it can be far more devastating. The copy of Fey's book *Bossypants* that I bought was the same size and shape and color of one of my favorite novels in college—*The Awakening* by Kate Chopin. So every time I started reading Fey, I thought about Chopin's heroine Edna Pontellier, a woman in New Orleans in the 1800s who comes to realize how limited her options are in life. As Edna begins to have a sense of herself as a human being seeking new possibilities, Chopin laments, "How few of us ever emerge from such beginning! How many souls perish in its tumult!" Like so many fictional heroines with an independent spirit seeking a role outside of wife and mother, Edna comes to a tragic end. Seeing no satisfying options in her closed society, she ultimately swims into the ocean, where "the voice of the sea speaks to the soul . . . enfolding the body in its soft, close embrace." I read that book over and over in college, unbearably moved by Edna's plight. It's overwhelmingly sad to imagine how many brave and original women we have lost over the years to the sea, to sexist producers, or to a restrictive society. When we limit our view of what men and women can do, everyone suffers.

Geniuses are always outliers, different from the average. Once you stop trying to slot people into a gender category, you can recognize their full talents in all their glory. Katherine Phillips, a professor at Columbia Business School who studies diversity, urges organizations to "fade gender into the background a bit." She found that after giving people an article to read with evidence that "at our core we are all the same," the women became more confident and the men more likely to give them opportunities. If you emphasize gender, the opposite happens—people focus on what they expect innate differences to be (even though they're usually wrong), which just reinforces stereotypes. And those don't help anyone to break away and be a star.

I don't underestimate how difficult it is to be brave and original and follow your own path. The mathematician Karen Uhlenbeck broke new ground in 2019 when she became the first woman to win the Abel Prize, considered one of the highest honors in international mathematics. The award has been presented (in a ceremony with the King of Norway) only since 2003, so we seem to be making progress— this time, it took only sixteen years for a woman to be noticed. In the many speeches and talks she gave after the award, Uhlenbeck called herself part of the first generation of women who could become mathematicians and obtain academic positions and so make the kinds of discoveries she did.[1] I have no doubt that she meant that to be inspiring and show how far we've come—but I also found it unbearably sad.

---

1 She pioneered a field called geometric analysis, and her work focused on the minimal surfaces of soap bubbles. I can't fully explain anything beyond that—but I invite you to read about it online.

Pause to think how tragic it is that one of the most admired mathematicians in the world right now was part of the *first generation of women*
who could have a normal career in math. Women's brains and abilities
did not magically change a generation ago. Previously, a woman with
Uhlenbeck's genius simply had no way to develop her talent and nobody to nurture her gifts. She had no place to direct her drive or even
to do her work in any formal setting. If ever you need proof that we
have no idea what a "natural woman" can do, that should be it.

Dr. Uhlenbeck spent most of her career as a professor at the University of Texas at Austin, then retired in her mid-seventies and
moved to the Institute for Advanced Study at Princeton to continue
solving interesting problems. In an impromptu celebration her colleagues threw after she won the Abel Prize, several people gave
speeches and toasts honoring the power of her work. When it was her
turn to speak, she wryly noted that, yes, from her current advanced
perspective, she could see that she had been impressive. Since there
weren't any women in the field for her to look up to when she started
out, she claimed her role model was chef Julia Child. "She knew how
to pick the turkey up off the floor and serve it," Dr. Uhlenbeck said.

You have to love that lesson. Genius is never a straight path, and
women are far less likely than men to get a second chance when something goes wrong. And something *always* goes wrong. In learning how
to cope with setbacks, Julia Child really is a good role model. When she
started out, everyone thought French cooking was too complicated for
Americans—and certainly above the capabilities of the nice women
who were cooking meals every night in the pre–Betty Friedan 1960s.
But Julia Child blundered on her TV shows and moved forward and
laughed about mistakes because for her cooking was joy and excitement and a commitment to the art. It doesn't matter if you drop the
turkey on the floor, as long as you pick it up and keep going. Nobody
gets it right every time—but if you don't let anyone discourage you,

then eventually you might create something deliciously wonderful. To me, that's a pretty good definition of the genius of a woman.

Despite the image of the solitary genius, it's hard to be a genius on your own. Somebody has to buy the groceries, make the bed, and take care of the kids (if there are any) so you can be free to let your talents roam.

The fabulous painter Sally Michel was born in 1902 and knew she wanted to be an artist from the age of six. Her paintings and watercolors are wonderful—original, sensuous, and brilliant, filled with simple forms that bring painting back to its most elemental meaning. Their warmth and ease pull you in immediately, and their style has had a significant impact on modern art. Some of the savviest art collectors I know are now snapping up her pictures, which have only recently become available. But at a recent exhibit of her paintings at a gallery in Boston, I noticed that almost all of her work was done when she was over sixty years old. Often *much* over—she lived to 100. So why did she do so little painting for the forty years that might otherwise have been her prime?

Michel married fellow artist Milton Avery when she was in her early twenties, and her style probably influenced his (and vice versa). They loved painting together, but as she described it later, "someone had to make some money." He was the genius, she thought, and she wanted to be sure that he "could devote himself completely to painting" without having any financial pressures. She abandoned her own ambitions and took up commercial art, doing fashion drawings for ad agencies and illustrating a column for *The New York Times Magazine* while also raising their daughter.

"I really thought that Milton's work was so much more important than mine," she explained.

Was his work more important? In truth, I like hers better. But Milton Avery is now a huge name in the art world, and you'd probably never heard of Sally Michel before. (As with Nobel laureate Donna Strickland, she has been ignored by the gatekeepers at *Wikipedia*.) If you're thinking of collecting, her paintings sell for a tiny fraction of the millions his can get—and I dare you to tell some of the pieces apart. I so fell in love with her style that I bought one of her watercolors of a woman sitting in a chair and hung it next to my bed. I look at it every morning and night now. It is soothing and beautiful—and it also reminds me how hard women have to work to find the balance in their lives, to let their genius emerge. Milton Avery definitely painted more pieces than his wife, which makes sense since he had a forty-year head start. She admitted that painting was "my main interest all my life," but for decades, she painted only occasionally when she and Milton were on summer vacations. The rest of the time she was hustling for work to pay the bills. No matter how much talent you start with, you can't grow into a star if you don't have the opportunity to develop your gifts. Or as she admitted, "Painting has to grow out of painting and not out of talk about painting."

Social messages are powerful, and Sally Michel's choice to support her husband is easy to understand. Remember the survey that said 90 percent of us think that geniuses tend to be male? It is difficult to stand up to patriarchal expectations under any conditions, and hard to imagine what it would take for a woman in a creative partnership in the early part of the twentieth century to demand her own celebrity. And yet think how powerfully different art, science, and so much of the world could be if we cultivated the genius of women. In his play about a powerful couple where the husband has been president of the United States and his wife is running for the same office, the playwright Lucas Hnath has his heroine musing one night about their respective roles. "One hundred, two hundred, three hundred years from now your name will be the name people know as they know the stars above," she says to her husband. "But what if it was the other way around? What if instead of me supporting you it was you supporting me? Did we ever consider that possibility?"

In a taped interview Sally Michel did for the Smithsonian archives shortly after her husband died, she was introduced as "Sally Michel or Mrs. Milton Avery." She laughed and interrupted to say that "they're both one in the same." But they're not. One subsumed the other for years. Mrs. Milton Avery put her own genius on hold to do commercial art and nurture her husband's talent. It probably never occurred to her that the roles could be flipped. Genius needs to be nurtured and genius needs to be recognized, and only after Milton Avery died in 1965 did Sally Michel emerge, a brilliant woman artist, able to put her own genius on display.

Tina Fey once joked that "talent is not sexually transmittable." But it's more than a joke because too many women still take their identity from the man they marry, date, or otherwise hook up with. You become great by developing your own unique abilities, not by hoping that someone else's talents will reflect on you. Your partner has to support and celebrate your genius—or it will be tough for it to flourish. But you can't always blame the guy when a woman's genius gets pushed aside. Social pressures are hard for anyone to ignore, and even the most talented women can get trapped by the myth of man as genius. They put themselves second (or third or fourth) in the family dynamic, and while they help their partner's genius flourish, their own begins to wilt.

After I framed and hung up my Sally Michel watercolor, I kept thinking about the idea of "Mrs. Milton Avery"—and how the very formulation shows how easily we wipe out a woman's existence. Where is Sally Michel in that name? She's not there at all. Something as simple as how we address people has a huge effect on how we see ourselves—and one another. If you invite "Mr. and Mrs. Milton Avery" to a wedding, you are asking the great artist to come—with wife as accessory. She is about as important as the tuxedo and shiny shoes he will wear. The egregious sexism of this seems so obvious to me that I would think it long gone. But then my husband and I got a wedding invitation in a fancy ecru envelope, addressed to "Dr. and Mrs. . . . ," with only his name.

"I'm actually a person, too," I said tossing down the invitation.

"It's just tradition," my husband said, trying to calm me down.

I get it. But tradition is not an excuse for making a woman disappear. If you can't say her name, how can you recognize her talent or genius or individuality? I find it appalling, outrageous, and heinous (do I make myself clear?) that anyone would still use this format. I love my husband. I am happy to attend weddings or other events with him. But a woman is not an appendage, thank you. If we want to recognize the genius of women, first we have to recognize that women actually exist.

Traditions that undermine women need to be abandoned. Girls at a charter school in North Carolina had to wear skirts until a federal judge ruled in 2019 that the policy was unconstitutional. The school had insisted that the ban on girls in pants was to uphold "traditional values," but the court essentially ruled that those traditional values hurt girls. When you're worried about keeping your skirt in place, you're distracted from studying and you "avoid certain activities altogether, such as climbing or playing sports during recess." The "traditional value" a dress code enforces isn't respect—it's keeping girls from competing with boys on any equal footing. I would call this court ruling encouraging, but there have been similar fights about pants versus skirts in schools back to the 1960s, and the concept that physical freedom is part of equality goes back even further. The earliest suffragists tossed away corsets and hoop skirts for less restrictive attire. You have to be able to move freely to think freely. I wear dresses a lot, but I would be furious if anyone tried to monitor my closet. The bigger point is that controlling what women wear or do with their bodies is demeaning, and whatever other excuses are given, it is ultimately an effort to constrain and undercut their talent, potential, and power.

The roboticist Cynthia Breazeal at the MIT Media Lab had told me that "we are in an age of a thousand nudges." What you are called, what you wear, what your teachers tell you, all nudge you in a particular direction. Breazeal's parents were both computer scientists and nudged her in the direction of science—but so many young women are nudged away from recognizing their genius and fulfilling their potential. What keeps women out of robotics or computer science or any other field now isn't blatant sexism so much as a subtle lack of encouragement. "It's harder to address because it's not overt and it's not necessarily intentional," Breazeal said. "A boy may be told that he's really good at math and should keep doing it, while a girl doesn't hear that as often so she drifts away to a different path."

The unconscious bias that permeates our language, our clothing, and our view of one another has ramifications far beyond making it harder for genius women to get noticed. It even makes it difficult for us to understand how babies get made. You thought you got that wrapped up in seventh grade, right? But amazingly, even the basic sperm-and-egg story is influenced by our sexist views of men and women. When anthropologist Emily Martin looked at years of research on reproduction, she found that early academic papers described the energetic sperm powerfully swimming toward the passively waiting egg. With thousands of sperm competing in the race to arrive first, the strongest and most robust would burst ahead, penetrate the barrier, and achieve victory. I admit that's what I always understood—and what most biology classes and sex-ed lectures teach. You could practically see the sperm as armored warrior, galloping in with lance drawn, while the waiting egg fluttered her fan and batted her eyelashes.

But the description turns out to be wildly inaccurate. The anthropomorphized assumption that the female (egg) would be passive and the male (sperm) aggressive probably kept scientists from recognizing the real interaction for longer than necessary. Most sperm are rather lackadaisical swimmers, and when they get to the egg, they don't so much penetrate as just hang on. The thick outer coating of the egg, the zona pellucida, determines which one will be let through. With this new information, the researchers and science writers simply turned to a different stereotype in the papers they wrote. Martin found that the more active egg was now perceived as a dangerous and aggressive femme fatale. The wily and devious egg lured and trapped the sperm, like some gold-digging divorcée cruising the streets of Palm Beach.

The truth is that sperm and egg are working together, cellular partners in the process of fertilization. They interact on mutual terms, with the male and female cells dancing equally together for the advantage of both. That the process rarely gets explained that way may be the ultimate example of unconscious bias. We are so driven by gender expectations that we attribute passive and aggressive traits to *cells*. Martin pointed out that attributing gender personality on a cellular level (where it doesn't exist at all) suggests that the traits are unalterable. Is it any wonder that when that collection of cells eventually becomes a living, breathing woman, male scientists see her as different from themselves? They've been making up characteristics about her since she was smaller than the head of a pin. If you can't even imagine an egg and sperm working compatibly, you're going to have a tough time seeing someone of a different gender as a colleague and friend.

Falling into the gender-stereotypes trap is dangerous and damaging, even when it's done to give a positive spin. On good days, I like to believe that we have moved beyond the stereotypes Emily Martin uncovered of female as either (a) meekly passive or (b) dangerously aggressive. But on bad days, I realize that, as with the descriptions of eggs and sperm, we have simply updated the stereotypes once again. Now we hear that women are collegial and collaborative, naturally nurturing, and interested in getting to solutions rather than in grabbing the spotlight. These traits get mentioned in explaining why we need more women in politics, academia, and corporations. While women seeking political office used to try to ignore gender altogether, now many run on platforms of *female is better.* Writing in *The New York Times,* editorial writer Michelle Cottle described one congresswoman in 2018 who sanctimoniously described herself and other women as facilitators and problem solvers whose maternal instincts would help them work for the common good.

Cottle's reply: "How uplifting. How stirring. How absurd."

Yes, how absurd. Many of the women elected to Congress in 2018 proved themselves combative, outspoken, and not willing to fall into line with the party standard-bearers. In other words, they didn't fit the stereotype of collegial female at all. The idea that women politicians are "less ragingly ambitious, more conciliatory or less partisan is insulting and contrary to the facts," Cottle said. We do need more women in politics, academia, and corporations, but the goal is diversity of experience, not some manufactured myth of how the Perfect Woman will save us all. Similarly, you don't become a genius in science or engineering or art or any other field by trying to fit into some newfangled stereotype that slots you as a collegial/nurturing/maternal wonder. Maybe you have developed those traits and maybe not. Once you decree what women *are,* you also decree what they *aren't.* And I dare you to tell any one of the genius women I met what she can't be.

Not every trailblazer or first woman in a field is a genius, but breaking glass ceilings requires genius-grade strength, tenacity, and intelligence. Geniuses change how we see the world and give us a new perception of what's possible. Hillary Clinton lost the electoral college in 2016, but by winning the popular vote, she inspired the many women candidates who stepped forward (and got elected) in 2018. By the time six women stepped onstage for the first 2020 Democratic presidential debate, you could feel that something had changed. As Elizabeth Warren and Kamala Harris emerged from the pack, neither seemed to worry about being stereotyped as the Woman Candidate. With their confidence, fresh voices, and distinctive ideas, they may define the new genius of women in politics. Harris likes to say that every time she seeks a position, she is told that nobody who looks like her has done that before. And so what? She has the political genius—the intelligence, talent, and celebrity—to change the rules.

Warren and Harris remind me of the many genius women I interviewed who do their work with great passion, so focused on what they want to achieve that they ignore the obstacles in their way. When asked if Americans have different criteria for male and female presidential candidates, Kamala Harris admitted early in her campaign that she didn't pay much attention. "How men are being treated compared to me . . . I don't let it distract me," she said. Warren also didn't let herself be distracted by the fact of being a woman candidate. Instead, she was busy issuing proposals on topics from health care to gun laws, attracting tens of thousands of people to her rallies, and winning over television audiences. Her approach definitely wins the vote as a mark of genius. Whether it can win her the next election is a different question. Women geniuses throughout history have battled male power issues and structural deterrents that have kept them from flourishing to their fullest potential. Whether we think of Fanny Mendelssohn Hensel, the women painters of the Renaissance, Lise Meitner, or Hillary Clinton, admiration for what they accomplished is mixed with the wistfulness of what might have been. I am in awe of the women geniuses in the arts, sciences, and politics who are making enormous breakthroughs right now— and I am also stunned by the continued misogyny that dogs them.

At a party I attended recently in Florida, an overly tanned man looked up smugly when I mentioned that I was researching women geniuses. "Have you found one yet?" he asked. Had I been looking for male geniuses, I expect he would not have been among them. But just by being male, he got to feel superior. Perhaps I should have repeated the comment that Simone de Beauvoir made, that "no one is more arrogant toward women, more aggressive or scornful, than the man who is anxious about his virility."

At the end of the party, I returned to the smug man and asked him if he knew how many countries had been led by a woman in the last few decades. He looked surprised, but then ticked a few off on his fingers. Germany had elected Angela Merkel, and the UK had Theresa May. ("And before that Margaret Thatcher," I offered.) And wasn't there that famous woman in Liberia? "So that's three countries," he said dismissively.

"Don't forget the terrific leaders in Australia and New Zealand," I said.

"Then five. I'll even double it and say ten," he said.

"Final answer?" I asked.

"Yup."

"You're way off," I said, trying not to sound similarly smug. "There have been sixty."

"That can't be!" he said.

"Oh, but it is," I said, enjoying myself now.

Yes, it is. I can't really blame the self-congratulating man for not knowing—I've asked the same question of many people, and nobody has guessed more than ten. Or known that in the six countries in the world with the largest populations, half have had women leaders. (Yes, the United States is among the have-nots.) The nice thing about political leaders is that we can actually tally the votes and watch them emerge. But the conversation only made me even more troubled, thinking about the women who have been stars and innovators in other spheres but didn't get counted because it was the men doing the counting. Perhaps we can all start counting differently now.

When I was invited to be a keynote speaker at a women's summit at the University of Southern California recently, I politely replied that it sounded great but I was too busy to come. The college junior inviting me responded immediately—and it was clear that she wasn't letting a small barrier like a rejection get in her way. She tried a different angle and a new approach, and her energy and passion made me smile. After a few more exchanges, my no turned to a yes. How could I not give her my support? Refusing to be deterred has been a constant for women geniuses through the centuries, so she was on the right path.

I flew out for the daylong event, which was dedicated to inspiring young women about all the possibilities in their lives. In person, the student organizers were as impressive and galvanizing as they'd been long distance. With their focused efforts, more than a thousand women (and some scattered men) filled the auditorium. Usually, I am wary of single-sex events, but on this otherwise well-integrated campus, there was a visceral power to the idea of women inspiring women. I thought of the time Ruth Bader Ginsburg was asked how many women she thought would be the right number on the Supreme Court and she responded—nine. People never thought it strange when there were nine men, so why would nine women be any different?

In the green room before my talk, I met two young entrepreneurs who were going to be on a panel about women starting their own companies. One had launched a successful online cosmetics company and the other had developed ice-cream stores around the country. Both were under thirty and could have passed as teenagers. Chatting with them, I had a tingle of hope about the genius of women being expressed in new ways in the next generation. The ice-cream CEO, Maryellis Bunn, was wearing a crepe white jumpsuit with red backless mules, and her long dark hair fell to her shoulders. Tiny and slim, she looked like a pop star—but the moment she started talking, I realized she was whip smart and had thought out every step of her business. Karissa Bodnar, the jeans-clad cosmetics exec, had such wisdom about her products that I wanted to start ordering them immediately.

When I told them about my interest in the genius of women, they nodded eagerly. In developing their companies, they had gone in original directions, focused on disrupting existing models and building new communities. Being female had been an obstacle—but they had figured out how to navigate around the negative messages. Bunn struggled to get a lease for her first store since the male rental agents didn't take her seriously. Now that she'd had some success, the power had turned and "they're all calling me and begging me to take properties," she said with some satisfaction. Bodnar had originally created the products herself in her kitchen, relying on her own knowledge of chemistry to formulate the lipsticks and mascara exactly the way she wanted. She launched without any venture capital money because none was offered.

"Do you think getting the lease and the investment money was a problem because you're a woman, you're young, or people didn't understand your business?" I asked.

"All three," they said in unison.

Neither had been too worried about the doubters. They believed in themselves, and the venture capitalists were the ones who would lose out, since many studies now show that women-led companies offer a better return on investment. They hadn't planned it to happen, but the staffs at their rapidly growing companies were almost all women.

"It's not that I'm looking to hire only women—it's just that the women are better," said Bunn. She paused, and when Bodnar nodded, she continued, "But we're looking for a man. Diversity is important."

I laughed. Carol Anderson had told me that we already have affirmative action for men in colleges, and it was interesting to reach a point where it was necessary (for at least a few companies) in the workplace. But it was also revelatory. Women aren't "just better," and neither are men. But Bunn's feeling that women are smarter, harder working, and more insightful was the flip side of the problem that has held women back for centuries. People in power naturally gravitate to others like themselves. For all the years and decades and centuries that men held the power, they hired their mirror images. They didn't necessarily think they were discriminating. They just looked at the people who went to school with them and played squash with them and dressed like them and figured they were "the best." There was no reason to take a chance on someone who wasn't just like them.

You want structural change? You're not going to convince some men that the women are just as good. They don't want to hear it or know it—and they have no particular reason to give up their power. One large and prestigious New York law firm proudly posted online the new partners it anointed at the end of 2018—and the pictures included eleven white men and one white woman. When people reacted loudly on social media, the chairman explained that they already had more women partners than other big firms. It sounded an awful lot like the we-already-invited-one syndrome. *The New York Times* called it "a stark illustration of what can happen when promotion decisions are . . . concentrated in the hands of white-male rainmakers." It doesn't matter how smart you are if the men in power want protégés who look just like them.

When women like Bodnar and Bunn start hiring, you don't have to convince them of the value of women. They naturally shake up the world because the people who make them comfortable and whom they are prepared to trust are women just like themselves. They can look at a woman who is beautiful and young and wearing pretty clothes and know that she can also be ambitious and smart and a business genius. They offer new mirrors. They understand that talking about "women" means talking about a broad range of people, older and younger and stylish and not, with different abilities and talents. Somewhere in that very large and varied group is the whiz with numbers who should run the business side and the genius at marketing who can get a company known around the world. Is there a guy who could do the job just as well? Well, maybe. But really— you don't want to take the chance.

In researching genius through the generations, I realized that certain times and places have been hubs of genius—Italy during the Renaissance, Silicon Valley in the 1970s, ancient Athens. For women geniuses, periods of upheaval may allow their talent to flourish and give them the courage to be heard. Remember Madame de Staël, who created her salons and stood up to Napoléon in the late eighteenth century in France? She had genius and fearlessness—but surely the energizing spark of the French Revolution gave her the sense that the world was open to change. The same was true for the women painters of the Renaissance who were part of that period's breathless creativity. Dr. Frances Arnold, who won the Nobel Prize in chemistry, grew up in suburban Pittsburgh, but she went to Washington, DC, as a teenager to be part of the antiwar protests of the seventies, and that renegade spirit never left her.

Women's genius has flourished in every time and place, but in moments of anxiety or retrenching, men's angst about losing out makes them look for someone to blame—and powerful women become a target. It's not a coincidence that right-wing commentators today are increasingly hostile to women, or that alt-right websites spew vitriolic theories about strong and successful women. I read an article by a politician who opposed co-ed sports for kids because the girls on his son's soccer team were bigger and stronger. Right you are, sir. He worried that the goal-scoring girls gained more confidence than the boys—but what could possibly be wrong with that? Encouraging female strength is exactly how we will make a better society. Because as Dr. Arnold said—without diversity, we go extinct.

Once you become aware of the deep biases and social expectations that permeate our lives, you become even more awed by the women whose genius has emerged. The Cambridge professor who defined genius for me as the spot where extraordinary ability meets celebrity was surely right. Since women with great talent were too often denied the visibility and attention they deserve, the extraordinary, varied, and powerful genius of women has been dramatically overlooked. But if my pollster friend Michael Berland does another survey on genius, maybe, just maybe, the 90 percent who previously said that geniuses are predominately male will start to change. If Mike comes your way, you'll tell him that geniuses include both men *and* women, and when asked to name a female genius, you'll mention Marie Curie first. But then you'll ask him to sit down—because you have a long list to share.

CHAPTER 18

The Game-Changing Power of Genius Women

While interviewing dozens of genius women for this book, I kept looking for what they had in common. Geniuses are by definition distinctive and individualistic—but some consistent traits did seem to hold true. Most had a supportive parent or encouraging mentor at some point in their lives, whether male or female. All had a tenaciousness and determination that let them pursue what they wanted, and most treated obstacles like Olympic track stars treat hurdles—as something to sail over on your way to a gold medal. They didn't accept labels or limits, and generally, their genius was field specific and not related to gender. I met women who were brilliant in astronomy, physics, painting, composing, microbiology, philosophy, neuroscience, theater . . . If those subjects seem unrelated, that's the point. Women's talents go in many directions. The women scientists had a lot more in common with the male scientists than they did with the women artists or composers.

On a personal level, most of the genius women I met were married and had children, and they raved about having a spouse or partner who shared equally—or sometimes even more—at home. They were happy to be devoted to their kids without giving up their own ambitions on the way. They didn't mind being a little different, resisting stereotypes, and setting their own rules. I don't think any of them would dress their children in princess costumes. Most had been fairly gender-blind as their careers took off—they were comfortable with both male and female colleagues. They seemed to have blinders to gender bias or else they just ignored it and found alternate paths. When they were finally in the position to fight entrenched sexism and support other women, they did exactly that. A few had been prodigies when young, and all of them—prodigies or not—understood that talent requires hard work and determination and resilience.

What is the magic that allowed them to face a resistant world with good humor, positivity, and power? Most weren't afraid of failure and they were all unusually good at bouncing back from adversity. They knew that trying and trying again was part of the genius game and that nobody gets it right the first time—or every time. Embracing that is a first step to success. Think of actress Halle Berry, who won an Academy Award as best actress one year and a Golden Raspberry Award as worst actress a few years later. She had the courage and good humor to show up and collect the Razzie in person. "I have so many people to thank because you don't win a Razzie without a lot of help from a lot of people!" she joked. She held her Oscar up high and said that she didn't have to give it back.[1]

Genius by its very definition is a talent that makes you different, special, and original, and what nurtures genius women may change over time. But here are the elements I discovered that help genius women flourish in any time or place.

---

1 The Academy Award was for *Monster's Ball* and the Razzie for *Catwoman*.

1. One supportive person

Genius needs to be nurtured and doesn't appear fully formed. Historically, women's potential withered because nobody was willing to recognize or encourage it, but social change brings powerful results. Roboticist Cynthia Breazeal's parents brought her to science museums when she was young and encouraged her to play with computers. Anne Wojcicki grew up with a supportive community of academics telling her she could succeed, and they gave her the confidence to go in her own direction and start the breakthrough company 23andMe. Mathematician Helen Wilson had one professor making an objective assessment that she had talent, and she went on to prove him right. In earlier centuries, women artists like Sofonisba Anguissola and Artemisia Gentileschi relied on a husband or parent to give them an opportunity to shine. For genius women, the whole world doesn't need to be on their side—and it almost never is. But one mentor, teacher, or parent offering encouragement is vital.

2. Blinders to bias

Women who see bias everywhere may be right—but they also hinder themselves. Genius women triumph when their focus and excitement about their own work allow them to ignore the doubters in their way. Working in the 1930s, Lise Meitner persisted despite being barred from science labs that didn't allow women. More recently, astrophysicist Jo Dunkley never noticed how few women were in her physics classes at Oxford, and when Meg Urry was racking up "first woman" positions at NASA and then Yale, she believed that all paths were open and she could do anything. Once Dunkley and Urry reached the top of their professions, they could look back and see the barriers they had faced—and now they are ardent about removing them for other women who follow. But sometimes you need to ignore the structural problems until you are in a position to do something about them.

3. Seeing beyond gender

Genius women refuse to limit and categorize themselves, and they reject the gender conventions that diminish and restrict what a woman should do. When Fei-Fei Li was growing up, her parents never expected her to conform to restrictive female stereotypes and they encouraged independent thinking. Her genius in artificial intelligence comes in part from her ability to think in broad, unbounded ways. Microbiologist and Princeton president Shirley Tilghman taught herself to close her eyes and think of a scientist—and picture a woman as often as she pictured a man. Genius women know that social messaging creates divisions far more intractable than any that could be explained by the overlapping mosaics that constitute men's and women's brains.

As a woman genius, you need to define yourself as an individual without the limitations of gender stereotypes and understand that your unique talent can stand alone. You need an ability to transcend the male-female dichotomy, not worry about being like others, and refuse to conform to expectations that narrow the world of possibility.

4. A positive approach

Whatever slights and rebuffs and bias they faced, almost all the genius women I spoke to had a way of reframing problems as opportunities. I have never heard fewer complaints than I did in speaking to them. Chemist Frances Arnold encourages women to face the world in a positive and powerful way rather than a negative and fearful one. Her own ability to see the good in any situation got her through tough personal times—and helped send her to Sweden to accept the Nobel Prize. African American studies expert Carol Anderson realized that women don't get second chances, and however unfair that may be, she stays upbeat and just makes sure that her work is beyond reproach. Genius women seem to have a joy about their work and an optimism that they can overcome negative social messaging about women's abilities with their own powerful and meaningful contributions.

5. A core belief that you belong

If you want other people to see and celebrate your genius, you can't be intimidated by those who want to undermine your talents or send you to the sidelines. You have to believe that you have a right to be in the game. Broadway phenom Tina Landau says that she isn't a woman director but rather a woman who directs—to make it clear that being a woman is just one part of who she is. Monica Mandelli left her small town in Italy with complete fearlessness to pursue a bigger life. She had a passion to succeed and an attitude that it was okay to be different. Madame de Staël had no rights as a woman back at the time of the French Revolution, but she had complete confidence in her positions on equality and freedom—and she found a way to be heard. It's always easy to find a reason to be stopped. Genius women refuse to accept the message that they are outsiders—whatever pop culture messages they receive—and they feel powerfully that they can play in the mainstream.

6. A multifaceted life

Genius women understand that, as Barnard president Sian Beilock discovered, sometimes you're making a world-changing breakthrough in research and sometimes you're a mom who forgets to pack lunch. Engineers Andrea Goldsmith and Daphne Koller brought game-changing innovations to their fields—and also flourished as role models and moms for their own children. Genius women have many complexities and levels of selves, and they won't be limited by undermining expectations of what women can do. Like actress Geena Davis, they discover the power of finding their own voice and do not try to define or limit themselves. They know the real joy of being a woman genius is that you contain multitudes.

Most of the genius women I met had a resolve and strength of character that I admired—and yet it would be excessively optimistic (even for me) to think that individual fortitude solves all problems. You can be confident and believe in yourself and focus so intently on your work that you don't see the barriers and biases—and still be tripped up by structural unfairness, social messages, and implicit bias. But genius women now and in the past help change the story. They become role models for a different way of approaching the world. Their refusal to conform to social expectations helps point out just how ridiculous some of those assumptions might be. Women aren't good in science? Please meet Nobel laureate Frances Arnold. Motherhood interferes with having a brilliant career? Practically every genius woman I met had children and family. Women don't make breakthrough inventions? You could ask social robot Jibo about that—and he will give a little bow to his creator, Cynthia Breazeal.

All the genius women I met compete—and star—in the same fields as men, and talking to them made me realize just how vital it is that boys and girls work together and trust each other from an early age. You can tell a girl, "You can be anything," but when you give her pink Legos and a chemistry set to make beauty products, the much louder message is that girls are in a separate category. The real goal should be to recognize that talent does not discriminate and how we see ourselves matters. Actress Mayim Bialik told me that you don't always know what you can be until you see it—and to every parent who buys her daughter a princess costume, I hope you will think about replacing it (or at least complementing it) with an astronaut outfit. Women reach great heights when doing so seems normal and expected.

Once we expect to see women's genius on display, the lack of it seems wrong and inexplicable. A critic for *The New York Times* recently reviewed the main galleries at the Museum of Modern Art and described the absence of women artists as "breathtaking." She suggested selling some of the works of Picasso to buy more important pieces by women. That we have come to the point where critics complain when women *aren't* on museum walls is . . . breathtakingly wonderful. The point isn't to be politically correct but to recognize the power of talent not defined by a male hierarchy. That power was clear when another museum in New York, the Guggenheim, did a solo show in 2019 of the artist Hilma af Klint, who had painted in the early 1900s and stipulated that her work not be seen until twenty years after her death. If her hope was that women artists would be treated differently by then, she was right. Her bold, radically abstract, and spiritual paintings were so astonishing that her show attracted the largest crowds in the history of the museum. I like to think that somewhere the great artists Clara Peeters, Judith Leyster, and Artemisia Gentileschi are feeling vindicated.

To the women geniuses like Ada Lovelace and Grace Hopper who helped launch the computer era, and to those who were early to make breakthroughs in science, including Lise Meitner, we are forever indebted. There remain so many who had the talent but not the celebrity. Henrietta Swan Leavitt, who worked at the Harvard College Observatory in the early 1900s, made discoveries about the brightness of stars that made it possible to more precisely measure the universe. She got no credit for her discovery at the time, but Edwin Hubble used her work to measure galactic distances and became so famous that the Hubble Space Telescope was named for him. If you've heard of any astronomer, it is probably Hubble. He owed a big debt to Leavitt. Maybe the next rocket to the moon will bear her name.

Women's discoveries have opened the world to us—and they continue to do so. As I approached the end of my research for this book and began discussing it in public, people I met began sending me articles about women who'd had brilliant breakthroughs or great triumphs that were appreciated only years later. Or they told me stories about an extraordinary woman they knew (or heard about) who was making waves as a musician or artist or scientist. Wouldn't I like to include her?

I would like to include all of them, and I hope that in a general way, I have done just that. We are starting to realize that women are half the world, and the real revelation in the individual stories is how powerful the combined talent and genius of women can be. So much talent from the past has been overlooked or not encouraged, and if we are recognizing it now, if we are excited by its potential, then I think the world will start to be very different in the years ahead.

Change occurs slowly, but it does occur. Our perceptions of what women can do are transforming, as is our understanding of all that has been lost from women of the past. One night as I was finishing this book, my husband got tickets to the Metropolitan Opera, and we sat in delight through a wonderful performance of Verdi's *Rigoletto.* I'm not a huge opera buff, but I loved every moment of the nineteenth-century masterpiece, and when the Duke sang his famous aria in the third act, I recognized the music immediately. (Trust me, you would, too.) The Met has screens with translations at the seats, so I was surprised when I saw what the charming and seductive song actually said. As my husband got into bed late that night, I mentioned the words.

"'Woman is fickle like a feather in the wind, she is always lying, always miserable,'" I said, repeating the lyrics I could remember. "That's what that glorious aria means?"

"What would you like it to say?" he asked.

"How about 'woman is powerful and strong, always brave, always bold, and the best are geniuses.'" I shrugged. Maybe it wasn't perfect, but the Met was always updating its productions—this one had been transposed from sixteenth-century Italy to 1960s Las Vegas. Couldn't they change a few words, too? If we wanted a different world that reflected hope and possibility and advancement, we had to lose the old stereotypes and take charge of a new narrative.

My husband had been getting updates on my research into women and genius for months now. He had heard my sympathy and outrage over Mozart's sister never having a chance, over Claire Foy not realizing how much she was worth, and over Lise Meitner and so many other brilliant women scientists never getting their much-deserved Nobel Prizes. He understood how much glorious potential has been lost and abandoned through the centuries and what all of us can gain by celebrating and encouraging the genius of women.

Now he rolled over. Opera evenings are long, and he was tired. Rather than discuss artistic depictions of women at close to midnight, he wanted to go to sleep. But he put his arm around me and pulled me close. As he closed his eyes, he murmured,

"What we really need is an opera written by Verdi's sister."

I slept well that night. I felt like we might be making progress.

Acknowledgments

What a profound pleasure to write this book with the support and encouragement of two genius women of publishing. I am extremely grateful to Alice Martell who is smart and tenacious and advocated for this subject from the first day; and also to Jill Schwartzman, an extraordinary and insightful editor who always makes my work better. I so appreciate the winning group at Dutton, including Christine Ball, John Parsley, Emily Canders, Rebecca Odell, Natalie Church, Marya Pasciuto, and Alice Dalrymple. A bow to Madeline McIntosh, Allison Dobson, and Ivan Held for leading a terrific team.

Given her talent and accomplishments, Susan Fine deserves to be one of the genius women in this book, but she is also my dear friend and advisor, and she has been my guiding star since fourth grade. Chris Darwall and Bob Kaplan were enormously generous with ideas, friendship, and support, and that we are related just makes it better. Robert Masello keeps me laughing and filled with writerly inspirations, and my longtime genius friend and mentor Henry Jarecki always offers insights and an original view. I learned a lot about leadership and strength from Anthea Disney, and I am grateful to have had her as a model early in my career and as a friend now. Thanks also to many friends, including Lisa Dell, Jean Hanff Korelitz, Karen Capelluto, Candy Gould, Lynn Schnurnberger, Wendy Hashmall, Beth Schermer, Leslie Berman, Nancy Kaplan, and Marsha Edell for their encouragement and good comments as I developed my ideas.

Many academics, scientists, artists, writers, and geniuses in the US and the UK shared their stories with me, and I am very grateful for their time and insights. To those I wrote about and those I didn't, your honesty, brilliance, and determination fill me with awe. Stanford genius Stephen Boyd was extremely thoughtful in introducing me to several extraordinary women, and I appreciate his kind help and magnanimous spirit. Many thanks to strategy consultant Michael Berland for encouraging me to write about genius and women. His poll findings, as I reported in the book, were key to my early interest in the subject, as was his enthusiasm and good perspective. Thanks also to librarian Christina Kasman at the Yale Club and assistant Debbie Nugent, who were always available to find references and to provide good cheer.

I am grateful to Jacob and Eli because after a day of writing, nothing is better than hearing their stories. Admiration and love to Zach, Annie, Matt, and Pauline for being inspirations of how to mix genius with joy. My husband, Ron Dennett, listened to me and helped me develop my ideas, and he offered wisdom and encouragement when I read draft after draft aloud to him. Readers of my other books know him as the handsome husband, but he is also the paradigm of a man strong enough to believe in equality. Author Tillie Olsen once said that a male writer can dedicate a book "to my wife, without whom . . ." but a woman writer never has that support. I had that support. So this is to my husband, Ron, without whom . . . nothing else really matters.

Notes

The Great Books curriculum began in the 1920s with a group of male academics, led by Columbia professor John Erskine, who believed in establishing a canon of books that would define an educated person. The works they selected by Homer, Chaucer, Thomas More, Shakespeare, Adam Smith, and others spanned literature, philosophy, and history—but there were no books by women in the top one hundred. In the century since then, many colleges have created classes around these lists, and Columbia University and the University of Chicago continue to have a required "core curriculum" for all students based on Great Books. Professors at both universities told me that battles to update the lists began in the 1980s and continue to right now. For Columbia undergraduates in 2019, the fall semester's literary requirement had thirteen books, with Sappho the only woman represented. The spring was a little better, with eleven titles that included three women—Jane Austen, Virginia Woolf, and Toni Morrison. One older professor explained to me that having women on the list is important, but it is outrageous to have replaced *King Lear*, *Gilgamesh*, and *Oedipus Rex*. He had been teaching the core curriculum for thirty years and said that the discussions about book choices during depart-ment meetings continue to range from loud to vicious.

Katherine Maher, the executive director of the nonprofit that runs *Wikipe-dia,* wrote an article for the *Los Angeles Times* on October 18, 2018, where she discussed the Donna Strickland matter and the underrepresentation of women on *Wikipedia* pages. In explaining why Strickland had been denied a *Wikipedia* page until she won the Nobel Prize, Maher admitted that "our contributors are majority Western and mostly male, and these gatekeepers apply their own judgment and prejudices. . . . We are working to correct biases in *Wikipedia*'s coverage."

Peter Schjeldahl's review of the Berthe Morisot show at the Barnes Foun-dation appeared in *The New Yorker* on October 29, 2018.

CHAPTER 1: Why You've Never Heard of Lise Meitner

The 2009 film *Agora* directed by Alejandro Amenábar starred Rachel Weisz as Hypatia.

The full story of the doomsday cult—and the people who refuse to change their beliefs—is in *When Prophecy Fails*, written by Leon Festinger, Henry Riecken, and Stanley Schachter. The 1956 book was reprinted in 2009 by Mar-tino Fine Books.

It seems appropriate that my earworm was from *Hamilton* since the show's creator and original star, Lin-Manuel Miranda, is the very definition of a mod-ern genius celebrity. In addition to Tony Awards and a Grammy and the Pulit-zer Prize, he got both the MacArthur Fellowship (often called the Genius Award) and a starring role in the movie *Mary Poppins Returns*.

Even though Lise Meitner was outrageously ignored by the Nobel Com-mittee on the basis of her gender, she wouldn't have been the first female win-ner in science. Marie Curie won the Nobel Prize in physics in 1903 for her discoveries in radiation—but that came with some help. Marie worked with her husband, Pierre, and the Nobel Committee initially planned to give the award to Pierre Curie and Henri Becquerel. When Pierre heard about it, he insisted that his wife's name be added. She won again in 1911 for chemistry. Meitner did not have a similar advocate at the time.

Meitnerium is the first element in the periodic table named exclusively for a real (as opposed to mythological) woman. There is also an element called Curium, but it was named for both Marie Curie and her husband, Pierre. I got a lot of information on the naming of the elements in the periodic table, as well as the comment about its being "the most iconic real estate in science" from a *Slate* column called "Blogging the Periodic Table" by science writer Sam Kean, posted July 12, 2010.

CHAPTER 2: The Outrageous Bias Against Mozart's Sister

An article in *The Atlantic* by Olga Khazan, "'Negative Physiological Impacts'? Why Saudi Women Aren't Allowed to Drive," on October 7, 2013, quoted Sheikh Saleh bin Saad al-Lohaidan of Saudi Arabia making the absurd connection between driving and fertility. He claimed "medical studies show that [driving] automatically affects the ovaries and pushes the pelvis upwards. . . . Those who regularly drive have children with clinical problems of varying degrees." The author suggested the sheikh might be confused about the definition of "medical study."

Among the many excellent books on Madame de Staël, I recommend *Madame de Staël: The First Modern Woman,* by Francine du Plessix Gray (Atlas and Company, 2008), and *Madame de Staël: The Dangerous Exile,* by Angelica Goodden (Oxford University Press, 2008). The Goodden quotes are from her book.

The Darrin McMahon quotes are from his excellent book *Divine Fury: A History of Genius,* published by Basic Books in 2013.

A traditional way of measuring retail success is dollars earned per square foot, and by that metric, the Apple stores are the most successful in the world. A 2017 report from eMarketer and CoStar has Apple as number one, earning about $5,500 per square foot—which is three times what the leading apparel retailer earns and way ahead of Tiffany & Co., which sells similarly pricey products and comes in at about $3,000. Obviously, many things other than the Genius Bar contribute to Apple's extraordinary retail success.

In reading about Francis Galton, I was particularly interested in a column by Subhadra Das, the curator of the Galton and Pathology Collections at University College London, posted on the UCL site in November 2015. She is the source of the quote that Galton was "bat guano crazy," and she also pointed out that "what is particularly hard to swallow is how influential he was."

Many studies support the contentions that IQ tests are unpredictive. The Terman experiment was just the start. In a 2012 study out of the UK that appeared in the journal *Neuron,* some 110,000 people took an online intelligence test, and the researchers found at least three different types of intelligence—reasoning, memory, and verbal skills. They concluded that no one test could measure them all. An example of that truth comes from Richard Feynman, one of the great geniuses of the twentieth century. Brilliant, original, and able to see things that nobody else ever did, he's usually hailed on par with Einstein. He solved the puzzle of what led to the *Challenger* disaster in 1986 and had a wildly open and creative mind. I recommend his charming and funny memoir, *"Surely You're Joking, Mr. Feynman!,"* which shows how a true genius thinks differently from the rest of us. He got the highest scores ever recorded on some famously difficult math tests. But he reported that his score on a school IQ test was a very modest 125.

CHAPTER 3: Einstein's Wife and the Theory of Relativity

Although I was on the Princeton University campus, Albert Einstein actually worked a few miles away at Princeton's Institute for Advanced Study.

Philosopher and novelist Rebecca Newberger Goldstein has touched beautifully on the subject of genius in many of her books. The quote here is from her article in 2016 for the online site Edge.org. Answering the question "What do you consider the most interesting recent scientific news?" she wrote about male-female perceptions of genius. Her piece "The En-Gendering of Genius" cites the work of Sarah-Jane Leslie and Andrei Cimpian and also points out that "for most of its history our species has systematically squandered its human capital by spurning the creative potential of half its members."

I recommend Jo Dunkley's book, *Our Universe: An Astronomer's Guide,* published in 2019 by Belknap Press. In addition to being an excellent introduction to cosmology, the book includes stories of many women scientists who have often been overlooked. "Astronomy has a particular history of women having great victories that made a big impact," she told me. "But their discoveries were never widely known outside the field."

Shirley Tilghman was president of Princeton University from 2001 to 2013. She told me that she got the position after she had been voted by the faculty in sciences as the representative to the search committee and traveled with trustees on the committee for several months interviewing candidates. They got to know her—and realized that they didn't have to look further. "Honestly, I think there was zero chance I would have been chosen if they didn't have those months to get comfortable with me as a human being," she said.

Chimamanda Ngozi Adichie's quotes are from her 2012 TEDx Talk, "We Should All Be Feminists." It was turned into a book of the same name, published by Anchor Books in 2014.

Amos Tversky's study on similarities and differences was done at the Hebrew University of Jerusalem. Tversky famously partnered with Daniel Kahneman for important work in behavioral economics that won the Nobel Prize in 2002. Sadly, Tversky died 1996 when he was just fifty-nine so didn't get to share the prize. An excellent overview of their work and ideas is Kahneman's *Thinking, Fast and Slow,* published by Farrar, Straus and Giroux in 2011.

CHAPTER 4: How a Teenage Nun Painted *The Last Supper*

A good oral history of the Guerrilla Girls appeared in *The New York Times* in August 2015: "The Guerrilla Girls, After 3 Decades, Still Rattling Art World Cages." The comment from the artist who calls herself Frida Kahlo is from this article.

Men's power over art history has been so pervasive that museums and galleries are only now beginning to reconsider the sexist images that get hailed as great. In her Netflix special *Nanette*, comic Hannah Gadsby notes the many female nudes in most museums. "If you go into a gallery with old paintings, there's a lot of evidence to suggest women have existed for a very long time. Longer than clothes," she says.

I recommend Linda Gordon's book *Dorothea Lange: A Life Beyond Limits,* published by W. W. Norton and Co. in 2009.

The information about the director of the Uffizi Gallery comes from an article in *USA Today,* on December 26, 2017, called "In Florence They're Bringing the Works of Women Artists Out of the Basement." The director, Eike Schmidt, plans to leave the Uffizi in 2020 to head up a museum in Vienna. Maybe he will bring more women out of the basement there, too.

The Ruth Asawa exhibit was at the David Zwirner gallery in New York City in 2017. The October 9, 2017, review in *The New Yorker* was by Andrea K. Scott and titled "Ruth Asawa Reshapes Art History."

The study by Claudia Goldin and Cecilia Rouse was called "Orchestrating Impartiality: The Impact of 'Blind' Auditions on Female Musicians" and appeared in the *American Economic Review* of September 2000 (pages 715–741), published by the American Economic Association.

The quotes from music critic Alex Ross are from his article in *The New Yorker,* "The Oceanic Music of Kaija Saariaho," which appeared in the October 31, 2016, issue.

CHAPTER 5: Why Italian Women Are Better than You at Math

Irene Adler appears in the story "A Scandal in Bohemia," the first story in *The Adventures of Sherlock Holmes,* which came out in 1892 and has been admired ever since. Irene Adler has been portrayed on-screen by actresses from Charlotte Rampling to Rachel McAdams.

The most comprehensive study showing what happens to pay scales when women enter a field was done by Paula England, Silver Professor of Arts and Science and professor of sociology at New York University. She looked at census data from 1950 to 2000 and found that when a field starts to attract a large number of women, its wages drop. She controlled for factors like work experience, education, and location—it didn't matter. The one constant variable in how a job paid was how many women were in it.

CHAPTER 6: Rosalind Franklin and the Truth About the Female Brain

The quote about Rosalind Franklin's X-rays is from John Desmond Bernal, who pioneered the use of X-rays in microbiology.

Daphna Joel has published many scientific papers on her research, including "Analysis of Human Brain Structure Reveals that the Brain 'Types' Typical of Males Are Also Typical of Females, and Vice Versa," in *Frontiers of Human Neuroscience,* October 18, 2018, written with six colleagues from Israel and Germany; and "Sex Beyond the Genitalia: The Human Brain Mosaic," published December 15, 2015, in *PNAS* (*Proceedings of the National Academy of Sciences of the United States of America*). That paper analyzed the MRIs of more than fourteen hundred brains and found "extensive overlap between the distributions of females and males for all gray matter, white matter, and connections assessed."

Joel and Cordelia Fine wrote an op-ed in *The New York Times,* "Can We Finally Stop Talking About 'Male' and 'Female' Brains?" on December 3, 2018.

CHAPTER 7: Why Fei-Fei Li Should Be on the Cover of *Vanity Fair*

Fei-Fei Li ran Google Cloud's AI division for a year, from 2017 to 2018. By the time we met, she was back at Stanford and had no ties to Google. She is now codirector of the Stanford Institute for Human-Centered Artificial Intelligence (hai.stanford.edu).

The Mary Wollstonecraft quotes are from *A Vindication of the Rights of Woman,* first published in 1792. There are many editions available.

The quote from Carolyn Gold Heilbrun is from her 1973 book *Toward a Recognition of Androgyny* (Alfred A. Knopf). I also recommend her excellent *Writing a Woman's Life* (W. W. Norton, 1988)—and the mystery novels she wrote under the pseudonym Amanda Cross, which are both entertaining and revelatory about the life of a woman academic.

CHAPTER 8: The Astrophysicist Who Does Not Need Tom Cruise

For an interesting perspective on Fanny Mendelssohn and other women who sought to be heard rather than silenced, I recommend *Jewish Women and Their Salons,* published by the Jewish Museum, New York, and Yale University Press in 2005.

I learned about Elizebeth Friedman's adventures as a cryptanalyst from Jason Fagone's terrific book *The Woman Who Smashed Codes,* published by HarperCollins in 2017. My explanation of Enigma machines is adapted from his descriptions.

The Women in Astronomy conference that Meg Urry organized produced the Baltimore Charter for Women in Astronomy in 1992.

Lera Boroditsky described her fascinating work in a talk at TEDWomen 2017 called "How Language Shapes the Way We Think." You can view it at the TED website.

CHAPTER 9: Broadway's Tina Landau Contains Multitudes

The research about moms' inaccurate assessments of what their eleven-month-old girls can do is from "Gender Bias in Mothers' Expectations about Infant Crawling," by Emily R. Mondschein, Karen E. Adolph, and Catherine S. Tamis-LeMonda, *Journal of Experimental Child Psychology,* December 2000.

CHAPTER 10: RBG and the Genius of Being a Cuddly Goat

I learned about the goats named Ruth, Bader, and Ginsburg from Jill Lepore's article in *The New Yorker,* "Ruth Bader Ginsburg's Unlikely Path to the Supreme Court," October 21, 2008. Lepore's insights were very helpful to my perspective, particularly her comment, "Ginsburg was and remains a scholar, an advocate, and a judge of formidable sophistication, complexity, and, not least, contradiction and limitation. It is no kindness to flatten her into a paper doll and sell her as partisan merch."

CHAPTER 11: The Dark Lord Trying to Kill Off Women Scientists

Christia Mercer was hired as a junior faculty member at Columbia and was the first woman to rise through the ranks in the philosophy department and get tenure. Columbia had previously brought in other tenured women from outside.

The historian whose name I didn't mention is Ernst Cassirer. In the early 1900s, he wrote a history of modern philosophy from the Renaissance through Kant, and no women appeared. Then he wrote a major work on developments in physics, and while he would have had to work hard to keep Émilie du Châtelet out of that one, he managed.

CHAPTER 12: Battling the Ariel-Cinderella Complex

Mary Beard's lectures became the basis for her excellent short book *Women & Power,* published by Liveright Publishing Corporation in 2017.

CHAPTER 13: Why Oprah Wanted to Be a Beauty Queen

"Oprah's Letter to Her Younger Self" is on Oprah.com. The designation of Oprah Winfrey as the first black woman billionaire comes from *Forbes.*

Jill Lepore spoke about her anger with the cartoon that appeared in *The Chronicle of Higher Education* when she spoke to the same publication for a November 13, 2018, article about her history book *These Truths.*

The quote from Kate Manne is from her book *Down Girl: The Logic of Misogyny,* published by Oxford University Press in 2017.

Deborah Rhode discussed the topics here in her book *The Beauty Bias,* published by Oxford University Press in 2000. I also reference her *New York Times* article of October 18, 2000, "Step, Wince, Step, Wince."

CHAPTER 14: Geena Davis and the Problem of Being Nice

When I met with Daphne Koller, the company she started, Coursera, had forty million users around the world and was valued at more than a billion dollars. She told me that she hadn't yet received bundles of money because Coursera was still not liquid.

The popularity of *Good Girls Revolt* comes from the *Deadline* article "'Good Girls Revolt' TV Series Eyes Season 2 Comeback As Its Relevance Rises," by Nellie Andreeva, November 9, 2017. The hoped-for second season didn't occur.

The number of prominent men to lose their jobs from #MeToo was based on reporting in *The New York Times* on October 29, 2018: "#MeToo Brought Down 201 Powerful Men. Nearly Half of Their Replacements Are Women," by Audrey Carlsen, Maya Salam, Claire Cain Miller, Denise Lu, Ash Ngu, Jugal K. Patel, and Zach Wichter.

The quote from Maggie Gyllenhaal comes from an interview in the *Independent* newspaper in the UK, "Maggie Gyllenhaal Interview: 'We Live in a Misogynistic World, As Much As We'd Like to Believe Otherwise,'" by Patrick H. J. Smith, March 6, 2019.

White Rage by Carol Anderson was published by Bloomsbury USA in 2016 and is a fascinating and original perspective on discrimination.

CHAPTER 15: Frances Arnold Knew She Was Right (and Then She Won the Nobel Prize)

Alice Waters's quote is from "Life's Work: An Interview with Alice Waters," by Alison Beard in the *Harvard Business Review*, May–June 2017 issue.

All of the quotes from Anne Wojcicki are from our personal interview and conversation. The information about Sergey Brin and Parkinson's disease comes from an article in *Wired* magazine: "Sergey Brin's Search for a Parkinson's Cure," by Thomas Goetz, June 22, 2010. According to the article, one study linked drinking coffee to a reduced risk of Parkinson's disease in young men.

CHAPTER 17: Why Sally Michel Was a Genius Painter and Mrs. Milton Avery Was Not

The Tina Fey quotes are from her speech accepting the Mark Twain Prize for American Humor at the Kennedy Center in 2010 and from her bestselling book *Bossypants*. The cover image I reference is from the mass-market paperback edition from Reagan Arthur / Little Brown in 2013. My similarly colored college copy of *The Awakening* by Kate Chopin may be hard to find now—but the book is worth reading in any edition. It was first published in 1899.

The Karen Uhlenbeck quotes are from "The Bubble Verse" by Siobhan Roberts, *The New York Times,* April 9, 2019.

The interview with Sally Michel is from the Smithsonian Archives of American Art, "Oral History Interview with Sally Michel Avery, 1967 November 3." The interview was conducted by Dorothy Seckler.

The Lucas Hnath play *Hillary and Clinton* premiered in Chicago in 2016 and on Broadway in 2019. It takes place in 2006, when Hillary was seeking the Democratic nomination, but the beginning of the play describes it as taking place in an alternate universe with some different Hillary than the one we know running for president. Hnath wants the themes to be universal—and the line I quote about who supports whom resonates, no matter what your political beliefs (or what universe).

Information about the North Carolina court case is from *The Washington Post,* "Girls Were Forced to Wear Skirts at School to 'Preserve Chivalry.' So They Sued—and Won," by Kayla Epstein, March 30, 2019.

The fascinating study of how sexism affects our views of reproduction is by Emily Martin: "The Egg and the Sperm: How Science Has Constructed a Romance Based on Stereotypical Male-Female Roles," *Signs,* Spring 1991, pages 485–501.

Michelle Cottle's excellent editorial "The Outspoken Women of the House" appeared in *The New York Times* on March 22, 2019.

The six countries in the world with the largest populations are China, India, the United States, Indonesia, Brazil, and Pakistan. The three that have had women leaders are India (Indira Gandhi), Brazil (Dilma Rousseff), and Pakistan (Benazir Bhutto). My statement that sixty countries have been led by women is an approximation. You can find one list of countries with women leaders at CNN Politics: "All the Countries That Had a Woman Leader Before the U.S.," by Amanda Wills, Jacque Smith, and Casey Hicks, updated January 28, 2019. Another insight comes from the Pew Research Center article of March 2017, "Number of Women Leaders Around the World Has Grown, but They're Still a Small Group," which says fifty-six countries have had a female head of government for at least one year, and another thirteen have had women leaders who held office for less than a year.

Karissa Bodnar founded Thrive Causemetics in 2015 with a plan to make beauty products with pure ingredients and to donate one product for each one sold. In 2019, she made *Forbes*'s list of "America's Richest Self-Made Women," and for her thirtieth birthday that year, the company made a $30 million donation to women's causes.

CHAPTER 18: The Game-Changing Power of Genius Women

Roberta Smith is cochief art critic at *The New York Times* and the first woman to hold that position. (It will be nice when the "first" designation isn't part of so many women's titles.) In her article on June 6, 2019, "Last Call: MoMA's Closing, and Changing," Smith noted that "the absence of art by women in the first six galleries is breathtaking. The only exception to the un-relieved maleness is [one painting by] Sonia Delaunay-Terk."

I hope and expect that there will soon be new and better exhibitions at MoMA and other important museums. Because as Smith and others under-stand, we can no longer tell the true story of modern art—or anything else—without including the genius of women.

Index

Abel Prize, 283

Academy Award, 30, 133, 301

Adichie, Chimamanda Ngozi,
 56, 315

Adler, Irene, 87, 317

affirmative action, 143, 244–245, 296

Agóca, Kati, 82

AI4ALL, 123

Alsop, Marin, 81–82, 84

Amour de Loin, L' (Saariaho), 85

Anderson, Carol, 239–240, 242–245, 246,
 296, 303, 321

Angelson, Genevieve, 239

Anguissola, Sofonisba, 73, 302

appearance
 children and, 220–223
 double standard of, 219–220
 effects of, 224–225, 228–230
 paradoxical effect of, 218–219
 social pressure and, 214–218
 as way of trivializing
  women, 226–228

Apple stores, 40–41, 314

Arbus, Diane, 27

Ariel, 200–203

Arnold, Frances, 249–255, 257–258, 298,
 303, 305

art, 67–78, 285–288, 306, 316, 323

artificial intelligence, 120–121, 123–124,
 126, 318

As Good As It Gets, 134

Asawa, Ruth, 77, 316

Association for Women in
 Mathematics, 276

astrophysics, 49–52, 141–144, 186

Austen, Jane, 311

Avery, Milton, 285–288

Awakening, The (Chopin), 282, 321

Bacon, Francis, 22–23

Baker Street Irregulars, 86–87

Baltimore Charter for Women in
 Astronomy, 318

Baltimore Symphony, 81–82

Barabási, Albert-László,
 265–266, 274

Barad, Jill, 100

Barbie, 99–100
Barnard College, 161–162
Barnes, Julian, 147
Barnes Foundation, 4–5
Beard, Mary, 206–208, 223, 225, 320
Beaser, Robert, 82–84
beauty
  map of, 43
  pageants, 215–217, 230–231
  pressures on girls, 221–223
  products, 94
  self-objectification and, 225–226
Beauvoir, Simone de, 14
Beethoven, 19, 83
Beilock, Sian, 161–165, 253, 304
belief in self, 249–250, 263, 271, 304
Bell, Jocelyn, 186–188, 199
Bell Jar, The (Plath), 27
Berland, Michael, 1–2, 7, 298–299
Berry, Halle, 301
Bhutto, Benazir, 322
Bialik, Mayim, 88–90, 93, 305
bias
  blinders to, 122, 142, 175–176, 301, 302
  confirmation, 22–23, 245–246
  in describing reproduction, 289–291
  implicit, 275–277
  unconscious, 104–105, 187, 289–290
Big Bang Theory, The, 87–90
Big Little Lies, 238
bikini study, 224–225
blind auditions
  for orchestras, 79–80
  for talk shows, 80–81
Blossom, 88
Bodnar, Karissa, 295–297, 323
Bodow, Steve, 80–81
body image. See appearance
Bohr, Niels, 25
Boroditsky, Lera, 148–149, 318
Bossypants (Fey), 282
Boston Marathon, 101–102

brain
  cerebral cortex in, 110
  hardwiring of, 110
  lack of gender differences in, 105–106,
    107–113
  mass of, 41–42
  structure of, 109–110, 112–113, 159
Breakthrough Prize, 181–182, 187
Breazeal, Cynthia, 170–176, 179, 200,
    217–218, 228, 289, 302, 305
Brin, Sergey, 260, 262, 321
Broad Institute, 183–185
Brontë, Anne, 27, 28
Brontë, Charlotte, 26–27, 28
Brontë, Emily, 27, 28
Brooks, Mel, 129
Brooks, Rodney, 171–172
Brzezinski, Mika, 220
Bunn, Maryellis, 295–297
Burnell, Dame Jocelyn Bell, 187–188

California Institute of Technology, 252
Calvo, Dana, 238
Cam, Helen, 35
Cambridge University, 18, 35, 51, 65, 91,
    206, 239, 298
Cassirer, Ernst, 319
Catwoman, 301
celebrity, 18–19, 21, 42, 75
Charpentier, Emmanuelle, 181–185
Chastenay, Madame de, 38
chefs, 256–257, 284–285
Chez Panisse, 256–257
Child, Julia, 284–285
choking under pressure, 161–163
Chopin, Kate, 282, 321
Chronicle of Higher Education, 227
Cimpian, Andrei, 94–96, 98, 315
Cinderella, 202–203
Civil Rights Act, 128
civil rights movement, 178

Clinton, Hillary, 220, 292, 322
clothes, 217–218, 288–289
Coleridge, Samuel Taylor, 132
collaboration
    in discovering theory of relativity, 47
    as element of genius, 155–156
    in mathematics, 276–278
Comfort, Nathaniel, 184
computer programming, 97
conductors, 81–82, 84–85
confidence, 249–250, 255, 263, 271
confirmation bias, 22–23, 245–246
confrontation, avoidance of, 240–242
Congress, pool of, 37. See also politics
Constitution, 128
convents, 17, 71
Conway, Anne, 191
cooking, 256–257, 284–285
Copernicus, 25
Cottle, Michelle, 291, 322
Coursera, 233–234, 320
Coyne, Petah, 70
crafts, 76–77
Crick, Francis, 106–107
CRISPR, 181, 183–185, 194–195
Cross, Amanda, 318
Crown, The, 78
Cruise, Tom, 133–134
cryptanalysis, 137–139, 275
Culinary Institute of America, 257
cultural expectations, effect of, 90–92,
    95–102, 99–100
Curie, Marie, 2, 178, 312–313
Curie, Pierre, 313

da Vinci, Leonardo, 72
Dabhoiwala, Faramerz, 55
Daily Show, The, 80–81
Damon, Matt, 29–30
Daniel Deronda (Eliot), 147
Davis, Geena, 236–238, 246, 273, 304

de la Parra, Alondra, 84
Delaunay-Terk, Sonia, 323
denial of entry, women
    to Congress's pool, 37
    to Faculty Club, 35–36
    to Yale Club pool, 36–37
deprecation, gendered language of,
    240–241
Descartes, 189–190
Didion, Joan, 26
directed evolution, 250
"Disappearing Ink" (O'Neill), 190
Disney Princesses, 200–205, 208
disrupters, 169–170
diversity
    importance of, 250–251
    ways to achieve, 283
Dixon, Maynard, 76
DNA, 106–107, 181–186, 259–260, 262
"domestic associations," 77
doomsday cult, 23
Double Helix, The (Watson), 106
Doudna, Jennifer, 181–186, 194–195
Doyle, Arthur Conan, 86
dress codes, 288–289
du Châtelet, Émilie, 192–194, 319
Dunkley, Jo, 49–52, 54–55, 63–64, 66,
    122, 123, 142, 211, 302, 315
Dupin, Aurore, 146–147
Dutch Golden Age, 67, 74–75

eBay, 60–61
education
    divided, 159–161
    lack of access to, 35, 38
    single-sex schools and, 160–162
Einstein, Albert, 25, 46–48, 314
Eisen, Michael, 184
Eliot, George, 147
Eliot, Lise, 106, 107–112, 159–160, 161
Elisabeth of Bohemia, Princess, 191

elliptic curve cryptography, 275
Emmy Award, 78, 238
encouragement/nurturing
    importance of, 45
    lack of for women, 35
    Matt Damon Problem and, 29–30
    Mozart and his sister and, 30–32
England, Paula, 317
Enigma machines, 137–138
Enlightenment, 40, 55
Ephron, Nora, 160
Equal Rights Amendment, 128
Erskine, John, 311
Evans, Mary Ann, 147
evolution
    directed, 250
    explanations of difference based on,
        55, 108
expectations, effect of cultural, 90–92,
    95–102, 99–100

Fagone, Jason, 318
Fallon, Jimmy, 281–282
Faust, Drew Gilpin, 37–38
fearlessness, 255–256, 257–259
fertility. See reproduction
Festinger, Leon, 23, 312
Fey, Tina, 150–151, 279, 281–282,
    287, 321
Feynman, Richard, 314
field-specific ability beliefs (FAB), 96
finance, 269–270
Fine, Cordelia, 113, 318
Fiorina, Carly, 220
fMRI scans, 109
Foster, Jodie, 87, 154
Fowler, Amy Farrah, 87–90
Foy, Claire, 78, 308
Frankfurter, Felix, 168
Franklin, Rosalind, 106–107, 121, 317
fraternities, 161

Fredrickson, Barbara, 224–226
Free to Be . . . You and Me (Thomas),
    129–130
Friedman, Elizebeth, 137–139, 275, 318
Friedman, William, 137
Frozen, 203–205

Gadsby, Hannah, 316
Galbraith, Robert, 146
Galton, Francis, 42–43, 266, 314
Gandhi, Indira, 322
Geena Davis Institute on Gender in
    Media, 237
gender-based distinctions
    as result of social learning, 118
    in language, 148–149
    not hardwired, 105–106, 107–113
    seeing beyond, 303
    unwarranted, 32–34, 41, 158–159
generalizations. See also stereotypes
    twisting of, 155–157
    uselessness of, 32–34, 56–57
genetics
    as explanation for genius, 42–43
    field of, 181. See also 23andMe
    as proposed basis for inequality, 43
genius
    as aberration of femaleness, 48–49
    as celebrity, 18–19, 21, 42
    characteristics of, 9
    commonalities for, 300
    defining, 40, 41–43
    elements that help, 302–305
    genetics as explanation for, 42–43
    spontaneous, 29–30
    survey on public perceptions of,
        1–2, 7
Genius Bar, 40–41, 314
Gentileschi, Artemisia, 73–74, 302, 306
geometric analysis, 283n1
Giacobassi, Julie Ann, 81

Ginsburg, Ruth Bader, 166–170, 178–179, 200, 295
Gloria: A Life, 6–7
Golden Globe Award, 78
Golden Raspberry Award ("Razzie"), 301
Goldin, Claudia, 79–80, 316
Goldsmith, Andrea, 208–212, 304
Goldstein, Rebecca Newberger, 48–49, 315
Good Girls Revolt, 238–239, 320
Good Will Hunting, 29
Goodden, Angelica, 39
Google, 260
Gordon, Linda, 75–76, 316
Gould, Stephen Jay, 43, 108
gratitude, 252
Gray, John, 157–159
Great Books, 1, 311–312
Grier, Rosey, 129
Guerrilla Girls, 69–70, 316
Guggenheim Museum, 306
Gutmann, Amy, 59n2
Gyllenhaal, Maggie, 241–242, 321

Hahn, Otto, 21–22, 24
halo effect, 218
Hals, Frans, 74–75
Hamilton, 25–26, 312
Hammer, Armie, 169
Handmaid's Tale, The, 238
hard work versus natural brilliance, 94–96
Harris, Kamala, 292
Harry Potter series, 146
Harvard University, 35, 37–38
heads of state, women as, 207, 293–294, 322. *See also* politics
Heilbrun, Carolyn Gold, 132, 318
Hensel, Fanny Mendelssohn, *See* Fanny Mendelssohn

Hereditary Genius (Galton), 42
Heti, Sheila, 10
Hidden Figures, 21
high heels, 80, 229
Hildegard of Bingen, 17, 199
Hillary and Clinton (Hnath), 286–287, 322
hippocampus size, 109
Hnath, Lucas, 286–287, 322
Holmes, Sherlock, 86–87
Homer, 206
Hoover, J. Edgar, 138–139
Hopkins, Nancy, 34
Hopper, Grace, 41, 306
House, 87
How Should a Person Be? (Heti), 10
Hubble, Edwin, 306–307
Hubble Space Telescope, 142, 306
Hughes, Howard, 8
Hunt, Helen, 134
Hypatia, 19–20, 312

ImageNet, 124
inequality, claims of genetic basis for, 43
intelligence, types of, 314
IQ tests, 43–45, 314
Isaacson, Walter, 9

Jane Eyre (Brontë), 26, 27
Jerry Maguire, 133–134
Jibo, 170, 174–175, 305
Joel, Daphna, 112–113, 317
Johnson, Katherine, 21
Johnson, Samuel, 190
Jolly Companions, The (Leyster), 74–75
Jones, Charles, 18–19, 239
Jones, Felicity, 169
Judith Beheading Holofernes (Gentileschi), 74
Just So Stories (Kipling), 108

Kagan, Elena, 166
Kahlo, Frida, 69
Kahneman, Daniel, 315
Kaling, Mindy, 202
Kant, Immanuel, 125
Kelly, Megyn, 219–220
Keohane, Nan, 59
King's College, 91
Kipling, Rudyard, 108
Kismet, 172–173
Klawe, Maria, 59n2
Klint, Hilma af, 306
Klum, Heidi, 220n3
Knightley, Keira, 202–203
Koller, Daphne, 233–235, 246–247,
    304, 320
Krasner, Lee, 68

Lady Margaret Hall, 16
Lahti, Christine, 7
Lamarr, Hedy, 8
Landau, Tina, 150–155, 157, 304
Lander, Eric, 183–185
Lange, Dorothea, 75–76
language
of deprecation, gendered, 240–241
effect of on perception, 148–149
gender in, 148–149
Last Supper (Nelli), 71–72
Lauter, Kristin, 275–277
leadership, 57–58
Lean In (Sandberg), 53
Leavitt, Henrietta Swan, 306–307
Lee, Jennifer, 203
Lepore, Jill, 226–228, 319, 320
Leslie, Sarah-Jane, 94–96, 98–99,
    222–223, 228, 315
Leyster, Judith, 74–75, 306
Li, Fei-Fei, 120–126, 127, 132, 142, 145,
    172, 179, 200, 211, 303, 318
Lionni, Leo, 277–278

Little Engine That Could, The, 271
Little Man Tate, 87
Little Mermaid, The, 200–203
looks, See appearance
Lovelace, Ada, 26–27, 306

MacArthur Genius Award, 233, 312
Maher, Katherine, 3–4, 312
makeup, 118, 221, 229
male anger and violence, 240–241
male-centrism, 237
Mandelli, Monica, 266–273, 304
Manne, Kate, 220, 320
mansplaining, 192
Maria Anna (Nannerl; Mozart's sister),
    31–32, 45
Marić, Mileva, 46–48
Mark Twain Prize for American
    Humor, 279
Martin, Emily, 289–291, 322
mathematicians, women, 275–277,
    283–284
Mattel, 100
Maurer, Dóra, 274
May, Theresa, 293
Mayer, Louis B., 8
McMahon, Darrin, 40, 42, 44, 313
Mehta, Zubin, 79
Meitner, Lise, 21–22, 23–25, 180, 199,
    302, 306, 308, 312
meitnerium, 25, 180, 313
men, viewed as the norm, 14–15
Men, Women, and Me concept, 120, 122,
    127, 132
Men Are from Mars, Women Are from
    Venus (Gray), 157–159
Mendelssohn, Abraham, 135
Mendelssohn, Fanny, 17, 134–137,
    199, 318
Mendelssohn, Felix, 134–137
Menzel, Idina, 204

Mercer, Christia, 188–192, 193, 195, 319
Merkel, Angela, 293
#MeToo movement, 5–6, 184, 238–239, 320–321
Michel, Sally, 285–288, 322
Michelangelo, 72
Middlemarch (Eliot), 147
Midwife's Tale, A (Ulrich), 177
Mill, John Stuart, 279–281
mind-set, power of, 92–93
misogyny, 37, 161, 200, 239, 246
Miranda, Lin-Manuel, 25–26, 312
Mismeasure of Man, The (Gould), 43
MIT Media Lab, 170–171
Mitchell, Joan, 68
Moana, 203
Molteni, Carla, 91–92, 267
Mona Lisa, 75, 76
More, Henry, 191
Morisot, Berthe, 4–5
Morrison, Toni, 311
motherhood, 48, 50, 54–55
Mozart, 29, 30–31, 45, 83
MRI scans, 109, 317
"Ms.," 130–131
Murdoch, Rupert, 157
Museum of Modern Art, 306
music and composers, 16–17, 18–19, 78–80, 81–85, 94, 134–137
Musk, Elon, 126
Myerson, Bess, 215–216

names, importance of, 288
Nanette, 316
Napoléon, 38, 39, 298
narrative, control of, 26
NASA, 21, 139, 302
National Gallery in London, 74
nature-versus-nurture debate, 43
Nelli, Plautilla, 71–72, 199
network theory, 265–266

networks, importance of, 265. *See also* encouragement/nurturing; supportive person
Neumann, John von, 29
New York Philharmonic, 80, 81
New York Times, The, 26–27
Ng, Andrew, 233–234
Nicholson, Jack, 134
Nixon, Richard, 130
Nobel Prize
    for Arnold, 249–251
    on *The Big Bang Theory*, 90
    for Curie, 312–313
    for Einstein, 47
    for Hahn, 21–22
    Meitner and, 21–22, 23
    for pulsar discovery, 186
    for Strickland, 3–4
    for Watson and Crick, 106
nonbinary designation, 128–129
norm, men viewing themselves as, 14–15
nuclear fission, 21–22
nudges, 289
nuns, 17, 71–72
nurturing genius. *See* encouragement/ nurturing

Odyssey (Homer), 206
"Oh Do Shut Up Dear!" (Beard), 206
O'Keeffe, Georgia, 68
On the Basis of Sex, 169
O'Neill, Eileen, 190–191
"Orchestrating Impartiality" (Goldin and Rouse), 79–80
orthogonal dimensions, 222, 224
"Overlooked" (*New York Times* series), 26–27
outsider status, advantages of, 173–174
Oxford University, 15–16, 35, 39, 50, 61, 123, 225–226, 232, 302
oxymoron problem, 190

Page, Larry, 260
Palin, Sarah, 216
parental leave, 128
Parkinson's disease, 262, 321
Parks, Rosa, 178–179
Patents
    for CRISPR, battle for, 183
    for women inventors, 212, 254, 275
patriarchy, 7–8, 215, 240
Paumgarten, Nick, 102
Paxson, Christina, 59n2
pay inequity, 78, 97, 317
Peeters, Clara, 67–68, 76, 306
perfectionism, 233
periodic table, 24–25, 313
Petrenko, Vasily, 82
Philharmonic Orchestra of the
    Americas, 84
Phillips, Katherine, 283
philosophy, 94–95, 188–192
Photo 51, 106
Picasso, 75
placebo effect, 92–93
Plath, Sylvia, 26–27
Plato, 9
Poets' Corner, Westminster Abbey, 28
politics, 291–294. See also heads of state,
    women as
Pollock, Jackson, 68
positive approach, 303–304
positive psychology, 226, 252
power
    of changing roles, 14
    men controlling, 2–3, 4, 7, 14, 42, 68,
        72, 97, 184, 187–188, 220, 238–239,
        266, 280
    vision of, 207–208
    women giving away, 6, 204, 206
    women gaining, 20, 38, 39, 48, 53, 69,
        102, 209, 215, 249, 296–297, 306
Prado Museum (Madrid), 67–68
presidential election, 292. See also heads
    of state, women as; politics

pressure, choking under, 161–163
Princeton University, 49, 50, 57, 58–59,
    61, 94, 122, 123, 185, 303, 314, 315
Principles of the Most Ancient and Modern
    Philosophy, The (Conway), 191
protactinium, 25
"protecting" women, 168–169
pseudonyms, 146–147
Pulitzer Prize, 27, 177, 232
pulsars, 186

Queensland Symphony Orchestra, 84

ramp experiment, 163
Randall, Lisa, 218–219
Rauch, Melissa, 89
Rehnquist, William, 169
relativity, theory of, 46–47
Renaissance, 73–74, 297–298
reproduction
    control of, 127
    as excuse for prohibitions, 34, 313
    sexist bias in describing, 289–291
reverse role models, 269
Rhode, Deborah, 228–229, 320
Ridgeway, Cecilia, 97, 245
Rigoletto (Verdi), 307–308
risk taking, 233–235
robotics, 170–176
Rome Prize, 82
Ross, Alex, 85, 316
Rouse, Cecilia, 79–80, 316
Rousseff, Dilma, 322
Rowling, J. K., 146
rule setting, power of, 2–3
Russakovsky, Olga, 123

Saariaho, Kaija, 85
Salke, Jennifer, 239
Sand, George, 146–147

Sandberg, Sheryl, 53–54
Sappho, 311
Sarandon, Susan, 236
Saturday Night Live, 279, 281–282
Saudi Arabia, driving in, 34, 313
Sawyer, Diane, 216
Scalia/Ginsburg, 166
Schjeldahl, Peter, 4–5
Schmidt, Eike, 69, 316
Schumann, Clara, 17
Scott, Andrea, 77
Second City (improv group), 282
self, belief in, 249–250, 263,
    271, 304
self-confidence deficit, 59
self-deprecation, 240–241
self-objectification, 225
self-perception, 7–8
Sesame Street, 62–63
setbacks, 284–285
sexiness, 55–56
sexual dimorphism, 112
sexual harassment, 238–239. See also
    #McToo movement
Shakespeare, William, 28
Shelley, Mary, 119n1
Shiffrin, Mikaela, 102
silencing women, 206
Silverstein, Shel, 271
single-sex schools, 160–162. See also
    education
Sirani, Elisabetta, 73, 75
Slater, Ethan, 152
Slaughter, Anne Marie, 59n2
Smith, Matt, 78
Smith, Roberta, 323
Smith, Valerie, 59n2
social learning, 110–111
social robots, 172–174
Socrates of Constantinople, 19–20
sororities, 161
Sotomayor, Sonia, 166
Southey, Robert, 27, 28

SpongeBob SquarePants: The Musical,
    151–152, 154
spontaneous genius, 29–30
sports, 101–102
Staël, Madame de, 38–40, 48, 199, 298,
    304, 313
"status belief," 97
Stanford University, 97, 120, 127, 183,
    208, 210, 228, 233–234, 245, 258, 318
Steinem, Gloria, 6–7, 49
STEM (science, technology, engineering,
    and math) subjects, 94
stereotypes. See also generalizations
    diversity and, 283
    early internalization of, 98–99
    ignoring, 119–120
    resistance to, 301, 303
stress relief, 162
Strickland, Donna, 3–4, 286, 312
Subjection of Women, The (Mill), 279–280
Suh, Rhea, 164–165
Summers, Larry, 33–34
supportive person, 300–301, 302
survey on public perceptions of genius,
    1–2, 7
Swimmy (Lionni), 277–278
Switzer, Kathrine, 101–102

Taylor, Harriet, 280–281
television, 80–81, 87–90, 150–151, 279
Tenant of Wildfell Hall, The (Brontë), 27
Teresa of Ávila, 189–190
Terman, Lewis, 44, 314
"That Swimsuit Becomes You"
    (Fredrickson), 224–225
Thatcher, Margaret, 293
Thelma & Louise, 236–237
Theon of Alexandria, 20
theory of relativity, 46–47
These Truths (Lepore), 226–228
Thomas, Marlo, 129–130
Thrive Causemetics, 323

Tilghman, Shirley, 57–60, 61, 64, 122, 145, 185, 254, 303, 315
Title VII, 128
tokenism, 276, 297
Tolstoy, Leo, 23
Tony Award, 152
Trump, Donald, 219–220
Tversky, Amos, 63, 315
23andMe, 259–261
Tyson, Neil deGrasse, 219

Uffizi museum (Florence), 69, 74, 316
Uhlenbeck, Karen, 283–284, 321
Ulrich, Laurle Thatcher, 176–179
unconscious bias, 104–105, 187, 289–290
University College London, 43, 64, 314
Urry, Meg, 139–146, 200, 208, 211, 254, 302, 318

van Gogh, Vincent, 74
Verdi, 307–308
Vergara, Alejandro, 67–68
Vindication of the Right of Woman, A (Wollstonecraft), 318
Voltaire, 193

Warren, Elizabeth, 292
Waters, Alice, 256–257, 321
Watson, James, 106–107
Well-Behaved Women Seldom Make History (Ulrich), 177–178
When Harry Met Sally, 160

White Rage (Anderson), 242, 321
Whitman, Meg, 60–61
Whitman, Walt, 153
Whitney Museum (New York), 68–69
Wikipedia, 3–4, 312
Wilde, Oscar, 216
Wilkins, Maurice, 106n1
Wilson, Helen, 64–66, 302
Winfrey, Oprah, 215, 216, 320
Wojcicki, Anne, 258–264, 302, 321
Wojcicki, Janet, 258
Wojcicki, Susan, 260
Wollenberg, Susan, 16–17, 83
Wollstonecraft, Mary, 119, 230, 318
Woman Who Smashed Codes, The (Fagone), 318
Women & Power (Beard), 320
Wonder Woman, 227
Woolf, Virginia, 2–3, 311
world leaders, women as, 207, 293–294, 322. See also politics
World War II, 137–139
writers' rooms, 80–81, 150–151, 279
Writing a Woman's Life (Heilbrun), 318
Wuthering Heights (Brontë), 27

Yale Club of New York City, 36–37
Yale University, 36, 41, 61, 62, 139–140, 143, 144–145, 154, 302
YouTube, 260

Zellweger, Renée, 133–134
Zhang, Feng, 182–183, 185

About the Author

Janice Kaplan has enjoyed wide success as a magazine editor, television producer, writer, and journalist. The former editor in chief of *Parade* magazine, she is the author or coauthor of fourteen books, including the *New York Times* bestsellers *The Gratitude Diaries* and *I'll See You Again.* She lives in New York City and Kent, Connecticut.